Harwood Fundamentals of Pure and Applied Economics

MARXIAN ECONOMICS
I

FUNDAMENTALS OF PURE AND APPLIED ECONOMICS

EDITORS IN CHIEF

J. LESOURNE, Conservatoire National des Arts et Métiers, Paris, France
H. SONNENSCHEIN, University of Pennsylvania, Philadelphia, PA, USA

ADVISORY BOARD

MARXIAN ECONOMICS I

MARXIAN ECONOMICS
I

Money, Accumulation and Crisis

Duncan K Foley

Value, Exploitation and Class

John E Roemer

Capitalist Imperialism, Crisis and the State

John Willoughby

First published in 1986, 1986 and 1986 by
Harwood Academic Publishers GmbH

Reprinted in 2001 by
Routledge
2 Park Square, Milton Park, Abingdon, Oxon, OX14 4RN

Transferred to Digital Printing 2007

Routledge is an imprint of the Taylor & Francis Group

The publishers have made every effort to contact authors/copyright holders
of the works reprinted in *Harwood Fundamentals of Pure & Applied Economics*.
This has not been possible in every case, however, and we would welcome
correspondence from those individuals/companies we have been unable to
trace.

These reprints are taken from original copies of each book. in many cases
the condition of these originals is not perfect. the publisher has gone to
great lengths to ensure the quality of these reprints, but wishes to point
out that certain characteristics of the original copies will, of necessity, be
apparent in reprints thereof.

British Library Cataloguing in Publication Data
A CIP catalogue record for this book
is available from the British Library

Marxian Economics I
ISBN 0-415-26983-0
Harwood Fundamentals of Pure & Applied Economics
ISBN 0-415-26907-5

MONEY, ACCUMULATION AND CRISIS

DUNCAN K FOLEY

Money, Accumulation and Crisis

Duncan K Foley

Barnard College of Columbia University, USA

A Volume in the Marxian Economics Section
edited by
John E Roemer
University of California, Davis, USA

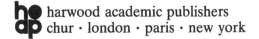 harwood academic publishers
chur · london · paris · new york

© 1986 by Harwood Academic Publishers GmbH, Poststrasse 22, 7000 Chur, Switzerland. All rights reserved.

Harwood Academic Publishers

P.O. Box 197
London WC2E 9PX
England

58, rue Lhomond
75005 Paris
France

P.O. Box 786
Cooper Station
New York, New York 10276
United States of America

Library of Congress Cataloging in Publication Data
Foley, Duncan K.
  Money, accumulation, and crisis.
  (Fundamentals of pure and applied economics,
ISSN 0883-2366; vol. 2. Marxian economics section)
  Bibliography: p.
  Includes index.
  1. Capitalism. 2. Marxian economics. 3. Social conflict. I. Title. II. Series:
Fundamentals of pure and applied economics; v. 2. III. Series: Fundamentals of pure and
applied economics. Marxian economics section.
HB501.F64   1986   330.12'2   86-3144
ISBN 3-7186-0280-6

CONTENTS

INTRODUCTION TO THE SERIES

Drawing on a personal network, an economist can still relatively easily stay well informed in the narrow field in which he works, but to keep up with the development of economics as a whole is a much more formidable challenge. Economists are confronted with difficulties associated with the rapid development of their discipline. There is a risk of "balkanisation" in economics, which may not be favourable to its development.

Fundamentals of Pure and Applied Economics has been created to meet this problem. The discipline of economics has been subdivided into sections (listed on the inside back cover). These sections include short books, each surveying the state of the art in a given area.

Each book starts with the basic elements and goes as far as the most advanced results. Each should be useful to professors needing material for lectures, to graduate students looking for a global view of a particular subject, to professional economists wishing to keep up with the development of their science, and to researchers seeking convenient information on questions that incidentally appear in their work.

Each book is thus a presentation of the state of the art in a particular field rather than a step by step analysis of the development of the literature. Each is a high level presentation but accessible to anyone with a solid background in economics, whether engaged in business, government, international organizations, teaching, or research in related fields.

Three aspects of *Fundamentals of Pure and Applied Economics* should be emphasized:

—First, the project covers the whole field of economics, not only theoretical or mathematical economics.

—Second, the project is open-ended and the number of books is not predetermined. If new interesting areas appear, they will generate additional books.
—Last, all the books making up each section will later be grouped to constitute one or several volumes of an Encyclopaedia of Economics.

The editors of the sections are outstanding economists who have selected as authors for the series some of the finest specialists in the world.

J Lesourne   H Sonnenschein

Money, accumulation, and crisis

DUNCAN K. FOLEY

1. INTRODUCTION

THIS ESSAY presents the outlines of a theory of macroeconomics based on Marx's theory of capitalist production and accumulation. The central unifying concept is the *circuit of capital*, which views the circular flow of commodities and money from the perspective of the income statements and balance sheets of capitalist firms. Capitals motivated by the pursuit of profits to accumulate, rather than households motivated by utility maximation through consumption, are the basic economic agents in this framework. Household and state economic behavior are included in the framework, but play a subsidiary role.

The essay begins by reconsidering the labor theory of value, explaining the relations in Marx's theory between commodities and money and between money prices and labor time. The key simplifying idea in this discussion is the notion that the aggregate value added in money terms produced by a system of capital is an expression of the aggregate labor time newly expended in production. The ratio of the labor time to money value added I call the *value of money*. This approach interprets the claims of the labor theory of value as applying exactly in the aggregate, but not necessarily to the prices of particular commodities, thus eliminating major problems in the traditional treatment of the relation between value and price. In this interpretation the labor theory of value becomes a natural and powerful foundation for macroeconomic theory, which is concerned precisely with these aggregate flows of value.

The essay continues by reviewing Marx's theory of capitalist production and of surplus value. The central idea here is that the emergence of labor-power as a commodity sold on the market for a wage creates a fundamental division of aggregate value added between wages and surplus value, and a parallel division of social labor time between paid and unpaid labor.

The ability of capital to appropriate surplus value is the foundation of the circuit of capital. Value moves continually from the form of money into means of production and labor-power, then into newly produced commodities containing surplus value, and back into money again through sale, thus preparing the next round of the circuit. The circular motion of the aggregate social capital is the object of analysis of a Marxist macroeconomic theory.

The development of a mathematical representation of the circuit of capital allows us to resolve questions of steady-state growth (which Marx calls *expanded reproduction*) and to pose the problem of the instability of capital accumulation. I make explicit within this framework the Keynesian notion that sources of money demand must be sought within the circuit of capital itself, in the capital outlays of capitalist firms. This analysis shows the close connection between the expansion of credit and the continued expansion of the circuit of capital. This link is studied both by comparing steady-state paths, and by examining arbitrary paths of the model. These results are extended to situations where the value of money varies over time in response to changes in the average tightness of the market for produced commodities.

In order to make the comparison of this labor theory of value based macroeconomics with Keynesian and neoclassical macroeconomic theory clearer, theories of credit, interest, and central bank policy that are consistent with circuit of capital macroeconomics are outlined.

The most intriguing aspect of the circuit of capital approach is the possibility of systematically modelling non-linearities in the system that could give rise to instabilities and crises in the accumulation of capital. The problems of proportionality between different Departments of production, of changes in the basic parameters of profitability with accumulation, and the specific nature of crises of capital accumulation are the subjects of the last sections.

The macroeconomic theory that emerges from this study has some technical features that are of interest.

In the circuit of capital model the availability of non-produced resources, including labor-power, enters only through the impact shortages or surpluses have on the parameters of profitability that govern the model. The proximate limit to capitalist production is the availability of capital, that is, accumulated surplus value. This point of view allows us to analyze the dynamics of capital coherently without the notion of full employment of labor, and without the confusions raised by the concepts of voluntary and involuntary unemployment. The circuit of capital models offer a more direct theory of the volume of employment itself.

The circuit of capital framework offers a unified and powerful method for dealing with the problems of stocks and flows (see Ref. 46 for a discussion of the difficulties in traditional treatments of these issues). The basic elements of analysis are flows of value and time lags in the various phases of the circuit. These time lags give rise to stocks of value in various forms as a consequence of the pattern of flows. This treatment can be applied uniformly to all stocks of value, to financial assets as well as to productive assets.

Finally, the circuit of capital theory replaces the concept of equilibrium, which has muddied macroeconomic thinking, with the more natural concept of determinate paths for the value flows in the capitalist economy. The system of capitals is seen as being in continuous but determinate motion, not as heading for some (possibly shifting) equilibrium state. It is possible to define properties of paths that have equilibrium-like characteristics, such as stationarity or stability of stock-flow ratios, but the analysis is not bound to such constructions.

In writing this essay I have tried to synthesize disparate strands of economic thought. The references in general indicate the broad sources which contribute to this synthesis rather than specific technical contributions. My aim is to chart a theory in which the main ideas of macroeconomics from different schools can find their proper places.

2. PRICE AND VALUE[1]

Because so much misunderstanding has collected around the idea of value, it may help to begin with the most elementary considerations.

In ordinary language a commodity has a price, the amount of something else (usually money) for which it can be exchanged. A collection of commodities whose prices are expressed in the same units have a value, the sum of the product of each commodity's price and the quantity of it in the collection. If v is value, p_j the price of commodity j, and q_j the quantity of commodity j,

$$v = p_1 q_1 + \dots + p_n q_n. \qquad (2.1)$$

There are two different ways of interpreting this relation. Modern economic theory tends to view prices and quantities as the fundamental objects of scientific explanation, and value merely as a way of summing up the prices of commodities.[2]

The classical economists and Marx, on the other hand, viewed value itself as a fundamental object of investigation, with its own laws and determinants that were prior to the determination of price. With this starting point prices appear as a device for *distributing* value over the commodities on the right-hand-side of equation (2.1). There is nothing "metaphysical" in this view as long as the theory specifies clearly what social laws the value concept is supposed to express.

In what follows particular interest attaches to the value newly produced in an economy in a period of time, the aggregate *value added*, or the value of the net product once the value of means of production used up has been deducted. If the economy is a national economy, this is the familiar Net National Product of national income accounting.

Very little can be said about the concept of value without introducing further theoretical ideas. If the concept of value is to have any meaning, however, it must exhibit some invariance

---

1. The argument of this section was developed in conversation with G. Dumenil.
2. Thus Debreu [3] explains value by investigating the determinants of price in a static market clearing framework.

properties. At a minimum, a uniform proportional change in all prices should leave the value unchanged (or equivalently, should alter the units in which we measure value in the inverse proportion). What other changes in prices and quantities leave value invariant is the subject of theories of value.

The value approach to economic theory essentially argues that we can distinguish between explanatory laws that govern the total value produced and those that determine the distribution of this value through prices to the commodities produced. This point of view may be contrasted with the notion that only prices are determinate, that is, that the only laws are those governing price.

3. COMMODITY, VALUE, AND MONEY

In a commodity producing society, products are the property of particular economic agents and are exchanged through bargaining. The commodity thus has two aspects: its usefulness, or, in Smith's language, use value, which makes it an object of interest to someone in the society, and is a necessary condition for it to exchange for other commodities; and its power to exchange for other commodities. The system of exchange establishes exchange ratios between all the commodities in the system: 1 bushel of wheat = 10 pounds of oranges, and so on.

The point of view of the theory of value hypothesizes that these exchange ratios express a common social substance, *value*, contained in or carried by the commodities. It is possible to see any collection of commodities as carrying a certain amount of value, which is distributed among the commodities in proportion to the exchange ratios. The exchange ratios express only the *relative* amounts of value assigned to the various commodities. In order to express the absolute amount of value it is necessary to construct some measure of value.

The values of all the commodities can be expressed in terms of a *general equivalent* (which may be a particular commodity, or an abstract standard). Marx proposes that money is a *socially accepted general equivalent*, a general equivalent commonly used in a commodity producing society to express the value of the commodities.

Money is thus an expression of value separate from particular commodities, or a form of value.

This proposal insists that money is inherent in the commodity form of production itself. This suggests that an attempt to develop a theory of commodity exchange without money (a "barter economy") and then to introduce money (as, for example, a device to minimize transaction costs (see Ref. 35, 37, and 40 for examples) involves a fallacy, since important functions of money are already posited in the barter economy (cf Ref. 2 for an account of models in which all commodities are implicitly assumed to be money).

This point of view also requires us to distinguish between the problem of the money form of value (how value can appear separately from particular commodities), and the problem of forms of money (what social devices, for example, the emergence of a money commodity, or of credit denominated in abstract monetary units, perform monetary functions in particular societies).

4. VALUE AND LABOR

Classical economic theory, reaching its high point in Ricardo, goes further and identifies the value in collections of commodities with the human labor expanded in their production. This idea arises from the global, social point of view of classical theory, which sees property rights and the commodity form of production as devices to organize and allocate human productive activity (labor). This idea makes no sense from a local or particular perspective, since there are many ways to secure value in a commodity producing society besides expending labor in production. The labor theory of value is the assertion that different explanatory principles govern the production of value at a social level (the expenditure of labor) and its distribution among various agents though prices.

The labour theory of value leads to many paradoxes unless the level of abstraction at which it holds is specified precisely. Marx undertook to clarify and refine Ricardo's formulation of the labor theory of value to eliminate these paradoxes. The important results of his critique are the following (see Ref. 44 for a full account of these critical results):

1. Although the forms of value, money and price appear pervasively throughout commodity producing societies, the origin of value is in the new production of commodities through the expenditure of labor. It is necessary to develop the principles governing the production of value before treating problems of the exchange of old or non-produced things (land, rare paintings, and so forth).

2. In considering the new production of value, the principle that value arises from the expenditure of labor applies at the level of the aggregate of newly produced commodities. Thus the aggregate value added in money terms in commodity production in a period is an expression of the total social labor expended in that period. The ratio of total productive social labor time to aggregate value added is called the *value of money* (or the *monetary expression of value*, see Ref. 1, 5, 7, 11, 25) and is denominated in hours of social labor per unit of money.

3. The fact that labor is expended in commodity production means that in addition to its concrete properties (as weaving, building, or information processing labor) labor has a general *abstract* property, its power to produce value.

4. Labor expended outside the system of commodity production produces no value in this sense (although it may in a larger social sense be necessary labor: see Ref. 10, 16, 21, 50). This is to say that *social* labor produces value.

5. The equalization of commodity prices in exchange implies that labor expended in the current socially most efficient methods of production governs the value of commodities. Thus labor expended in excess of what is socially necessary does not produce value.

We may sum up these points by saying that the aggregate money value added in a commodity producing society is an expression of the aggregate abstract, social, necessary labor expended in producing the net commodity product. In what follows I will assume that the reader recalls these important qualifications, and will write 'labor' for 'abstract, social, necessary labor'.

The labor theory of value in Marx's interpretation argues that the principles governing the production of new value lie in the amount and mode of utilization of social labor in a commodity producing society.

This value may be redistributed in the exchange of the commodities produced. The price of a particular commodity less the costs of non-labor inputs to its production (its value added) may, given the monetary expression of value, be the equivalent of more or less labor time than was actually bestowed on the commodity in its production. This gives rise to *unequal exchange*, in which a commodity has a price that is the equivalent of more or less labor time than is actually contained in it. Unequal exchange arises from differences in the bargaining positions of commodity owners and especially the degree of competition on both sides of the market for a commodity. In the aggregate, value added is proportional to the total labor expended.

Claims to part of the newly produced value may be exchanged against property rights in old or non-produced things. For example, the ownership of land, the right to exclude other agents from it, because it allows the owner to collect a rent from the stream of newly produced value, will exchange for a claim to part of that newly produced value. Land has a price, though it has no value.

5.   CAPITALIST PRODUCTION

Marx conceives of *capital* as self-expanding value. In contrast with the behavior of agents who exchange commodities through the medium of money to achieve a more satisfactory consumption of use-values, a capital buys and sells commodities for the sake of the increment in value it can appropriate in that process. Capital begins with money (in some form or other, including financially denominated claims), which it uses to buy means of production and labor power. The expenditure of labor in production transforms the means of production into a new qualitatively different use-value, a finished commodity that carries the value of those means of production and the value added by the labor expended. This finished commodity is then sold for money, returning the costs of means of production and labor power together with an incremental value, or *surplus value*. The surplus value together with the wages paid to purchase labor power comprise the value added. The money value added in this sense corresponds in the aggregate to the total social labor expended in the production of commodities, although any particular commodity may have a price that deviates from the direct and indirect labor expended in the production of that commodity.

The labor theory of value implies that the value added in the aggregate is an expression of expended social labor. Workers receive only a part of this value added in the form of wages. The wage is the price of labor power. If we multiply the wage by the monetary expression of value, we express the wage in terms of hours of abstract labor received by workers per hour of labor power sold, which Marx calls the *value of labor-power*. (Here I assume that one hour of labor-power sold corresponds to one hour of labor expended. The value of labor-power is normalized to an hour of labor-power.) The proximate source of surplus value is the fact that the value of labor-power is less than unity, so that productive workers as a class receive an equivalent in wages for only a fraction of the labor time they actually expend. The ratio of surplus value to wages, which is an alternative method of describing the division of social labor time between wages and surplus value, Marx calls the *rate of exploitation* or the *rate of surplus value*.

The labor theory of value also requires us to distinguish between wages and the costs of other means of production. The value of other means of production than labor power reappears unchanged in the total value of output, and is thus, from the point of view of the labor theory of value, a non-expanding or *constant capital*. The value of wages reappears in the value of output sold augmented by the addition of the surplus value and is thus expanding or *variable capital*. One of the main explanatory claims of the labor theory of value is that changes in constant capital and variable capital have different effects on the amount of surplus value produced.

The aggregate surplus value is paid out in a variety of forms: as the wages and salaries of administrative and sales employees; as fees for legal and financial business services; as interest payments on borrowed money capital; as direct and indirect taxes; and finally as the profit of the capital itself.

The level of the value of labor-power is obviously a variable of critical importance to a capitalist economic system. The general level of the value of labor-power must reflect the relation between the standard of living of workers and average labor productivity in the system. Capitalist economic systems normally function with a margin of potentially employable workers, which Marx calls the *reserve army of labor*. In Marx's view the exhaustion of this reserve, if it occurs, will be automatically offset by the contraction in surplus value and hence capital accumulation and demand for labor-power that results from a rise in the value of labor-power. Here is a main point of contrast with neoclassical general equilibrium theory, which assumes full utilization of all resources, including labor, and sees the limiting factor in the rise of the value of labor-power with full employment as the psychological reluctance of capitalists to accumulate rather than consume as the rate of profit falls.

Capital is self-expanding value, but the secret of its expansion is the exploitation of labor through the mechanism of the wage.

6. THE CIRCUIT OF CAPITAL

The flow of value through a capitalist enterprise, or group of enterprises, can be thought of as a circuit. In qualitative terms this circuit shows the sequence of forms value takes in capitalist production:

$$M - C\{(MP, LP) \ldots (P) \ldots C' - M'\} = M + \Delta M \qquad (6.1)$$

where value in the form of money (M) is used to purchase commodities (C), namely means of production and labor-power (MP, LP) which pass through the production process (P) to become a new commodity (C') which in turn is sold for money (M') which comprises the return of the original money capital, M, and a surplus value (ΔM).

This motion of value is also summarized in the income or profit-and-loss statement of capitalist accounting practice:

Sales	$M' = M + \Delta M$
less labor costs	LP
less nonlabor costs	MP
(including depreciation)	
equals gross profit on sales	ΔM
or surplus value	(6.2)

The aim of the circuit of capital is the expansion of value, in contrast with the circuit of commodity exchange

$$C - M - C' \qquad (6.3)$$

where commodities of a given value are sold for money to purchase a different bundle of commodities of the same value. In particular the $C - M - C'$ circuit comes to an end with the purchase of the final bundle C', since the economic agent has transformed its value into the most desirable attainable collection of use-values. The $C - M - C'$ circuit can be renewed only by an external recreation of its initial conditions, where the economic agent possesses a group of commodities that is not its most desired collection among all those of the same value. The $M - C \ldots (P) \ldots C' - M'$ circuit, on the other hand, recreates its own initial conditions, namely a mass of money value in tension with its own possibility of expansion through the circuit of capital.[3]

The fundamental object of study of Marxist economic theory is an ensemble of capitals traversing the circuit of capital. The problem is to understand the characteristic behavior of such a system driven proximately by the pursuit of surplus value. Each capital may, of course, have many value flows in different phases of the circuit at any one moment.

---

3. Neoclassical economic theory, since it acknowledges only the pursuit of use-value as an ultimately rational end of human activity, cannot conceptualize capital accumulation as a self-determined phenomenon, and in its place studies economic growth driven by changes in external variables like population or resource availability. Patinkin [40] exemplifies the dilemmas of the C–M–C' approach in his parable of "manna".

Each phase of the circuit of capital takes some time for its completion. A certain period elapses between the hiring of labor-power and the purchase of means of production to begin the process and the emergence of a finished commodity at its end. Likewise, a finished commodity waits for a certain length of time before it is sold for money, and the money proceeds from sales stay in the hands of the firm for a period in the form of money before being spent to purchase labor-power and means of production to start a new phase of the circuit. Thus at any moment in time we would find certain stocks of value in each of the phases of the circuit of capital. The asset side of the balance sheet of a capitalist firm measures these stocks:

Assets
Financial assets   } Money capital
Inventories of raw materials
    and partly finished goods   } Productive capital
Undepreciated long-lived assets
Inventories of finished goods
    awaiting sale   } Commercial capital   (6.4)

The size of these stocks of value depend on the historical flows of value through the circuit and on the structure of time lags in production. In this conception the flows of value are fundamental, the stocks arising as an incidental consequence of the fact that it takes some time for value to traverse each phase of the circuit of capital.

A convenient way of modelling the circuit of capital mathematically is to use convolutions to link flows of value in different parts of the circuit. For example, we can regard a dollar laid out to purchase labor-power and means of production at a certain time t as emerging in the form of finished commodities at later times, perhaps distributed over a whole interval of the future. The pattern of output may be a simple time delay of duration T in production. A dollar of capital outlay at time 0 waits for the period T and then emerges all at once in the form of a finished commodity. On the other hand, more general cases exist in which the value of the capital outlay at time 0 emerges gradually and continuously over the future. The integral of the distribution describing this time pattern over the whole positive half line must be equal to 1, since all the value laid out as capital must emerge sooner or later from production. This method can describe quite general temporal patterns of input-output relations. For example, some of the capital outlay may experience a simple time delay (circulating capital) and some may emerge uniformly in the value of finished products over a period (uniformly depreciating fixed capital) (cf Ref. 54).

To construct a model of the circuit of aggregate social capital, let $C(t)$ be the flow of value of capital outlays at time t: $P(t)$ the flow of value of finished commodities emerging from production at time t, including surplus value; $R(t)$ the flow of value of realization, including surplus value at time t; $a(., t')$ the time profile of production lags for capital laid out at time t'; $b(., t')$ the time profile of realization lags for finished commodities emerging at time t'; $c(., t')$ the time profile of lags in the recommital of money realized at time t' to production; $q(t')$ the value markup (the ratio of surplus value to costs of production) on capital laid out at time t'; and $p(t')$ the proportion of surplus value realized at time t' that is recommited to production.

According to the labor theory of value, in the aggregate value is created only by the expenditure of social labor. If the money wage at time t' is $w(t')$, the monetary expression of value $m(t')$ (the ratio that expresses the labor time equivalent to an hour's labor), and the fraction of capital outlays going to the purchase of labor-power at time t' is $k(t')$, the total labor hours set in motion at time t' are $(k(t')C(t'))/w(t')$. This labor time has the money equivalent at time $t'(k(t')C(t')/w(t')m(t')$, since $1/m(t')$ is the monetary expression of the value added by an hour of labor at time t'. The surplus value arising from this labor time is just $(1 - w(t')m(t'))(k(t')C(t')/w(t')m(t'))$, and the markup $q(t')$ is

$$q(t') = \frac{(1 - w)mk}{wm} = ek \qquad (6.5)$$

where $e(t')$ is the rate of surplus value at time t'. The money surplus value realized by capital may be larger or smaller than this if the monetary expression of value changes between the time capital is laid out and time of realization of the finished commodity. For the moment assume that the value of money is constant through time.

The parameter p is necessary because not all of the surplus value realized is recommitted to production. Some part is spent on the consumption of capitalists, is taxed and spend by the State, or is used up in unproductive expenditures of capitalist firms.

Given these basic parameters, the flows in the circuit of capital are related by the convolutions:

$$P(t) = \int_{-\infty}^{t} C(t')(1 + q(t'))a(t - t'; t') \, dt' \quad (6.6a)$$

$$Q(t) = \int_{-\infty}^{t} C(t')a(t - t'; t') \, dt' \quad (6.6b)$$

$$R(t) = \int_{-\infty}^{t} P(t')b(t - t'; t') \, dt' \quad (6.7a)$$

$$R'(t) = \int_{-\infty}^{t} Q(t')b(t - t'; t') \, dt' \quad (6.7b)$$

$$R''(t) = \int_{-\infty}^{t} (P(t') - Q(t')b(t - t'; t') \, dt' \quad (6.7c)$$

$$C(t) = \int_{-\infty}^{t} (R'(t') + p(t')R''(t'))c(t - t'; t') \, dt'$$

$$(6.8)$$

Here $R'(t')$ is the part of realization that corresponds to the recovery of capital outlays, and $R''(t')$ is the part that corresponds to the realization of surplus value. $Q(t')$ is the flow of the value of finished commodities at cost.

If $F(t)$ is aggregate financial capital, $N(t)$ aggregate productive capital, and $X(t)$ aggregate commodity capital, we have the relations:

$$dF(t)/dt = R'(t) + p(t)R''(t) - C(t) \quad (6.9)$$

$$dN(t)/dt = C(t) - Q(t) \quad (6.10)$$

$$dX(t)/dt = P(t) - S(t) \quad (6.11)$$

The relations (6.6)–(6.11) describe the flow of value through the aggregate social circuit of capital in a completely general fashion, since the time lag profiles may vary arbitrarily over time.

7. SIMPLE AND EXPANDED REPRODUCTION

In a real capitalist economy the reinvestment of surplus value in production constantly expands the aggregate social capital, which is the phenomenon of *accumulation*. Real accumulation involves the constant revolutionizing of the production process: the adoption of new techniques of production, often on a larger scale, the creation of new products, the reorganization of capitals, and so on. These qualitative changes in production find their reflection in changes in the parameters that govern the circuit of capital, the composition of capital outlays (k in the notation of the last section), the value of labor-power (wm, or e) which determine the value markup (q), the rate of capitalization (p), and the production, realization and finance lags.

As a first step toward analyzing these complex, and necessarily nonlinear problems, let us consider the imaginary situation of a capitalist economy that reproduces itself without changes in the underlying parameters. This is the exercise Marx, Ref. 28, II, ch XX, XXI, calls the analysis of the *simple* and *expanded* reproduction of capital. Marx's analysis there focusses on the problem of proportionality between production of means of production and means of subsistence. To begin with I will abstract from this problem and look at the aggregate value conditions for reproduction.

Analytically the assumption of simple and expanded reproduction requires that the parameters p, q, and the lag functions $a(.)$, $b(.)$ and $c(.)$ of the model set out above be constant through time. When this is true the basic equations become:

$$P(t) = (1 + q) \int_{-\infty}^{t} C(t')a(t - t') \, dt' \tag{7.1a}$$

$$Q(t) = \int_{-\infty}^{t} C(t')a(t - t') \, dt \tag{7.1b}$$

$$R(t) = \int_{-\infty}^{t} P(t')b(t-t')\, dt \tag{7.2a}$$

$$R'(t) = \int_{-\infty}^{t} Q(t')b(t-t')\, dt' \tag{7.2b}$$

$$R''(t) = \int_{-\infty}^{t} (P(t') - Q(t'))b(t-t')\, dt \tag{7.2c}$$

$$C(t) = \int_{-\infty}^{t} (R'(t') + pR''(t'))c(t-t')\, dt' \tag{7.3}$$

Simple or expanded reproduction correspond to exponential growth paths for all the flows of value. Since the system is homogeneous of first degree in the absolute size of the flow $C(t)$, normalize by assuming $C(0) = 1$, so that $C(t) = \exp(gt)$ for an unknown growth rate g on an exponential path. By successive substitution we reach:

$$P(0) = (1+q)a^*(g) \tag{7.4a}$$

$$Q(0) = a^*(g) \tag{7.4b}$$

$$R(0)\ (1+q)a^*(g)b^*(g) \tag{7.5a}$$

$$R'(0) = a^*(g)b^*(g) \tag{7.5b}$$

$$R''(0) = qa^*(g)b^*(g) \tag{7.5c}$$

$$C(0) = 1 = (1+pq)a^*(g)b^*(g)c^*(g) \tag{7.6}$$

where

$$a^*(s) = \int_{0}^{\infty} \exp(-st')a(t')\, dt' \tag{7.7}$$

which is the Laplace transform of the transfer function $a(.)$, and similarly for $b^*(s)$ and $c^*(s)$. Since the lag functions are nonnegative and integrate to 1 over the positive half-line, we have (assuming that the lags are not instantaneous):

$$a^*(0) = b^*(0) = c^*(0) = 1 \tag{7.8a}$$

$$da^*(s)/ds,\ db^*(s)/ds,\ dc^*(s)/ds < 0 \tag{7.8b}$$

$$\lim_{s\to} a^*(s) = \lim_{s\to} b^*(s) = \lim_{s\to} c^*(s) = 0 \tag{7.8c}$$

Equation (7.6) is the characteristic equation of the system. It has a unique positive real root g, the *expanded reproduction mode* of the system. When $g = 0$ the right hand side of (7.6) is $(1 + pq) > 1$ unless $pq = 0$. If $pq = 0$ the rate of growth is zero, corresponding to what Marx calls *simple reproduction*. If $pq > 0$, the right hand side of (7.6) is greater than 1 for $g = 0$, but declines monotonically to zero as g increases. Thus there will be a unique positive g for which (7.6) is satisfied.

Solution of (6.9)–(6.11) yields the aggregate balance sheet ratios of the system:

$$F(0) = (1 + pq)a^*(g)b^*(g)(1 - c^*(g))/g \qquad (7.9)$$

$$N(0) = (1 - a^*(g))/g \qquad (7.10)$$

$$X(0) = a^*(g)(1 - b^*(g))/g \qquad (7.11)$$

These are all positive at the growth rate g and show the ratio of the assets to the current flow of capital outlays.

Conventional national income accounting focusses on the flows of value added, wages plus surplus value, in a national system of capitals. If $Y(t)$ is the value of net product including the markup, we have:

$$Y(t) = P(t) - \int_{-\infty}^{t} (1 - k(t'))C(t')a(t - t'; t') \, dt' \qquad (7.12)$$

In the case of simple or expanded reproduction this simplifies to:

$$Y(0) = P(0) - (1 - k)Q(0) = (k + q)a^*(g) \qquad (7.13)$$

The dependence of the growth rate on the parameters of the system is easy to see from (7.6). A rise in pq raises the growth rate; any shift of $a(.)$ that lowers $a^*(s)$ for all s will also raise g, and similarly for $b(.)$ and $c(.)$.

The *rate of profit*, r, is the ratio of the realized surplus value to the total capital tied up in the system. On an exponential path this is:

$$r = R''/(F + N + X) = g/p \qquad (7.14)$$

This is the "Cambridge equation" linking the growth rate of the system, the profit rate, and the rate of capitalization of surplus value. (These results have a close relation to the growth theory results in Ref. 6. 20 and 22. See also Ref. 42. The relation between the profit rate and the growth rate has been given an elegant exposition in Ref 38.)

8. AGGREGATE DEMAND IN THE CIRCUIT OF CAPITAL

The model of expanded reproduction developed in the last section abstracts from the problem of the source of aggregate money demand to realize produced commodities. It does this in assuming that the realization lag $b(.)$ is a given parameter of the system; sales are determined by production in this model.

In a closed capitalist economy (such as the world capitalist economy) the ultimate sources of aggregate demand are the capital outlays of firms to begin production, and realized surplus value. Capital outlays provide the demand for produced means of production and the wage incomes of worker households. Other household income arises from the wages of administrative, sales, and business services employees who do not produce new value, and from the dividends and interest paid to capitalist households (remembering that some households may have both labor and property income), both paid out of realized surplus value. State expenditure is ultimately financed by taxes on surplus value or incomes, or from the surplus value appropriated by State enterprises. There may be time lags in the spending of households or the State as well. The "life-cycle" and "permanent income" theories of household consumption can be expressed in terms of linear or nonlinear lags in consumption spending. See Ref. 23 and 14.

We can model aggregate demand in the circuit of capital by allowing the realization lag $b(.)$ to become a determined variable and specifying the dependence of aggregate demand on the flows of value in the circuit.

The sources of demand are:

$$D(t) = (1 - k(t))C(t) + \int_{-\infty}^{t} k(t')C(t')\, \mathrm{d}(t - t';\, t')\, \mathrm{d}t'$$

$$+ \int_{-\infty}^{t} (1 - p(t'))R''(t')e(t - t';\, t')\, \mathrm{d}t' + B'(t) \quad (8.1)$$

where the first term represents purchases of means of production, including gross investment in fixed capital, the second, workers' spending of wages (passed through the lag function $d(.)$), the third consumption and State spending out of surplus value (passed through the spending lag $e(.)$), and the last, $B'(t)$, household and State spending financed by new borrowing. The lags $d(.)$ and $e(.)$ have the same properties as we assumed for $a(.)$ in (7.8).

If $B'(t) = 0$, and capitals finance new production only out of past sales (as is implied by (6.8)), there will be insufficient aggregate demand on a path of expanded reproduction with a positive growth rate unless all the spending lags are zero. To see this, assume that $C(t) = \exp(gt)$, and that k, g, p, and the lag functions $a(.)$, $b(.)$, $c(.)$, $d(.)$, and $e(.)$ are all invariant through time. Then:

$$
\begin{aligned}
D(0) &= (1 - k) + kd^*(g) + q(1 - p)e^*(g)a^*(g)b^*(g) \\
&= (1 - k(1 - d^*(g)))(1 + pq)a^*(g)b^*(g)c^*(g) \\
&\quad + q(1 - p)e^*(g)a^*(g)b^*(g) \\
&= a^*(g)b^*((g)[(1 - k(1 - d^*(g)))c^*(g) \\
&\quad + q(p(1 - k(1 - d^*(g)))c^*(g) + (1 - p)e^*(g))] \\
&< a^*(g)b^*(g)(1 + q) = R(0) \hspace{2cm} (8.2)
\end{aligned}
$$

since $d^*(g)$, $c^*(g)$, and $e^*(g) < 1$ for $g > 0$. On a path of expanded reproduction with no borrowing past sales are insufficient to realize current production because of lags in spending.

This problem has two practical solutions (see Ref. 26, 27, 28, II, ch XXI, and 13). First, in an economy where money is a produced commodity, like gold, the money commodity need not be sold in order to be realized as money value, since it is already in the money form of value. Thus the gap between aggregate money demand and the realization of produced commodities can be filled by gold production at the appropriate scale. If $S(t)$ is the value of the flow of sales at time t, and $G(t)$ is the value of the flow of gold production at time t:

$$
R(t) = S(t) + G(t) = D(t) + G(t) \hspace{2cm} (8.3)
$$

On a path of expanded reproduction without borrowing we have $S(0) = D(0)$, and:

$$G(0) = R(0) - S(0)$$
$$= k(1 - d^*(g)) + q[(1 - (p(1 - k(1 - d^*(g)))) + (1 - p)e^*(g)] \tag{8.4}$$

Second, this gap can be filled by new borrowing, either by capitals to finance capital outlays, by households to finance consumption spending, or by the State to finance its expenditure. To allow for capital outlays financed by debt, we reformulate (6.8) as:

$$C(t) = \int_{-\infty}^{t} (R'(t) + p(t')R''(t))c(t - t'; t') \, dt' + B(t) \tag{8.5}$$

where $B(t)$ is new capitalist borrowing.

The steady-state growth rate in expanded reproduction now corresponds to the size of new borrowing, since we have from (8.3) and (8.1):

$$R(0) = D(0) + G(0)$$
$$= [(1 - k(1 - d^*(g))) + B'(0) + G(0)](1 + q)/$$
$$[1 + q(1 - (1 - p)e^*(g))] \tag{8.6}$$

$$C(0) = 1 = (R'(0) + pR''(0))c^*(g) + B(0) \text{ or} \tag{8.7a}$$

$$1 - B(0) = c^*(g)R(0)[(1 + pq)/(1 + q)] \text{ or} \tag{8.7b}$$

$$1 = B(0) + \frac{c^*(g)[(1 - k(1 - d^*(g))) + B'(0) + G(0)](1 + pg)}{1 + q(1 - (1 - p)e^*(g))} \tag{8.7c}$$

The higher is g, the smaller is the right hand side of (8.7c) for given values of $B(0)$, $B'(0)$, $G(0)$, p, q, and the spending lag functions $c(.)$, $d(.)$ and $e(.)$. This expression shows that new non-capitalist borrowing and gold production play the same role in linking realization and production in the circuit of capital. The larger are B or $(B' + G)$ the higher will be the realized rate of expansion g.

But there is a limit to how high this rate of expansion can

become, imposed by the time lag in production and the social limits to the appropriation of surplus value. A higher g is achieved by reducing the realization lag, and in that fashion accelerating the motion of value around the circuit. This reduction in realization time cannot proceed beyond the point where the realization lag is zero.

To study this limit mathematically, we need an explicit expression for the realization lag $b(.)$. The simplest way to make $b(.)$ endogenous is to assume that this lag is a simple time delay T, so that inventories of finished commodities awaiting sale are accounted for in the model on a first-in first-out basis. A commodity sold at time t has waited a period $T(t)$ to be sold. Given a path of production $Q(.)$ and a path of sales $S(.)$, the function $T(t)$ must satisfy the first-in first-out relation:

$$\int_{t-T(t)}^{t+\Delta t - T(t+\Delta t)} Q(t')\, dt' = \int_{t}^{t+\Delta t} S(t')\, dt' \qquad (8.8)$$

The mean value theorem assures us that:

$$Q(t')\left[t - T(t + \Delta t) - T(t)\right] = S(t'')\Delta t \qquad (8.9)$$

for t', t'' in the relevant intervals. Dividing by t and taking the limit as $t - > 0$, we get:

$$Q(t - T(t))\left[1 - dT/dt\right] = S(t) \text{ or} \qquad (8.10a)$$

$$\frac{dT}{dt} = 1 - \frac{S(t)}{Q(t - T(t))} \qquad (8.10b)$$

The speed of expansion of the system is limited by the requirement that T be nonnegative. On a steady-state path T is a constant, so we have from (8.10):

$$Q(t - T(t)) = S(t) \text{ or} \qquad (8.11a)$$

$$Q(0)\exp(-gT) = S(0) \text{ or, from} \qquad (8.11b)$$

$$T = (1/g)\ln(P(0)/S(0)) \geqslant 0, \qquad (8.11c)$$

$$(1 + q(1 - (1 - p)e^*(g)))a^*(g) \geqslant (1 - k(1 - d^*(g)))$$
$$+ B'(0) + (q/(1 + q))e^*(g)(1 - p)G(0) \qquad (8.11d)$$

When $d^*(g) = e^*(g) = 1$ identically, and $G(0) = B'(0) = 0$, this simplifies to:

$$(1 + pq)a^*(g) \geqslant 1 \qquad (8.12)$$

The g^* for which $(1 + pq)a^*(g^*) = 1$ is a *limiting rate* of accumulation, given technology and the social relations of production.

A higher rate of gold production or of new borrowing raises the realized rate of expansion of this system by facilitating realization (which is, in effect, Keynes' discovery [23]) but this process ultimately runs into the barrier constituted by the most rapid growth rate compatible with the time lags in production and the rate of exploitation (the object of von Neumann's analysis [56]).

There is no immediate reason to think that a capitalist economy operating according to these principles will tend to create a demand for labor-power equal to the amount of labor-power the population can and will supply. In other words, there is no presumption that the capitalist system will reach a state of full employment, even when it is expanding at its maximal rate.

The rate for labor-power in the circuit of capital depends on the total capital circulating, the proportion, k, that is spent on labor-power and the wage, w. If L is the total demand for labor-power:

$$L(t) = kC(t)/w(t) \qquad (8.13)$$

A fall in money wages would increase the demand for labor-power instantaneously only if k were to fall by a smaller proportion. Since k reflects, in the short-run, primarily the technical proportions between labor and non-labor inputs to production required by the currently adopted techniques of production, it is likely that a fall in w will be matched by a fall in k, so that the demand for labor-power would not increase.

A fall in money wages, if the value of money remains stable, or rises by a smaller proportion, corresponds to a fall in the value of labor-power, and a rise in the rate of exploitation of productive labor. This change has two effects. By raising the rate of profit it may induce a switch in the techniques used to produce output, which would be reflected in a change in the technical proportions in which labor and nonlabor inputs enter production, as well as a revaluation of the nonlabor inputs themselves. This effect is studied in the literature on distribution, pricing, and choice of technique (see Ref. 15, 39 and 53). An important conclusion of this literature is that a rise in the rate of profit may not increase the demand for labor-power for a given flow of capital value.

The rise in the rate of profit that follows from a rise in the rate of exploitation has another, more certain, consequence for the demand for labor-power. An increase in the markup, q, resulting from a rise in the rate of exploitation, leads, if the capitalization rate does not fall in the same proportion, to a higher rate of accumulation of capital, and hence, for given k and w, to a more rapid growth of the demand for labor-power.

Thus the problem of the degree to which labor is employed in a capitalist system is complex and historical. It depends on the interaction of accumulation, technical change, and the movement of the value of labor-power, and on historical, sociological, and political factors that influence the potential labor-power available to the system. There is in this theory no presumption that accumulation and wage flexibility will lead to full employment of the potential available labor force, only a set of relations that can be used to investigate this question in a specific historical context.

Despite the possible irrelevance of a full-employment limit to capital accumulation, we have seen that there is another, internal limit to the accumulation of capital that arises from the inter-action of the rate of exploitation of labor and the time lags in production.

9. ACCUMULATION AND REALIZATION OUT OF THE STEADY STATE

The relations between new borrowing and the actual rate of growth of capitalist system derived in the last section were of a comparative dynamic type in that they compared fully realized steady-state paths of expanded reproduction.

These relations suggest that there is an intimate connection between aggregate demand and realized rates of increase in sales and production on arbitrary paths in the circuit of capital model. This connection brings us to the heart of classic Keynesian analyses, which emphasize the role of aggregate demand in governing the path of production in a capitalist economy.

The demand parameters on which Keynes focusses attention are propensities to consume, which govern household spending out of wage and nonwage income, and liquidity preference, which indirectly governs capitalist firms' spending on new investment. These parameters appear in the circuit of capital model as the spending lags $c(.)$, $d(.)$ and $e(.)$. The effect of aggregate demand on production in Keynesian models depends on the relation between sales and production, and the resulting movements of inventories of finished commodities awaiting sale. These effects are summed up in the circuit of capital model in the variable realization lag T. As T becomes larger capitals experience greater difficulty in selling their product, and a growth in inventories of finished commodities awaiting sale.

As Keynes argues in a static equilibrium framework, there is a close connection between the parameters governing aggregate demand and the state of realization in a capitalist economy.

To simplify the mathematical expressions involved, assume that the spending lags $c(.)$, $d(.)$ and $e(.)$ are all simple time delays with time constants T_f, T_w, and T_p respectively: a finance delay in capital spending, a wage delay in workers' household spending, and a profit delay in the spending of household revenues that arise from the flow of surplus value. The same first-in first-out reasoning as supported (8.10) leads, assuming no household or state borrowing, to the relations:

$$\frac{dT}{dt} = 1 - \frac{S(t)}{P(t-T)} \tag{9.1}$$

$$\frac{dT_w}{dt} = 1 - \frac{E_w(t)}{W(t-T_w)} = 1 - \frac{E_w(t)}{kC(t-T_w)} \tag{9.2}$$

$$\frac{dT_p}{dt} = 1 - \frac{E_p}{(1-p)R''(t-T_p)} \tag{9.3}$$

$$\frac{dT_f}{dt} = 1 - \frac{C(t) - B(t)}{R'(t-T_f) + pR''(t-T_f)} \tag{9.4}$$

In this analysis, assume gold production is zero (or a monetary system not based on a commodity money), so that realization, R, is equal to sales, S. E_w is workers' household spending, W is wages, and E_p is household spending derived from revenues that are part of surplus value.

Suppose that an economy is on an arbitrary path consistent with the basic circuit of capital relations (6.6)–(6.8). We have, from (8.1) and (9.2)–(9.4):

$$S(t) = D(t) = E_w(t) + E_p(t) + (1 - k)C(t)$$

$$= [(1 - dT_w/dt)kC(t - T_w) + (1 - dT_p/dt)(1 - p) S''(t - T_p)$$

$$+ (1 - k)(1 - dT_f/dt)(S'(t - F_f) + pS''(t - T_f)) + (1 - k) B(t)$$

$$\tag{9.5}$$

so that

$$dT/dt = 1 - [(1 - dT_w/dt)kC(t - T_w)$$

$$+ (1 - dT_p/dt)(1 - p) S''(t - T_p)$$

$$+ (1 - dT_f/dt)(1 - k)(S'(t - T_f) + pS''(t - T_f))$$

$$+ (1 - k) B(t)]/P(t - T) \tag{9.6}$$

Thus on a path where spending lags are becoming longer (the derivatives of T_w, T_p, and T_f are negative) the realization lag T will also be rising faster than it would have if the spending delays were stable. Note also the important role that $B(t)$, capital outlays financed by new borrowing, plays in determining the path of the realization delay T.

Capital outlays financed by new borrowing create a flow of value to finance that new borrowing by realizing finished commodities held in inventory. If capitals borrow without spending the borrowed value on capital outlays, the finance time delay T_f will be increasing, by (9.4). If spending time delays are constant, an increase in capital outlays financed by new borrowing creates the flow of money value necessary to finance itself. This is a version of the Keynesian principle that the expansion of investment creates the saving necessary to finance itself.

The process of self-finance does, however, have a limit, namely the exhaustion of inventories of finished goods awaiting sale or (more broadly) of excess productive capacity. It is striking that this limit is internal to the circuit of capital, and need have no relation to the state of labor markets.

10. CHANGES IN THE VALUE OF MONEY

Upto this point I have abstracted from changes in the value of money, the ratio of aggregate labor time to aggregate value added.

In a commodity money system, one of the produced commodities, say, gold, becomes the socially accepted general equivalent. In this case the monetary unit (dollar, franc or whatever) is defined as being a certain amount of the money commodity (one U.S. dollar was originally 1/20th of an ounce of gold, for instance).

The gold price of a commodity in such a system tends to reflect the ratio between the price of production of that commodity (costs of inputs plus the average profit rate on the capital values tied up in production) and the price of production of gold. (Of course, further factors influencing the price of commodities, such as monopoly power or State intervention, may alter this relation.) In such a system the value of money tends to be equal to the aggregate labor time divided by the value added at the gold prices of commodities.

It sometimes happens that the State, especially under the fiscal pressures of war, issues paper "fiat" money that has no guaranteed rate of convertibility into gold. Leading examples are the British government's issue of paper pounds during the Napoleonic Wars, and the U.S. government's issue of greenback dollars during the Civil War. This paper money often goes to a discount against gold (a paper greenback dollar might be worth, say, only 50¢ in gold) because more paper is issued than could be absorbed by the circulation of currency in immediate transactions, or because of speculation on the military fortunes of the issuing State. In these cases the value of gold money continues to be determined by the price of production of gold relative to the price of production of other commodities. The existence of the fiat money merely raises the additional problem of the determinants of the discount between paper and gold.

In the twentieth century a new monetary situation evolved in which the relations between national monetary units (dollar, pound, franc, mark, etc.) and gold became weaker and weaker. This is different from the fiat money case, since now there is no gold money against which the dollar or pound or franc can be valued. In these circumstances the value of money is determined historically, by the inherited level of money prices assigned to commodities by producers on average, and by the average changes in those prices induced by the pricing strategies of capitals faced with a series of concrete conditions of demand. The value of money in this kind of system changes because on average the ensemble of capitalist firms raises or lowers the money prices of their products.

Such changes in the value of money may or may not lead to changes in the value of labor-power and the rate of exploitation, depending on the effectiveness with which workers defend the purchasing power of their wages.

Proximately, then, in such a system two important factors combine to determine the rate of change in the value of money. First, growth in average labor productivity tends to reduce the value of money, because less labor is expended per unit of use values produced. Second, average conditions of demand may permit capitals to raise the price per unit of use values, or may force them to lower prices per unit of use values. We can see these two factors if we write the value of money as the product of the price level and an index of average labor productivity:

$$m = \frac{\text{aggregate labor time}}{\text{aggregate value added}}$$

$$= \frac{\text{labor time}}{\text{index of use values produced}}$$

$$\times \frac{\text{index of use values produced}}{\text{value added}} \qquad (10.1)$$

Two problems arise in treating changes in the value of money within the circuit of capital framework. First, we need to distinguish between value flows measured in money terms and value flows measured in terms of social labor. Second, we need to propose some hypothesis as to what governs the historical evolution of the value of money.

The first problem is easily resolved conceptually. Adopt the convention that a variable prefixed with an asterisk is measured in money terms, and one without an asterisk is measured in terms of labor time. For example:

$$*C(t) = C(t)/m(t) \qquad (10.2)$$

We can write the aggregate demand as:

$$
\begin{aligned}
*D(t) = {} & (1 - k(t))*C(t) \\
& + \int_{-\infty}^{t} k(t')*C(t') \, \mathrm{d}(t - t'; t') \, \mathrm{d}t' \\
& + \int_{-\infty}^{t} (1 - p(t'))*R''(t')e(t - t'; t') \, \mathrm{d}t' \\
& + *B'(t) \qquad (10.3)
\end{aligned}
$$

This formulation implicitly assumes that the time profile of household spending streams depend on the time profile of money incomes. In other words, as the value of money changes households accept the labor value loss or gain on the principal value of their stocks of financial assets, and continue to spend the remainder in the same time pattern. An alternative conception would treat the changes in the value of money as current income, which would enter the households' spending lag process at the time it occurred.

We have, by a similar argument for firms:

$$*C(t) = \int_{-\infty}^{t} (*R'(t') + p(t')*R''(t'))c(t - t'; t') \, \mathrm{d}t + *B(t) \qquad (10.4)$$

The aggregate demand dynamics now are modelled in money terms. We can translate these money flows, given a path of m, back into labor value flows by multiplying by the value of money.

$$C(t) = *C(t)m(t) \qquad (10.5)$$

$$R(t) = *R(t)m(t) \qquad (10.6)$$

What determines the path of the value of money? In a non-commodity-money system, the change in the value of money over a period depends on the average price change for commodities and the change in labor productivity over the same period. Suppose for the moment that we abstract from changes in labor productivity. It seems likely that the average change in money prices of commodities will depend on the average difficulty capitals have in selling commodities, which is conveniently measured by the time delay in selling commodities, T. A large T will signal difficulties in selling, so that capitals will not raise prices rapidly, and may be forced to lower them, and the value of money will be stable or rising. A small T signals ease in selling, conditions of strong demand on markets, rising prices, and a falling value of money.

$$\mathrm{d}m(t)/\mathrm{d}t = u(T), \text{ with } u' > 0 \tag{10.7}$$

Notice that this formulation has no necessary connection with the state of the labor market. Changes in the value of money are a reflection of the underlying limits to the rate of accumulation imposed by the value of labor-power, the composition of capital, the capitalization rate, and the time lags of the system expressed by (8.11).

In the case of expanded reproduction we can easily see explicitly the relation between the value and money accounting categories. Suppose that $*R'(t)$ is the recovery of historic money costs in realization at time t, and $*R''(t)$ the realization of surplus value in money terms, which now includes money gains or losses due to the change in the value of money in the production and realization periods. Then, if we write the money markup as $*q$, and the value markup as q, we have:

$$*R(0) = R(0) = (1 + *q)*R'(0) = (1 + q)R'(0) \tag{10.8}$$

The recovery of money costs corresponds to capital outlays in the past:

$$*R'(0) = \int_{-\infty}^{0} *C(t')a(t - t') \, \mathrm{d}t'$$

$$= a*(*g)\exp(-*gT) \tag{10.9}$$

and similarly

$$R'(0) = a^*(g)\exp(-gT) \tag{10.10}$$

Thus we have

$$(1 + {}^*q)/(1 + q) = R'(0)/^*R'(0) = a^*(g)\exp(uT)/a^*(g + u) \tag{10.11}$$

where $u = {}^*g - g$, the difference between the rate of expansion of capital measured in money and the rate of expansion measured in labor value. The money markup exceeds the value markup by two factors, the change in the value of money during the production period, measured by the ratio of $a^*(g)$ to $a^*(g + u)$, and the change in the value of money during the realization period, measured by $\exp(uT) = \exp((g + u)T)/\exp(gT)$.

With this link we can move from the money accounting scheme to the value accounting scheme and back. The actual money rate of growth, $^*g$, will be determined by the money analog to (8.7):

$$1 = {}^*B(0) + \frac{c^*({}^*g)\,(1 + {}^*gp)\,[1 - k(1 - d^*({}^*g)) + {}^*B'(0)]}{1 + {}^*q(1 - (1 - p)e^*({}^*g))} \tag{10.12}$$

The division of this rate of expansion between changes in the value of money and real accumulation are given by

$$u = u(T) \tag{10.13}$$

where T is determined by the money analog to (8.11c).

$$T = \frac{1}{g}\ln\left\{\frac{a^*({}^*g)\,(1 + {}^*g(1 - (1 - p)e^*({}^*g)))}{1 - k(1 - d^*({}^*g)) + B'(0)}\right\} \tag{10.14}$$

With this method of treating changes in the value of money we have a system where the realized money rate of growth depends on the strength of aggregate demand. As this realized rate approaches the maximal rate of expansion of the system, a larger and large part of the monetary expansion takes the form of a depreciation in the value of money.

11. CREDIT AND INTEREST

The recommittal of money capital to production in the circuit of capital may take place directly, as in the cases of the recovery of capital outlays and the retention of profit by a capitalist firm, or indirectly, as in the case when a firm or household lends money realized in sales to another firm. This lending involves new forms of value, and of surplus value, although it changes nothing in the aggregate analysis of the preceding sections.

In a loan transaction an owner of money capital, the lender, places that money at the disposal of another agent, the borrower, under an enforceable agreement specifying how much money value the borrower will transfer back to the lender at particular future times or in particular future circumstances. If the total money value to be transferred back to the lender exceeds the amount lent, the difference is clearly a form of surplus value, called *interest*.

Loans and interest have probably existed in every society that has developed commodity relations and the money form of value. From the point of view of the labor theory of value, interest is always based on exploitation, since the lender receives command over social labor for which he has given no equivalent. This exploitation may be direct, in cases where the borrower pays the interest out of his or her own labor, like poor peasants who borrow to avoid starving in a bad year, or indirect, when the borrower pays the interest out of revenues derived from some other form of exploitation, like landowners who pay interest out of rents, or capitalists who pay interest out of profit.

In the context of the study of capitalist accumulation, the case of capitalist borrowing is of special significance. In this situation the motive of the capitalist in borrowing is not to ensure his physical survival, nor to alter his consumption pattern. The capitalist either wants to use the borrowed money as money capital in the circuit of capital to appropriate surplus values, or to ensure his economic survival by paying previous debts to avoid bankruptcy. Although borrowing by households to finance consumption and housing expenditures and by the State are quantitatively important in developed capitalist economies, it makes sense as a first step to focus our attention on specifically capitalist borrowing. The interest on loans made to capitalist firms is then ultimately a part of the surplus value appropriated when the loan is used as money capital to initiate capitalist production.

Marx expresses this by extending the diagram of the circuit of capital to include an original loan and the payment of principal and interest.

$$M^* - M - C\{(MP, LP)\ldots(P)\ldots C' - M' - M^{*'} \quad (11.1)$$

Here M^* is the money capital of the *financial capitalist*, which is lent to the *industrial capitalist*, passes through the circuit of capital and expands into M', and $M^{*'}$ is the payment of principal and interest (part of the surplus value) to the financial capitalist.

The "industrial" capitalist, or borrower, and the "financial" capitalist, or lender, are agents playing particular roles in a particular transaction. The same capitalist firm may find itself for one reason or another borrowing in one credit market and lending in another, thus performing the role of financial capitalist in one transaction, and the role of industrial capitalist in another. There is, of course, a tendency toward specialization of capitals in these roles.

The sequence of borrowing and lending may be layered even further because of the informational complexities of credit transactions. Agent A may lend to B, who, in turn, lends to the industrial capitalist, C, perhaps pooling A's funds with those of other lenders. This type of *financial intermediation* becomes highly developed in advanced capitalist societies. The intermediary takes some part of the interest paid by the ultimate borrower. Though intermediation adds greatly to the apparent complexity of financial arrangements, it does not fundamentally alter the source of capitalist interest in surplus value, nor the flows of value in the circuit of capital.

The level of the interest rate is determined by the bargain struck between borrowers and lenders as to what share of the surplus value appropriated through the use of a money capital will be returned to the lender. The analysis of this bargain rests on the nature of the agents involved, whether the marginal borrower and lender are capitalists, or worker or capitalist households, or the State. The central place of capitalist production and capital accumulation in capitalist society suggests that lending by capitalist firms to capitalist firms plays the dominant role in the formation of the interest rate. The problems of the theory of the level of the interest rate appear particularly sharply if we consider the case where there is no household or State borrowing or lending, so that all borrowers and lenders are capitalist firms.

If we abstract from the uncertainty of realization and the possibility of bankruptcy, capitalist firms would bid the interest rate to equality with the average rate of profit. No capitalist firm would lend for less than this, since it could use the funds in its own production to reap the average rate of profit, and no firm would borrow at a higher rate.

In reality, capitalist firms face uncertainty about their sales and face the risk of bankruptcy. At any moment different firms find themselves in different positions with regard to cash flow and the risk of bankruptcy. Some firms experience a shortage of money capital, and others a surplus. The interest rate is formed under these circumstances in the bargaining between the financially strong lenders and financially weak borrowers. Depending on how firms are distributed between these groups, the interest rate may be high or low relative to the average rate of profit (see Ref. 31, 32 on the concept of financial fragility).

These effects cannot be modeled directly in the circuit of capital framework, because they involve higher moments of the distribution of capitalist firms in the space of flows and stocks of value. The circuit of capital model, since it accounts for the social aggregate capital, reflects only changes in the first moment of these distributions.

The borrowing and lending of households and the State, if quantitatively large, can in this view influence the relation between the interest rate and the profit rate by changing the supply of loanable funds to capitalist firms. But since the financial position of the State and of households is largely determined by the circuit of capital, it would be a mistake to think of household or State behavior as fundamentally determining the interest rate (or through it the profit rate) as in neoclassical intertemporal equilibrium theories of the profit rate (as in Ref. 3 and 30).

The same factors that influence the level of the interest rate, the distribution of capitalist firms in the space of flows and stocks of value, also influence the average rate of spending on capital outlays for the system of capitals as a whole. Capitals that are in a weak financial position will conserve money capital by reducing the rate of their capital outlays as well as through borrowing. Capitals that are in a strong financial position will increase their capital outlays as well as their lending, other things being equal. But because the bankruptcy constraint is asymmetrical, a shift of the distribution of capitals toward financial weakness, even if the mean financial position of the aggregate capital is unchanged, will both raise the interest rate relative to the profit rate, and reduce the average rate of capital outlays. This effect is important in understanding the mechanism of crises in the accumulation process.

12. CENTRAL BANK POLICY

The Marxian view that sees the interest rate as the price of money capital within the framework of the circuit of capital is in sharp contrast to the Keynesian view that sees the interest rate as the price of liquidity. In particular, the Marxian view leads us to see central banks as regulating only a part of the spectrum of credit transactions. This in turn implies that central bank policy affects the *difference* between interest rates formed in unregulated markets ("the" interest rate of the last section) and interest rates offered borrowers and lenders by the financial intermediaries that are regulated by the central bank and influences by its policies. The central bank has no direct control over the average level of free market interest rates.

A simplified model of the banking system and central bank control, constructed so as to parallel standard Keynesian models as much as possible, may help to clarify these points.

In this model there are two ways for lending and borrowing to take place. First, lenders and borrowers may meet directly, without intermediation, and negotiate a loan contract at an interest rate r, the open market interest rate (which might be thought of as corresponding to the commercial paper rate in the U.S. financial system). Second, lenders may deposit their funds in banks at a deposit rate r_D. The banks then lend these funds to borrowers at the rate r_B. The banks' only liabilities are deposits, D (abstracting from the bank net worth account) and their assets are loans, L, and reserve deposits at the central bank, R. Assume that there is no hand-to-hand currency issued by the government, so that all transactions are paid by checks, and the quantity of money is just equal to the volume of bank deposits D. Suppose that banks are subject to a reserve requirement t, so that they must hold a fraction t of their deposits as reserves. Furthermore, assume that banks can lend and borrow reserves among themselves (as in the U.S. Federal Funds market) and that the interest rate formed in this market is r_F. The central bank creates reserves by buying direct placement loans, either those issued by private firms, or by the government, but does not lend directly to the banks, so that there is no interest rate in the model corresponding to the discount rate of the U.S. Federal Reserve System.

Suppose, then, that the cost to banks of servicing a loan is proportional to the size of the loan with the constant of proportionality c. Suppose further that, because of transaction costs experienced by some borrowers and lenders, deposits are not perfect substitutes for open market paper as assets for lenders, and bank loans are not perfect substitutes for open market paper to borrowers.

The direct cost to a bank of making a loan arises from its loss of reserves when the borrower uses the loan, since it will either lose the interest r_F it was earning on those reserves, or have to borrow reserves at the interest rate r_F, plus the cost of servicing the loan, c. Competition among banks in the loan market will force r_B to reflect these costs.

$$r_B = r_F + c \qquad (12.1)$$

If the reserve requirement is binding, banks will expand their loans and deposits by the familiar multiplier process until

$$R = tD \qquad (12.2)$$

Since the banks' balance sheets imply

$$D = R + L, \qquad (12.3)$$

we find

$$L = R((1/t) - 1) = aR \qquad (12.4)$$

where $a = ((1/t) - 1)$ is the bank loan multiplier.

The banks will be willing to expand to the limits set by reserves only if the rate they pay on deposits, r_D plus the direct cost of servicing deposits, d, is below their earnings on the excess reserves the deposit gives them.

$$r_D + d \leqslant r_F(1 - t) \qquad (12.5)$$

Finally, the banks must compete with the open market. If F is the total flow of credit, then the ratio of bank lending and deposit rates to the open market rate r would depend on the size of bank lending and borrowing relative to the total.

$$r_B = g(L/F)r, \text{ with } g' < 0 \qquad (12.6)$$

$$r_D = h(L/F)r, \text{ with } h' > 0 \qquad (12.7)$$

The five equations (12.1)–(12.3), (12.6)–(12.7) determine the five variables D, L, r_B, r_D, r_F, given R, r, F, and t, as long as the inequality in (12.5) is satisfied. This solution implicitly assumes some limitation on the competition of banks for deposits, since if banks competed freely, (12.5) would have to hold with equality. This equality could be achieved by allowing d to become an endogenous variable, reflecting the costs banks would incur in competing for deposits.

In this model the central bank has control of the quantity of money through its control over the supply of reserves, but not over the open market interest rate, r, which could be determined by the factors discussed in the last section. The effect of changes in reserves is exhausted by changes in the market price of reserves, r_F, and by changes in the interest rate differential between bank loans and open market paper.

The Keynesian and monetarist models of this process abstract from the possibility of differences between bank lending rates and open market rates, and thus make it appear that the only way the system can adjust to an altered supply of reserves is through changes in the open market rate itself. The Keynesian and monetarist view essentially forces equality in (12.6), and introduces a demand for money function to determine the level of r.

13. PROPORTIONALITY IN SIMPLE AND EXPANDED REPRODUCTION

In Ref. 28, II, ch XXI, Marx sets out a model of *expanded reproduction*. His aim is to find conditions under which a capitalist economy could expand smoothly, assuming that it is not disturbed, as all real capitalist economies are, by changes in techniques of production and the value of labor-power. Two issues especially concern Marx in this analysis: first, the problem of realization, or the source of demand in such an economy, which we have treated in section 8 above; and second, the problem of the proper division of the social capital between the production of elements of constant capital, means of production (which Marx calls Department I) and production of the substance of variable capital, means of subsistence, (which Marx calls Department II).

Although this model is the starting point for the theory of consistent sectoral production planning (as in Leontiev's input-output analysis), Marx's conception differs from the sectoral models in important ways. Marx's Departments are not sectors, because they are defined with reference to the function their output plays in the expanded reproduction of capital, not by the physical characteristics of the output. The same output, structural steel, for example, may be partly used as means of production in building factories, and partly used as means of subsistence in building apartment houses. Thus the steel sector would be divided between Department I and Department II. Furthermore, the motive for a sectoral division of production in an input-output table is primarily to understand the *technical* requirements of achieving a certain production plan. Marx's division corresponds to the division of capital as value between constant and variable capital, a distinction that arises specifically from the labor theory of value. Thus Marx's motive is to understand the *social* conditions for the reproduction of capital. The technical requirements reflected in the input-output table apply to any system of social production, but the division between constant and variable capital, and hence the distinction between Departments I and II reflects a specifically capitalist organization of social production.

We can treat this problem by using the methods already

developed to study the aggregate circuit of capital in section 7 above separately for each Department. We will allow each Department to have its own lag functions for production and finance, its own capitalization rate, composition of capital outlays, and rate of exploitation (to allow for possible deviations of price from value) and hence its own markup.

Two new issues are raised by the division of capital between the two Departments. First, if markups, time lags, and capitalization rates differ between the Departments, it is not certain that they will both be capable of growing at the same exponential rate when each Department finances its expansion out of its own surplus value. Marx handles this problem by adjusting the capitalization rates in the two Departments [28] II, p. 512 so as to be consistent. The other approach to this problem would be to allow borrowing and lending between the two Departments at an interest rate equal to a common profit rate.

This second approach is closer to the institutional reality of modern capital accumulation, but it leads to some unhappy analytical outcomes. If capitalists in Department I, for example, have a higher capitalization rate, so that they accumulate more value than is necessary to finance Department I accumulation, and lend the surplus to Department II, they will gradually come to own the whole social capital. The social capitalization rate would converge over time to the Department I capitalization rate. Because these effects are tangential to the problem of proportionality in reproduction, we will assume that the profit rates and capitalization rates in the two Departments are the same, and that each Department finances its own expansion.

Second, we now face the question of equalizing output and the social demand for output in each Department separately. This problem Marx tried to solve numerically in his schemes of reproduction [28] II, ch XXI.

To simplify the analysis, assume also that households and the State have no spending lags and do not borrow.

If we rewrite (7.4), (7.5) and (8.7) separately for each Department, we have (suppressing the Department subscripts)

$$P(0) = (1 + q)a^*(g)C(0) \qquad (13.1)$$

$$R(0) = (1 + q)a^*(g)b^*(g)C(0) \tag{13.2a}$$

$$R'(0) = a^*(g)b^*(g)C(0) \tag{13.2b}$$

$$R''(0) = qa^*(g)b^*(g)C(0) \tag{13.2c}$$

$$C(0) = (R'(0) + pR''(0))c^*(g)C(0) + B(0)$$
$$= (1 + pq)a^*(g)b^*(g)c^*(g)C(0) + B(0) \tag{13.3}$$

The demand for Department I's output arises from the constant capital outlays of the two Departments. The demand for Department II's output arises from the variable capital outlays of the Departments and capitalist consumption out of surplus value. In each Department, this demand must be the value actually realized on a consistent path of expanded reproduction.

$$D_I = (1 - k_I)C_I(0) + (1 - k_{II})C_{II}(0)$$
$$= R_I(0) \tag{13.4a}$$

$$D_{II} = (k_I C_I(0) + k_{II} C_{II}(0) + (1 - p)(R_I(0) + R_{II}(0))$$
$$= R_{II}(0) \tag{13.4b}$$

Furthermore, on a path of expanded reproduction,

$$g_I = g_{II} = g \tag{13.5}$$

since the two Departments must expand at the same rate.

If we sum (13.4a) and (13.4b) and use (13.5), we get one condition that links the growth rate g and the relative sizes of the two Departments, as expressed by the ratio of each capital outlay to the total.

$$1 = (1 + pq_I)a_I^*(g)b_I^*(g) [(C_I(0)/C(0)]$$
$$+ (1 + pq_{II})(a_{II}^*(g)b_{II}^*(g)[C_{II}(0)/C(0)] \tag{13.6}$$

We can also solve (13.4a) directly to get a second relation linking the growth rate g and the relative sizes of the two Departments as expressed by the ratio of their capital outlays.

$$\frac{C_I(0)}{C_{II}(0)} = \frac{1 - k_{II}}{(1 + q_I)a_I^*(g)b_I^*(g) - (1 - k_I)} \tag{13.7}$$

These two equations together jointly determine g and the ratio

$C_I(0)/C_{II}(0)$, and hence, assuming that $C(0) = C_I(0) + C_{II}(0) = 1$, $C_I(0)$ and $C_{II}(0)$.

Equation (13.3) then serves to determine the borrowing levels in each Department required to sustain expanded reproduction.

Equation (13.7) has several important special cases. Suppose, first, that we are studying simple reproduction, so that $p_I = p_{II} = 0$, and the growth rate g is also 0. Then equation (8.10) becomes

$$\frac{C_I(0)}{C_{II}(0)} = \frac{1 - k_{II}}{q_I + k_I} \qquad (13.8)$$

or

$$(q_I + k_I)C_I(0) = (1 - k_{II})C_{II}(0) \qquad (13.9)$$

If we translate equation (13.9) back into Marx's notation, we see that it says that the sum of surplus value and variable capital in Department I must equal the constant capital in Department II. This is Marx's basic result in the analysis of simple reproduction. Department I reproduces its own constant capital, so that the rest of the value of its product, equal to its variable capital plus surplus value, must take the form of the constant capital necessary for Department II.

$$s_I + v_I = c_{II} \qquad (13.10)$$

But equation (13.7) also tells us the necessary proportions to maintain expanded reproduction in both Departments.

Marx implicitly treats the problem of expanded reproduction as a period model, with periods that he refers to as "years". Capital outlays take place at the beginning of a year, and production is completed within the year. The product is realized at the beginning of the next year by the sale of the output. In the notation that we have been using, $C_I(t)$ is capital outlays at the beginning of year t, $Q_I(t)$ is the flow of finished product at the end of year t valued at its cost of production, and $R_I(t)$ is the sales at the beginning of year t, all for Department I, and similarly for Department II. Marx's assumptions in working out his schema of reproduction are

$$Q(t) = C(t) \qquad (13.11)$$

$$R(t) = (1 + q)Q(t - 1) \tag{13.12}$$

$$C(t) = R'(t) + pR''(t) \tag{13.13}$$

for each Department. The balance condition he proposes is that the output of Department I be realized through the capital outlays for constant capital in the two Departments.

$$R_I(t) = (1 - k_I)C_I(t) + (1 - k_{II})C_{II}(t) \tag{13.14}$$

Marx's system is a set of difference equations, but a comparison of (13.11)–(13.14) with (13.1)–(13.14) shows that they are exactly the same as the circuit of capital equations, with simple time delay lags, where the time delays are $T_P = T_F = 0$ and $T_R = 1$. Thus (13.7) also gives the necessary initial conditions for balanced growth in Marx's schemas. Since $(1 + pq) = \exp(g)$ (for either Department), we can write (13.7) as

$$\frac{C_I(0)}{C_{II}(0)} = \frac{(1 - K_{II})(1 + p_I q_I)}{(1 + q_I) - (1 - k_I)(1 + p_I q_I)} \tag{13.15}$$

The significance of (13.15) in terms of Marx's schemas is simple. If one begins with the capitals in the two Departments in the proportions indicated by (13.15), it is possible for the system to continue smoothly along a path of balanced expanded reproduction. If one starts with any different proportions, it will be impossible to meet all the conditions for expanded reproduction. For example, consider Marx's first attempt to develop a consistent schema of expanded reproduction [28] II, pp 505 ff. He sets up the following tableau:

	c	v	s	$c + v + s$
I	4,000	1,000	1,000	6,000
II	1,500	376	376	2,252

Marx assumes that each Department converts half its surplus value into capital, so that, in the circuit of capital notation, $p_I = p_{II} = 1/2$. He apparently wants to have the same composition of capital $k_I = k_{II} = 0.2$ in both Departments, though to achieve this the variable capital and surplus value in Department II ought to be 375, not 376. The rate of exploitation is the same, 1, in each Department, so that they have the same markups, $q_I = q_{II} = 0.2$.

If we follow Marx in trying to follow through the consequences of these assumptions, we find that the demand for the output of Department I consists of the replacement of its own constant capital, the replacement of Department II's constant capital, and the provision of additional constant capital to allow each Department to expand its operations in the original proportions. This demand is

$$c_I + c_{II} + p_I(1 + k_I)s_I + p_{II}(1 - k_{II})s_{II} =$$
$$4{,}000 + 1{,}500 + 400 + 150 \qquad = 6{,}050$$

which is 50 more than the actual output of Department I in the tableau. A similar calculation shows that the demand for the output of Department II is 50 too small. The discrepancy annoyed Marx, and he devotes several pages of his notes to trying to find a schema that will exhibit proportional expanded reproduction.

We can see what is wrong if we use equation (13.15). If we use the parameters assumed by Marx in equation (13.15) we can see that the proper ratio of C_I to C_{II} is 2.75 to permit balanced expanded reproduction. Marx's initial ratio, however, is $5{,}000/1{,}875 = 2.6667$, which is not equal to 2.75. If Marx had started with a capital of 1818.18 in Department II, instead of 1975, he would have found that the balancing conditions were satisfied.

Thus the general conditions for proportionality in expanded reproduction is given by (13.6) and (13.7). These results complete the discussion of the problems raised by Marx in his study of expanded reproduction.

14. ACCUMULATION

Accumulation in real capitalist economies does not resemble the models of expanded reproduction very closely. We see an uneven pattern of historical accumulation, marked by crises of aggregate demand, chronic emergence of disproportionality, and continual changes in the underlying parameters of capital accumulation.

Real accumulation, then, is not just a quantitative increase in the scale of production, but a continuing process of qualitative change, as new techniques and products emerge, and the sociological context of the economic system is transformed. From Marx's point of view, many of the changes that conventional economic theory sees as external shocks to the economy are in fact the systematic consequencies of the accumulation of capital.

These qualitative changes are reflected quantitatively in changes in the underlying parameters of the circuit of capital. The real process of capital accumulation, then, must be represented by a non-linear model in which the parameters of the circuit of capital depend explicitly on the path of capital accumulation. Such models are, of course, considerably less tractable to mathematical analysis than the linear models we have developed up to this point.

Considerable importance also attaches to what the specific non-linearities are, and what are their relative importances. Take, for example, the "Pigou effect", the contention that the level of consumption spending will rise, other things being equal, if the "real" value of household money balances increases through price deflation. In the context of the circuit of capital, this idea must link household money balances, the value of money, the spending lags of worker and capitalist households, and the captalization rate. In a similar fashion, many of Keynes' claims about critical aspects of the dynamics of income determination translate into non-linearities in the circuit of capital framework. The notion of liquidity preference, to take another example, must refer to a dependence of capital spending lags on the relation between the interest rate and the profit rate.

Marx himself put forward several conjectures about the importance of non-linearities in real capital accumulation. The most famous of these is the interconnected set of ideas associated with the "tendency for the rate of profit to fall" with capital accumulation. This nexus of ideas (among which the actual fall in the rate of profit may be the least important) is Marx's characteristic contribution to our understanding of the essential nature of capitalist economic systems.

Marx's central idea is that capitalism, as a technically progressive mode of production, exhibits a characteristic profile in the historical development of the parameters of the circuit of capital. Capital accumulation, in Marx's vision, starts with the transformation of relatively unproductive labor processes inherited from other forms of production into capitalist production. Because of the low productivity of these processes the surplus labor time available from them is small. In terms of the circuit of capital model this corresponds to a relatively high level of the value of labor-power and consequently a low rate of surplus value, e. On the other hand, these techniques require relatively small amounts of means of production and have short production periods. Thus the composition of capital outlays, k, is high, and the production time lag short. We might speculate that the rapid turnover of productive capital in the early stages of capitalist development was offset by relatively slow turnover of commercial and money capital. The markup and the limiting rate of profit could be quite high under these circumstances, because of the high level of the composition of capital outlays, despite the low rate of surplus value.

Capital itself, in its pursuit of surplus value, will revolutionize the processes of production to achieve higher levels of labor productivity and hence higher rates of surplus value. But, Marx argues, this technical progress must systematically tend to lower the composition of capital outlays, and lower the turnover of productive capital as more massive and longer-lived means of production come into use. This argument does not claim that every innovation must lower the composition of capital outlays, but does require a tendency for this fall to take place on average over time. Thus Marx expected to find higher levels of labor productivity, higher rates of surplus value, and lower compositions of capital and longer turnover times for productive capital after a significant period of capital accumulation. We might suspect that the turnover of commercial and money capital might be accelerated by this same process of development. Marx argued that this nexus of developments, by which capitalist production defeats diminishing returns to fixed resources through technical change, provides a rational explanation for the tendency of the profit rate to fall with capital accumulation. The lower composition of capital outlays and slower turnover of productive capital could outweigh the rise in rates of surplus value. Marx found this analysis particularly attractive compared to what he viewed as Ricardo's irrational attempt to explain falling rates of profit as a reflection of diminishing returns, thereby obscuring what Marx viewed as the essential character of capitalist production, its technical progressiveness (see also Ref. 19).

There is little doubt that several of the elements of this conception do describe pervasive historical tendencies of capital accumulation (see Ref. 8, 9, 17, 29, 50 and 51). No one disputes the claim that capitalism is a technically progressive mode of production, nor that an essential dynamic in capitalist development is a growth of labor productivity more rapid than the growth of the real wage. It is easy to demonstrate empirically that the average composition of capital outlays, k, has fallen over long historical periods, though the evidence on the rates of turnover of capital is less reliable and less clear-cut. There is also reason to believe that the average rate of profit has fallen over long epochs of capital accumulation, though this fall seems to have been reversed in periods of extremely rapid technical progress like the Second World War and its aftermath.

Considerable attention (see for example Ref. 36, 43, 55) has been focussed on the analytical finding that if capitalist firms adopt only new techniques that raise profits at existing prices, and real wages remain constant in a completely closed economic system, then capitals will never adopt new techniques that lower the system-wide average rate of profit. From a practical point of view this result is not of much relevance. Real capital accumulation involves a rising real wage, even as it generally leads to a rising rate of exploitation. If labor productivity is rising, workers may be able to produce a higher standard of living for themselves with shorter labor times. Marx's own argument acknowledges this by taking (in his discussion of the tendency of the rate of profit to fall) the value of labor-power, and not the real wage, as constant.

If one holds the value of labor-power (that is, the wage share of value added) constant, then there are viable techniques that lower costs at existing prices but which lead to lower general rates of profit when they are universally adopted. It is possible to exhibit examples of this in a one-commodity model of production. Suppose production of one unit of the commodity initially requires a units of the commodity and n units of labor, that capital turns over completely in one period, and that labor is paid at the beginning of the period at a money wage w. Assume also that the value of money is 1, so that one unit of money is equivalent to one unit of labor time. Then the labor value (and price) of the commodity will be

$$v = n + av \qquad (14.1)$$

or

$$v = n/(1 - a) \qquad (14.1a)$$

The equilibrium rate of profit will be

$$r = \frac{v - av - wn}{av + wn} = \frac{(1 - w)n}{(a/(1 - a) + w)n} = \frac{(1 - w)}{(a/(1 - a) + w)} \qquad (14.2)$$

Clearly any new technique that raises a will lower the equilibrium rate of profit, holding the money wage and the value of money, and hence the value of labor-power, constant. But the viable, cost reducing, techniques, given w and v are those for which

$$va' + wn' < va + wn \qquad (14.3)$$

Among these there will obviously be some for which $a' > a$, as long as

$$\frac{a' - a}{1 - 1'} < \frac{w}{v} \qquad (14.4)$$

In this example we have held the value of labor-power constant by stipulating that the value of money is 1 unit of labor time per monetary unit, and holding the money wage constant. The Okishio method would assume a constant real wage b, so that

$$\frac{w}{v} = b \qquad (14.5)$$

in equilibrium. In this case the equilibrium rate of profit can be written

$$r = \frac{v - av - wn}{av + wn} = \frac{v(1 - a - bn)}{v(a + bn)} = \frac{1 - (a + bn)}{a + bn} \qquad (14.6)$$

In this case any alternative technique (a', n') such that

$$va' + wn' = v(a' + bn') < v(a + bn) \qquad (14.7)$$

has

$$a' + bn' < a + bn \qquad . \qquad (14.8)$$

and this must raise the equilibrium rate of profit, as the Okishio argument claims.

The critique of the theory of the tendency of the rate of profit to fall based on the Okishio theorem is perhaps a fair rejoinder to Marx, who was extremely reluctant to admit explicitly that rising labor productivity with a constant value of labor-power implies a rising real wage. This same critique, on the other hand, is of little relevance to our understanding of the historical evolution of real capitalist economies, which generally exhibit a rising real wage and a falling value of labor-power (or rising rate of surplus value). Thus the real economies fall into the class of cases where the movement of the rate of profit cannot be predicted on a priori theoretical grounds.

The behavior of the rate of profit in the short and long period is one of the most important non-linear phenomena in the accumulation process. Careful studies of this non-linearity are a crucial element in a research program for understanding the dynamics of capital accumulation.

15. ECONOMIC CRISIS

Real capital accumulation, in sharp contrast to the fiction of expanded reproduction, is marked by periods of economic crisis. These crises begin with symptoms of overrapid expansion of the economy: rising money prices of commodities, shortages of certain commodities and certain types of labor-power, and high interest rates. The economy then reaches a turning point at which aggregate demand and output turn down sharply, and the demand for labor-power falls. The interest rate is very high relative to rates of profit at the turning point, and prices often continue to rise in many sectors for some time after the turning point. Output, profits, and employment continue to fall for some time, usually followed by a substantial decline in the rate of price increase and a fall in the level of interest rates relative to profit rates. The decline sooner or later comes to an end and the accumulation process resumes its upward course (see Ref. 34).

The length of the different phases of these periodic crises and the amplitudes of the motions are far from regular. There is no apparent relation between the length of one phase and that of succeeding ones, nor between the magnitude of contractions and succeeding expansions. Despite the fascination of macroeconomists with linear difference and differential equations which have cyclic modes among their solutions (see for example Ref. 45), the instabilities of capital accumulation do not seem to have the characteristics of physical linear oscillators.

Marx views capitalist crisis as an historic phenomenon in the sense that each crisis manifests the maturing of the particular contradictions of a particular wave of accumulation. The accumulation process is seen as poisoning itself by gradually destroying its own preconditions. In the circuit of capital framework, this idea can be expressed as systematic changes in the underlying parameters of the accumulation process, the markup, capitalization rate, and time lags in production, realization, and finance. These changes in parameters must force the system off its path of steady expansion (see Ref. 49, 57 and 58).

In mathematical terms, this type of explanation of crisis involves studying the non-linear relations among the parameters of the circuit of capital and between those parameters and capital accumulation itself. This is not an easy analytical task, and is made more difficult because the range of possible non-linearities is very large, and empirical exploration of them very tentative.

Furthermore, it seems likely that the exploration of these problems will require a shift from the study of aggregates, or averages, as in the present formulations of this model, to an explicit representation of the ensemble of individual capitals. Such a representation would allow for the analysis of higher moments of key distributions describing this ensemble (in terms of balance sheet stocks and income statement flows) than the means studied in the aggregate circuit of capital. Pending the development of such a theory the discussion of capitalist crisis must remain at the level of conjecture.

It is possible, however, to develop a quasi-dynamic analysis of the circuit of capital model which shows the reaction of that model to single shocks in the basic parameters.

Suppose that we study the circuit of capital model as described in section 8, assuming that the basic parameters of the model have had constant values, p_0, q_0, $a_0()$, $c_0()$, $d_0()$, $e_0()$, B_0, B'_0, g_0 up to time zero and that the system suddenly shifts to a new parameter set p, q, $a()$, $c()$, $c()$, $d()$, $e()$, B, B', g at time zero. The new path of borrowing must be consistent with the new steady state growth rate; in other words the new parameter set must satisfy (8.7c) and (8.11d).

The paths of the variables from time zero onward will be determined, first, by what is left "in the pipeline" as a result of capital outlays made before time zero, and, second, by the dynamic interactions of the new parameters after time zero. The path of the system up to time zero constitutes a set of initial conditions for its motion after time zero.

We can write the basic equations for capital outlays, realization (assuming no gold production) and value of output as follows:

$$C(t) = \int_0^t (R'(t') + pR''(t'))c(t - t')\ \mathrm{d}t' + B(t)$$

$$+ \int_{-\infty}^0 (R'(t') + p_0 R''(t'))c_0(t - t')\ \mathrm{d}t' \qquad (15.1)$$

$$R(t) = D(t) = (1 - k)C(t) + \int_0^t kC(t')d(t - t')\ \mathrm{d}t' \quad (15.2)$$

$$+ \int_0^t (1 - p)R''(t7)e(t - t')\ \mathrm{d}t' + B'(t)$$

$$+ \int_{-\infty}^{0} k_0 C(t') d_0(t - t') \, dt'$$

$$+ \int_{-\infty}^{0} (1 - p_0) R''(t') e_0(t - t') \, dt' \tag{15.2}$$

$$P(t) = (1 + q) \int_{0}^{t} C(t') a(t - t') \, dt'$$

$$+ (1 + q_0) \int_{-\infty}^{0} C(t') a_0(t - t') \, dt' \tag{15.3}$$

The paths of the other variables, including the stocks of value in financial, productive, and commercial capital, and the realization time lag, can be recovered once we know the paths of these basic variables.

It is convenient to express the solution of these equations in the form of Laplace transforms, using the assumption that, up to time zero, the variables all follow exponential paths at the common growth rate g_0. The initial conditions terms (those with integral limits from $-\infty$ to 0) all have the same form, an exponential function convoluted with a transfer function. The transform of such expressions can be illustrated by working out the simplest equation, (15.3).

If $P^*(s)$ is the Laplace transform of $P(t)$, defined by

$$P^*(s) = \int_{0}^{t} \exp(-st) P(t) \, dt \tag{15.4}$$

with the property that the transform of convolutions is equal to the product of the transforms of the convoluted functions, we have, from (15.3)

$$P^*(s) = (1 + q) a^*(s) C^*(s)$$

$$+ (1 + q_0) \int_{0}^{\infty} \exp(-st) \int_{-\infty}^{\infty} \exp(g_0 t') a_0(t - t') \, dt' \, dt \tag{15.5}$$

The integral in this equation can be simplified by letting $t'' = t - t'$, and the result is

$$P^*(s) = (1 + q) a^*(s) C^*(s) + (1 + q_0) \frac{a_0^*(g_0) - a_0^*(s)}{s - g_0} \tag{15.6}$$

since the transform of an exponential growing at rate g is just $1/(s - g)$.

By similar manipulations we find

$$C^*(s) = c^*(s)[R'^*(s) + pR''^*(s)] + B^*(s)$$

$$+ [R'(0) + p_0R''(0)] \frac{[c_0^*(g_0) - c_0^*(s)]}{s - g_0} \quad (15.7)$$

$$R^*(s) = (1 - k)C^*(s) + kd^*(s)C^*(s) + (1 - p)e^*(s)R''^*(s) + B'^*(s)$$

$$+ \frac{k_0[d_0^*(g_0) - d_0^*(s)]}{s - g_0}$$

$$+ \frac{(1 - p_0)R''(0)[e_0^*(g_0) - e_0^*(s)]}{s - g_0} \quad (15.8)$$

The reader can verify that if none of the parameters change, continued exponential growth at rate g_0 is a solution to these equations.

If one or more of the parameters do change, the flows of value will undergo a transient motion before converging to the new steady state path at growth rate g.

In this general model a difficulty arises from the necessity of distinguishing the two components of realization, R', the recovery of capital outlays, and R'', the realization of surplus value. If the markup changes at time zero, the proportions of surplus value and recovery of capital outlays in sales will not change until the vintage zero output passes through the sales lag and is actually sold. Since the sales lag, T, will vary in the transient motion, this introduces a non-linearity into the process. In order to avoid this complication, we will confine our analysis to the case where $p = p_0 = 1$, so that all surplus value is reinvested. With this assumption, (15.7) and (15.8) become

$$C^*(s) = c^*(s)R^*(s) + B^*(s)$$

$$+ \frac{R(0)[c_0^*(g_0) - c_0^*(s)]}{s - g_0} \quad (15.9)$$

$$R^*(s) = (1 - k(1 - d^*(s))C^*(s) + B'^*(s)$$
$$+ \frac{k_0[d_0^*(g_0) - d_0^*(s)]}{s - g_0} \qquad (15.10)$$

These two equations can be solved to give the transform of the transient path after the parameter change at time zero. The expression for $C^*(s)$ is, for example,

$$C^*(s) = [(s - g_0)(c^*(s)B'^*(s) + B^*(s))$$
$$+ c^*(s)k_0(d_0^*(g_0) - d_0^*(s))$$
$$+ R(0)(c_0^*(g_0) - c_0^*(s))]]$$
$$[s - g_0][1 - (1 - k(1 - d^*(s)))c^*(s)] \qquad (15.11)$$

The transient motion of the capital outlays can be recovered from this transform, and the motion of the other stock and flow variables can be derived from it.

For example, to simplify let us assume that workers spend their wages instantly, so that $d^*(s) = 1$, that the spending lag $c()$ is an exponential lag with parameter c ($c(t) = c\exp(-ct)$), so that $c^*(s) = c/(s + c)$, that $B'(t) = 0$, and that $B(t)$ after time zero is equal to $B(0)\exp(gt)$ where g is the new steady state accumulation rate, given, from (8.7c) by

$$g = \frac{c}{1 - B(0)} - c = \frac{cB(0)}{1 - B(0)} \qquad (15.12)$$

Under these assumptions $R(0) = 1$, from (8.6) so that

$$C^*(s) = \frac{(s - g_0)B^*(s) + [c_0^*(g_0) - c_0^*(s)]}{(s - g_0)(1 - c^*(s))}$$
$$= \frac{g(s + c)}{(g + c)s(s - g)} + \frac{c_0(s + c)}{(g_0 + c_0)s(s + c_0)} \qquad (15.13)$$

using the fact that $B^*(s) = g/[(g + c)(s - g)]$ and simplifying.

First note that only the growth rate and the spending lag appear in this expression. A fall in the markup, as we have seen already in section 8, if the path of borrowing remains unchanged, will not affect the growth rate, but will be absorbed by changes in inventories of finished commodities as reflected by the realization lag T.

Using the method of residues, or expanding the fractions in (15.13) directly, we can write the time path of $C(t)$ as

$$C(t) = \exp(gt) - \frac{c - c_0}{g_0 + c_0} \exp(-c_0 t) + c\left(\frac{1}{g_0 + c_0} - \frac{1}{g + c}\right)$$
$$+ \frac{c[(g - g_0) + (c - c_0)]}{(g_0 + c_0)(g + c)} \tag{15.14}$$

so that

$$C(0) = 1 + \frac{c_0 g - c g_0}{(g_0 + c_0)(g + c)} \tag{15.15}$$

Capital outlays, C, jump upward or downward at time zero depending on whether $c_0/c > < g_0/g$, and then smoothly converge to the new steady state path. Thus a crisis-like motion, involving a fall in capital outlays and output, could be the result of either a fall in the rate of borrowing, or a rise in the capitalist spending lag (which corresponds to a fall in the parameter c). A fall in the markup would produce such a crisis only through its effects on the spending lag $c()$ or on the path of new borrowing $B()$.

It is thus possible to get some insights into the dynamic behavior of circuit of capital models with these methods.

16. CONCLUSION

The investigation of Marx's conception of the circuit of capital reveals important connections between money, accumulation, and capitalist crisis.

Within the framework of the circuit of capital we can see the integral role money capital plays in the reproduction and expansion of capitalist production. We also see that the provision of financial assets is itself an incident in the circuit of capital. This places the role of the monetary policy of the central bank in a subordinate place. It also suggests that disturbances in the financial system reflect disturbances in capital accumulation.

Furthermore, because there is a close connection between the scale of capital outlays, aggregate demand, and new borrowing, it seems likely that the financial system plays a crucial role in transforming changes in the underlying parameters of accumulation like the markup into crises. Without feedback through financial variables to capital outlays there is no reason why the system could not adapt smoothly and gradually to a lower markup without a crisis. This suggests further that the persistence of crises depends strongly on the persistence of financial imbalance that have grown during periods of accumulation (see Ref. 32).

These conclusions have important ramifications for the Marxist theory of crises. Classical Marxism argued that capitalist crises were rooted in the fundamentally contradictory character of the capitalist mode of production. Thus it is impossible to avoid crises as long as production remains organized on capitalist principles. Furthermore, classical Marxism taught that crises would worsen as the contradictions of capitalism matured, leading to a final or ultimate crisis in which a revolutionary transformation of capitalism would become unavoidable.

Capitalist crisis certainly reflects the contradiction between exchange value and use value on which commodity production systems rest, since it exhibits a simultaneous increase of unfilled need and of unused capacity to meet need. Crises are inherent in a system where the proximate motive for production is surplus value, and the meeting of need is achieved as a contingent byproduct of the pursuit of profit. This analysis cannot, however, support the conclusion that the capitalist mode of production is contradictory in the sense of posing logically inconsistent requirements for its own reproduction, of being, in fact impossible. Crisis must be seen as part of the normal pattern of successful reproduction of capitalism.

Finance appears to be a critical mediating channel between changes in underlying parameters of accumulation like the markup and the ebbing of aggregate demand associated with the realization phase of crises. The disruption of the financial system is itself one of the most dramatic manifestations of such crises. But the circuit of capital analysis tends to confirm the view that financial problems have their origin in systematic effects of capital accumulation. Crises are not primarily financial, and no reform of the financial system alone can eliminate the tendency to crisis.

The circuit of capital models suggest, however, a much wider spectrum of effects of crisis than those identified by classical Marxism. The possibility that a fall in the markup might lead to higher rates of price inflation, rather than to a classic recessionary downturn, depending on the financial system and its behavior, is one example.

Furthermore, if the persistence and severity of crises depend on the persistence of financial imbalances, there are presumably strong state measures available to avoid systemic catastrophe. The financial system is a system of promises, and a financial crisis is a situation where a large number of such promises cannot be met consistently. If the state can achieve an orderly dissolution of enough financial promises, it can create a situation where accumulation can proceed, as long as there is a surplus value potentially available in the unpaid labor of productive workers.

This last remark calls into serious question the idea of a final or ultimate crisis of capitalist production arising purely from the predictable effects of accumulation. Economic crises may become more severe in their social impact as larger parts of the population depend on capitalist production to meet a larger part of their need. But if social labor is capable of producing a surplus, it is hard to see why a society that agreed on capitalist principles could not arrange to have that potential surplus take the form of a surplus value.

The investigation of problems within the circuit of capital framework has been only slightly developed. In particular, the study of systems with an ensemble of capitals distributed in the space of balance sheet and income statement variables is likely to provide a large number of important problems that can be attacked with modern statistical and modelling methods.

Barnard College, Columbia University

REFERENCES

*1. Aglietta, N. *A Theory of Capitalist regulation: The U.S. Experience*. London: NLB, 1979.
2. Clower, R. W. The foundations of monetary theory, *Western Economic Journal*, **6 (1969), 1–9, reprinted in *Monetary Theory*, ed. by R. W. Clower. Harmondsworth: Penguin, 1969.

**3. Debreu, G. *Theory of Value: An Axiomatic Analysis of Economic Equilibrium.* New Haven: Yale University Press, 1959.

*4. deBrunhoff, S. *Marx on Money.* New York: Urizen, 1976.

**5. deVroey, M.: "Value, Production and Exchange" in *The Value Controversy.* London: Verso and NLB, 1981.

6. Domar, E. "Capital Expansion, Rate of Growth, and Employment", *Econometrica*, **14 (1946), 137–147.

*7. Dumenil, G.: *De la Valeur aux Prix de Production.* Paris: Economica, 1980.

8. Dumenil, G. and M. Glick: "La Basse de la Rentabilite Aux Etats Unis: Inventaire de Recherches et Mise en Perspective Historique", *Observations et Diagnostics Economiques*, **6 (January 1984), 69–92.

**9. Dumenil, G. and M. Glick: "The Tendency of the Rate of Profit to Fall in the United States", *Contemporary Marxism*, forthcoming, 1984.

*10. Fine, B. and L. Harris: *Rereading Capital.* New York: Columbia University Press, 1979.

*11. Foley, D. K.: "The Value of Money, the Value of Labor Power, and the Marxian Transformation Problem", *Review of Radical Political Economics*, **14** (2) (1982), 37–47.

12. Foley, D. K.: "Realization and Accumulation in a Marxian Model of the Circuit of Capital", *Journal of Economic Theory*, **28(2) (1982) 300–319.

**13. Foley, D. K.: "Say's Law in Marx and Keynes", *Cahiers d'Economie Politique*, forthcoming.

**14. Friedman, M.: *A Theory of the Consumption Function.* Princeton: Princeton University Press, 1957.

15. Garegnani, P.: "Heterogenous Capital, the Production Function, and the Theory of Distribution", *Review of Economic Studies*, **37 (1970), 407–436.

16. Gerstein, I.: "Domestic Work and Capitalism", *Radical America*, **7 (4 and 5) (1973).

**17. Gillman, J. M.: *The Falling Rate of Profit.* New York: Cameron Associates, 1957.

18. Harris, D. J.: "On Marx's Scheme of Reproduction and Accumulation", *Journal of Political Economy*, 80 (1972), 505–522, reprinted in *The Economics of Marx*, ed. by M. C. Howard and J. E. King. Harmondsworth: Penguin, 1976.

**19. Harris, D. J.: "Are There Macroeconomic Laws? The Law of the Falling Rate of Profit Reconsidered", in *The Economic Law of Motion of Modern Society: A Marx-Keynes-Schumpeter Centennial*, ed. by M. J. Wagener and J. W. Drukker. Cambridge: Cambridge University Press, 1984.

**20. Harrod, R.: *Towards a Dynamic Economics.* London: Macmillan, 1948.

21. Himmelweit, S. and S. Mohun: "Domestic Labour and Capital", *Cambridge Journal of Economics*, **1(1) (1977), 15–32.

*22. Kalecki, M.: *Studies in the Theory of Business Cycles.* New York: Kelley, 1969.

*23. Keynes, J. M.: *The General Theory of Employment, Interest, and Money.* New York: Harcourt, Brace and World, 1964.

**24. Leontiev, W.: *The Structure of the American Economy*, 2nd edition. New York: Oxford University Press, 1951.

25. Lipietz, A.: "The So-Called 'Transformation Problem' Revisited", *Journal of Economic Theory*, **26 (1982), 59–88.

**26. Luxemburg, R.: *The Accumulation of Capital*. New York: Modern Reader, 1968.

**27. Luxemburg, R.: *The Accumulation of Capital, an Anti-Critique*, and Bukharin, N. *Imperialism and the Accumulation of Capital*. New York: Monthly Review, 1972.

*28. Marx, K.: *Capital*, Volumes I, II, III. New York: International Publishers, 1967.

**29. Mage, S.: "The 'Law of the Tendency of the Falling Rate of Profit': its Place in the Marxian Theoretical System and Relevance to the U.S. Economy, 1900–1960", Ph.D dissertation, Columbia University, 1963.

**30. Malinvaud, E.: *Lectures on Microeconomic Theory*. North-Holland, 1976.

*31. Minsky, H.: *John Maynard Keynes*. New York: Columbia University Press, 1975.

**32. Minsky, H.: *Can it Happen Again?* New York: M. E. Sharpe, 1982.

33. Modigliani, F.: "The Life-Cycle Hypothesis of Saving, the Demand for Wealth, and the Supply of Capital", *Social Research* **33(2) (1966), 160–217.

*34. Moore, G. H.: *Business Cycles, Inflation, and Forecasting*, 2nd edition. Cambridge, Massachusetts: NBER, Ballinger, 1983.

**35. Niehans, J.: *The Theory of Money*. Baltimore: Johns Hopkins University Press, 1978.

*36. Okishio, N.: "Technical Change and the Rate of Profit", *Kobe University Economic Review* **7** (1961), 86–99.

37. Ostroy, J. and R. M. Starr: "Money and the Decentralization of Exchange", *Econometrica*, **42(6) (1974), 1093–1113.

*38. Pasinetti, L.: *Growth and Income Distribution: Essays in Economic Theory*. Cambridge: Cambridge University Press, 1974.

*39. Pasinetti, L.: *Lectures in the Theory of Production*. New York: Columbia University Press, 1977.

**40. Patinkin, D.: *Money, Interest and Prices*, 2nd Edition. New York: Harper and Row, 1965.

*41. Ricardo, D.: *Principles of Political Economy and Taxation*. Harmondsworth: Penguin, 1971.

**42. Robinson, J.: *Essays in the Theory of Economic Growth*. London: Macmillan, 1962.

43. Roemer, J.: "Technical Change and the Tendency for the Rate of Profit to Fall", *Journal of Economic Theory*, **16 (1977), 403–424.

*44. Rubin, I. I.: *Essays in Marx's Theory of Value*. Detroit: Red and Black, 1972.

**45. Samuelson, P.: *Foundations of Economic Analysis*. Cambridge, Mass.: Harvard University Press, 1963.

**46. Schoenman, J.-C.: *An Analog of Short-Period Economic Change*. Stockholm: University of Stockholm and Almquist and Wicksell, 1966.

**47. Schoenman, J.-C.: "Interactions of the Marshallian Period as Privileged Base for Positive Theory", unpublished, 1984.

**48. Senchak, A.: "Capital Accumulation and the Duration of the Production, Sales, and Expenditure Processes: the U.S. Non-financial Corporate Business Sector 1963–1977", Ph.D. dissertation, Columbia University, 1982.

*49. Shaikh, A. "An Introduction to the History of Crisis Theories" in *U.S. Capitalism in Crisis*. New York: Union for Radical Political Economy, 1978.

**50. Shaikh, A.: *Marxian Economic Analysis*. Oxford: Blackwell, 1985.
**51. Shaikh, A.: "Profitability and the Current Economic Crisis", *Science and Society*, forthcoming.
**52. Smith, A.: *An Inquiry into the Nature and Causes of The Wealth of Nations*. New York: Modern Library, 1937.
 *53. Sraffa, P.: *Production of Commodities by Means of Commodities*. Cambridge: Cambridge University Press, 1972.
**54. tenRaa, T.: "Dynamic Input-output Analysis with Distributed Activities", unpublished, 1983.
55. van Parijs, P.: "The Falling-Rate-of-Profit Theory of Crisis: A Rational Reconstruction by Way of Obituary", *Review of Radical Political Economics* **12(1) (1980), 1–16.
 *56. von Neumann, J.: "A Model of General Equilibrium", *Review of Economic Studies*, (1945), 1–9.
**57. Weisskopf, T.: "Marxist Perspectives on Cyclical Crisis" in *U.S. Capitalism in Crisis*. New York: Union for Radical Political Economy, 1978.
58. Weisskopf, T.: "Marxian Crisis Theory and the Rate of Profit in the Postwar U.S. Economy", *Cambridge Journal of Economics* **3(4) (1979), 341–378.

INDEX

VALUE, EXPLOITATION AND CLASS

JOHN E ROEMER

Value, Exploitation
and Class

John E Roemer
University of California, Davis, USA

A Volume in the Marxian Economics Section
edited by
John E Roemer
University of California, Davis, USA

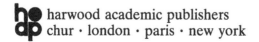
harwood academic publishers
chur · london · paris · new york

Harwood Academic Publishers

P.O. Box 197
London WC2E 9PX
England

58, rue Lhomond
75005 Paris
France

P.O. Box 786
Cooper Station
New York, New York 10276
United States of America

Library of Congress Cataloging in Publication Data
Roemer, John E.
    Value, exploitation, and class.
    (Fundamentals of pure and applied economics,
ISSN 0883-2366; vol. 4. Marxian economics section)
    Bibliography: p.
    Includes index.
    1. Labor theory of value. 2. Marxian economics. 3. Social
conflict. I. Title. II. Series: Fundamentals of pure and applied economics; v.
4. III. Series: Fundamentals of pure and applied economics. Marxian economics section.
HB206.R64   1986   335.4'12   86-3143
ISBN 3-7186-0278-4

CONTENTS

INTRODUCTION TO THE SERIES

Drawing on a personal network, an economist can still relatively easily stay well informed in the narrow field in which he works, but to keep up with the development of economics as a whole is a much more formidable challenge. Economists are confronted with difficulties associated with the rapid development of their discipline. There is a risk of "balkanisation" in economics, which may not be favourable to its development.

Fundamentals of Pure and Applied Economics has been created to meet this problem. The discipline of economics has been subdivided into sections (listed on the inside back cover). These sections include short books, each surveying the state of the art in a given area.

Each book starts with the basic elements and goes as far as the most advanced results. Each should be useful to professors needing material for lectures, to graduate students looking for a global view of a particular subject, to professional economists wishing to keep up with the development of their science, and to researchers seeking convenient information on questions that incidentally appear in their work.

Each book is thus a presentation of the state of the art in a particular field rather than a step by step analysis of the development of the literature. Each is a high level presentation but accessible to anyone with a solid background in economics, whether engaged in business, government, international organizations, teaching, or research in related fields.

Three aspects of *Fundamentals of Pure and Applied Economics* should be emphasized:

—First, the project covers the whole field of economics, not only theoretical or mathematical economics.

—Second, the project is open-ended and the number of books is not predetermined. If new interesting areas appear, they will generate additional books.

—Last, all the books making up each section will later be grouped to constitute one or several volumes of an Encyclopaedia of Economics.

The editors of the sections are outstanding economists who have selected as authors for the series some of the finest specialists in the world.

J Lesourne   H Sonnenschein

Value, exploitation, and class

JOHN E. ROEMER

INTRODUCTION

MARXIAN MICROECONOMICS has long been thought to consist primarily of the labor theory of value and its associated puzzles, such as the transformation problem. In this monograph, I maintain this view is obsolete. I claim Marxian microeconomics is interesting mainly for what it enables us to say about class formation and exploitation. Class formation is interesting as a sociological category, if one thinks that members of a class learn to behave in similar ways, that classes at certain times in history have overcome the collective action problem and become important historical actors. (The sociology and psychology of class action are not discussed here, but economic analysis for making a definition of class precise is provided.) Exploitation is important, in my view, as a normative category: it is a type of distributive injustice. Marxian economics has much to say about exploitation: within modern economics, it has remained the most unabashedly moral voice, claiming that positive and normative analysis, or scientific and ethical work, can be done together. (Albert Hirschman [26] attributes the apparent intellectual tenacity of Marxism to its attempted combination of moral commitment and scientific analysis.)

Marxian microeconomics, then, is not interesting primarily as *economics*, narrowly interpreted as the theory of price formation, but rather as a foundation for important *sociological* and *ethical* categories. There is, I think, no specifically Marxian theory of price under capitalism. Within neoclassical economics, the standard theory of price is the competitive or Walrasian theory, which I adopt in this monograph. (There are, of course, competing theories of disequilibrium prices, oligopoly, monopolistic competition, and so on. The version of Marxian microeconomics I present is, so to speak, the perfectly competitive version.) Similarly, Marxists have not developed any special insights into what constitutes 'real capitalist competition,' although many Marxists are critical of the passive form of competition which is assumed in the perfectly competitive model. (See for instance Shaikh [62].) The aggressive, ruthless competition which Marxists have in mind is the subject of much work in contemporary 'neoclassical' economics. I refer to the modern literature on oligopoly, game theory, and evolutionary models of firm growth and survival.

The labor theory of value has played two roles in Marxian economics. First, it has been claimed to be, at some level of abstraction, a theory of prices. Second, the concept of embodied labor time has been used to define exploitation. In its first role, the labor theory of value is useless. It is a mystical Hegelian enterprise which claims that regardless of the actual deviations of equilibrium market prices from embodied labor values, nevertheless the latter represent the true phenomenon while the former are the epiphenomenon. I think the tenacity of this dogma is the single greatest chalice which Marxian economics be ars. In the following pages, theorems are proved which show the labor theory of value is false. In fact, prices determine labor values (see Section 7.2), not the other way around. Having discarded labor values as a theory of price, however, they can still be used to define the concept of exploitation. This is, at first pass, more fruitful. Marx's project was to use the labor value theory of price to define his theory of exploitation: but, as is shown, the labor theory of exploitation is cogent even when the labor theory of prices is discarded and replaced by the conventional supply and demand theory of price determination.

Nevertheless, there are deep problems with the labor theory of exploitation—of defining exploitation in terms of the expropriation of surplus labor, and measuring the degree of exploitation by the amount of social labor expropriated by the capitalist class. After developing the labor theory of exploitation, I show in Section 8 how these problems emerge and in Section 9 I outline how the Marxian concept of exploitation can be redefined without any reference to labor value. Exploitation emerges as a concept defined purely in terms of property relations. Thus the labor theory of value, which in Marx's conception was the key to developing the theory of exploitation, turns out to be a false start. Nevertheless, the final insights, the theory of exploitation and class, remain valuable but are not built on the classical Marxian foundation.

One could ask: What remains, in this reconstruction, which merits the label 'Marxian?' The labor theory of value, and the falling rate of profit theory are claimed to be false; the transformation problem is an irrelevancy. A rigorous foundation remains for two concepts, class and exploitation, which are of sociological, ethical, and above all of historical importance. These concepts are not ones that have been of traditional interest to non-Marxian economists. They may come increasingly into their own in economics as economists struggle more seriously with problems of collective action and distributive justice. But even if one estimates that not very much is left of Marxian microeconomics, or that what is left is not particularly Marxian, that is not damaging, to this enterprise at least. The success of Marxism must in large part be evaluated by the extent to which it produces ideas that are viewed as coherent and important by all social scientists, not simply by those who have some privileged access to the mysteries of dialectics.

Such success requires, among other things, that Marxism be done with the standards of logic which are expected of contemporary social science. In economics, these standards require the use of mathematics and models; the method has been highly refined since the cumbersome algebra which Marx (and many of his generation of economists) employed. I therefore make no effort to write using classical Marxian notation, but use only modern notation. Nor do I view this monograph as a document in the history of thought, and so no effort is made to reference the vast literature of the past one hundred years on these topics. Classical ideas are presented, but in a way which (I hope) makes sense to the modern reader.

A fairly detailed overview of the monograph is provided by the Table of Contents. Section 1 presents the input–output theory of embodied labor value. Section 2.1 defines Marxian prices of production, and shows how they are equilibrium prices of a competitive model. Section 2.2 presents a simple example which highlights the main issues in the debate concerning the origin of profits. Section 3 defines exploitation in terms of embodied labor value, and demonstrates the formal link between exploitation of labor and profits. In Section 3.2, it is argued that the significance of this link has been overstated. Section 3.3 presents a model of the Marxian conjecture of a 'falling rate of profit' and shows the conjecture to be false. In Sections 4 and 5 the transformation problem of labor values into prices is discussed, and it is shown that this transformation makes sense only in a metaphorical sense. Labor value pricing is shown to coincide with non-exploitative regimes, and so the 'transformation' of labor values into equilibrium prices can be thought of as indicating the transformation of property relations from non-exploitative to exploitative ones.

Section 6 presents a formal definition of class, and shows how classes arise endogenously from given property relations, in a competitive equilibrium model. The relationship between class and wealth, and between class and domination, is made precise. In Section 7, two main concepts of Marxian economics are related to each other, class and exploitation, in a theorem called the Class Exploitation Correspondence Principle. This theorem proves that members of classes who hire labor are exploiters and members of classes who sell labor are exploited. While this may seem to be definitional, in the models here it is not. Class and exploitation are each endogenously determined features of agents, given their initial endowments and preferences, and so a relationship between the two features is not obvious. Sections 6 and 7 provide microfoundations for the classical concepts of class and exploitation using standard equilibrium models.

Sections 8 and 9 summarize the political philosophy which lies behind the notion of exploitation. In Section 8, it is asked: What phenomenon is exploitation a proxy for? Why be interested in the particular calculation of labor accounts, and the comparison of embodied labor times, which defines Marxian exploitation? Section 9 shows that Marxian exploitation is best understood as a type of distributive injustice, which results from unequal and unjust distribution of society's alienable productive assets. Section

10 proposes a model designed to study what the annihilation of exploitation would entail. In particular, it is claimed that the equality of opportunity which would be required to eliminate exploitation may not be achievable with an equal-division redistribution of society's alienable productive assets, even under the standard assumptions of perfectly competitive models. From Sections 9 and 10, it becomes apparent that the problems facing contemporary Marxists are similar to the questions of non-Marxian egalitarian political philosophy. What today distinguishes Marxism, at least with reference to the set of questions which this monograph leads to, from these other approaches, is not easy to define. The final section discusses the merging of research programs somewhat more explicitly.

Many writers, internationally, are contributing to the topics which are discussed in this monograph. Indeed, the number seems to be increasing exponentially. My bibliography is far from complete, and I apologize to the many authors whose work is not mentioned. Rather than a survey of all the work in the area, this monograph is intended as a condensed but quite self-contained development of the 'analytical Marxian microeconomics' which has emerged in the last ten to fifteen years.

1. LABOR VALUE

1.1 Linear models

The modern theory of labor value is developed using linear input–output theory. Early applications to Marxian economics of input–output theory were due to Morishima and Seton [38], Okishio [43], Schwartz [59], Brody [8]. A fairly complete development is contained in Morishima [35]. Since Morishima's book, there has been a veritable explosion in the use of these techniques to generalize and refine the labor theory of value and exploitation. Books on the subject include those by Steedman [64], Broome [9], Maarek [30], Pasinetti [44], Wolfstetter [76], Desai [15], Vegara [71], Morishima and Catephores [37], Fujimori [25], Flaschel [23], Roemer [49], Roemer [50], Lippi [29] and Krause [27]. There are, as well, writers who shun the use of mathematical models in developing the Marxian theory of value, believing that the essence of Marx's insight is lost with mathematical modelling. This position is reflected, for example, in Weeks [73], and Benetti, Berthomieu and Cartelier [3]. As noted in the introductory section, the former viewpoint is adopted in this monograph.

To develop a precise formulation of embodied labor time, we postulate a linear technology which can produce n commodities. Labor is the unique primary factor. Let:

$A = (a_{ij})$ be the $n \times n$ input coefficient matrix

L be the $1 \times n$ vector of direct labor coefficients.

The jth column of A, called $A_{.j}$, is the vector of inputs required to operate the jth activity at unit level, which in this case produces one unit of good j. The jth component of L, called L_j, specifies the direct labor required to produce one unit of good j. All labor is assumed to be homogeneous.

Let Λ_j be the amount of labor embodied in one unit of good j: Λ_j is the amount of labor required to produce one unit of good j, net of reproduction of the inputs consumed in the production of that unit of j. Represent one unit of good j as the unit column vector with one in the jth place and zeros in other components. Λ_j can be thought of as the amount of labor that would be required to produce e_j from scratch. To produce e_j as a net output, the technology (A, L) must be operated at activity levels x, where x is the column vector solving the input–output equation:

$$x = Ax + e_j \qquad (1.1)$$

Assuming (1.1) can be inverted, we solve:

$$x = (I - A)^{-1} e_j$$

and so the labor required to produce e_j as net output is:

$$\Lambda_j \equiv Lx = L(I - A)^{-1} e_j \qquad (1.2)$$

But the right hand side of (1.2) is simply the inner product of L with the jth column of the matrix $(I - A)^{-1}$; thus, the vector of embodied labor time for all commodities is given by:

$$\Lambda = L(I - A)^{-1} \qquad (1.3)$$

Two other interpretations of (1.3) are available. If $(I - A)^{-1}$ exists then it can be represented as the geometric series $(I + A + A^2 + \ldots)$, and so (1.3) becomes:

$$\Lambda = L + LA + LA^2 \ldots \tag{1.4}$$

Thus the embodied labor time of a vector of goods f is

$$\Lambda f = Lf + LAf + LA^2 f + \ldots \tag{1.5}$$

In (1.5), $A^i f$ may be interpreted as the vector of material inputs required "i stages ago" required to produce f today. Thus $LA^i f$ is the direct labor i periods ago expended to produce the inputs which eventually were used to produce f. Equation (1.5) expresses the labor embodied in f as the undiscounted sum of past labor expended. It expresses the labor required to produce f from scratch.

Alternatively we can begin with the unknown vector of labor values Λ, and note that if it exists, it satisfies the equation:

$$\Lambda = \Lambda A + L \tag{1.6}$$

where the term $\Lambda A_{.j}$ is the labor time embodied in the material inputs used to produce one unit of good j, and L_j is the direct labor. Equation (1.6) expresses labor value Λ as the sum of 'dead labor' ΛA and 'living labor' L.

The validity of (1.3) is conditional on the invertibility of $(I - A)$. Moreover, $(I - A)^{-1}$ should be non-negative, for otherwise we could specify an L which would produce negative labor values. A reasonable economic condition will guarantee that $(I - A)^{-1}$ exists and is non-negative.

Definition 1.1 A is a *productive* matrix if there exists a vector† $x \geqslant 0$ such that $x > Ax$.

A productive input matrix is capable of producing a strictly

---

†For vectors, $x > y$ means $x_i > y_i$ in all components i; $x \geqq y$ means $x_i \geqq y_i$ for all i; $x \geqslant y$ means $x \geqq y$ and $x_i > y_i$ for some i.

positive vector of net outputs. That is, the input–output equation

$$x = Ax + f$$

can be solved for some $f > 0$, with $x \geqslant 0$.

Theorem 1.1   If A is productive, then $(I - A)^{-1}$ exists and $(I - A)^{-1} \geqslant 0$. (This is sometimes known as Arrow's inversion lemma.)

Proof:
We show first that $(I - A)^{-1}$ exists. By the productiveness of A, there is pair $(\hat{x}, \hat{f})$ solving:

$$\hat{x} = A\hat{x} + \hat{f}, \quad \hat{f} > 0, \quad \hat{x} \geqslant 0 \tag{1.7}$$

Note $\hat{x} > 0$, since by (1.7) $\hat{x}$ is the sum of the positive vector $\hat{f}$ and the non-negative vector $A\hat{x}$. If $(I - A)$ is not invertible, choose a non-zero vector k in kernel $(I - A)$. k can be chosen to have at least one negative component; scale k so that the vector $(\hat{x} + k)$ is zero in some component i and negative in none, which can be done since $\hat{x} \geqslant 0$. Since k ε kernel $(I - A)$, $(I - A)(\hat{x} + k) = \hat{f}$. In particular,

$$(\hat{x} + k)_i = (A(\hat{x} + k))_i + \hat{f}_i \tag{1.8}$$

But (1.8) is impossible, since $(\hat{x} + k)_i = 0$ by choice; but $A(\hat{x} + k) \geqslant 0$, since $(\hat{x} + k) \geqslant 0$, and $\hat{f}_i > 0$. Thus $(I - A)^{-1}$ exists.

To prove $(I - A)^{-1} \geqslant 0$, recall that $\hat{x} > 0$. Suppose $(I - A)^{-1}$ has a negative element. Then there is a solution pair (x', f') such that:

$$x' = Ax' + f', \quad f' \geqslant 0, \quad x'_i < 0, \quad \text{some } i \tag{1.9}$$

Consider convex combinations $(\lambda f' + (1 - \lambda)\hat{f})$ and note that they correspond to solutions of the input–output equation $(\lambda x' + (1 - \lambda)\hat{x})$. Since $x > 0$ and $x'_i < 0$, there is a λ ε $(0, 1)$ such that $[\lambda x' + (1 - \lambda)\hat{x}]$ is zero in some component (call it i) and negative in none. Hence

$$0 = (\lambda x' + (1 - \lambda)\hat{x})_i$$
$$= (A(\lambda x' + (1 - \lambda)\hat{x}))_i + (\lambda f' + (1 - \lambda)\hat{f})_i \tag{1.10}$$

But the second term on the right of (1.10) is positive and the first is non-negative, a contradiction.

Therefore $(I - A)^{-1} \geqslant 0$ q.e.d.

It follows from (1.3) that the productivity of A assures the existence and non-negativity of the labor value vector Λ.

Sometimes, one is interested in systems where labor values are strictly positive. This is assured if A is an *indecomposable* matrix, for then $(I - A)^{-1} > 0$ and the positivity of Λ follows from (1.3). For a discussion of indecomposability, see Morishima [35] or Schwartz [59] or Takayama [68], for instance.

1.2 Joint production

Equation (1.3) can be called the additive model of labor value. With the introduction of joint production, the additive model in general fails, and a more general approach to labor valuation is required. Joint production is a convenient way to model fixed capital, differential turnover times among production processes, and the choice of techniques among many possible Leontief input–output technologies. As such it is desirable to extend the definition of embodied labor to the case of joint production, if there is to be a theory of labor exploitation for that case. For a discussion of how joint production encompasses these various apparently disparate economic phenomena, see Morishima [34].

Let

      B be an $m \times n$ output matrix

      A be an $m \times n$ input matrix

      L be a $1 \times n$ vector of direct labor inputs.

The technology (B, A, L) is a von Neumann Technology, with n processes and m goods. If the jth process is operated at unit level, the vector $B_{.j}$ of outputs is produced, and the vector $A_{.j}$ of inputs and L_j amount of labor are consumed. The joint production model is important in part because fixed capital which depreciates over time is most easily treated as a joint product (see Morishima [34]). In the model of Section 1.1, all capital was circulating, and depreciated completely each period of production.

We might try to derive the labor value of good j as we did in

Section 1.1. Thus we would seek a solution x to

$$Bx = Ax + e_j \tag{1.11}$$

and would define

$$\Lambda_j = Lx. \tag{1.12}$$

There are a variety of problems. In general $(B - A)^{-1}$ does not exist as $(B - A)$ is not even a square matrix. But even if (1.11) can be solved uniquely for x, it is quite possible that Λ_j, so defined, will be negative. This occurrence is not ruled out by the productiveness of the system (B, A). For example, consider the 2 process, 2 good productive system:

$$B = \begin{pmatrix} 6 & 3 \\ 1 & 12 \end{pmatrix} \qquad A = \begin{pmatrix} 5 & 0 \\ 0 & 10 \end{pmatrix}$$

$L = (1, 1)$.

To produce one unit of good 1 as a net output, we solve

$$(B - A)x = \begin{pmatrix} 1 \\ 0 \end{pmatrix} \tag{1.13}$$

which has a unique solution $x = \begin{pmatrix} 1 \\ -2 \end{pmatrix}$. Hence the labor embodied in good 1 is, according to (1.12), $1 \cdot 1 + 1(-2) = -1$.

Geometry provides some explanation. In Figure 1, the two net

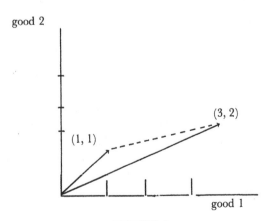

FIGURE 1

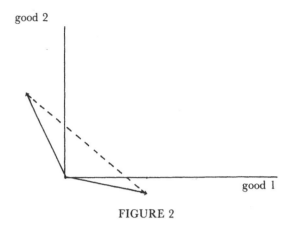

FIGURE 2

output vectors from operating the two processes at unit level are graphed.

To solve the Eq. (1.13), we are asking for a linear combination of the two net output vectors equal to $\begin{pmatrix} 1 \\ 0 \end{pmatrix}$. The cone generated by the two net output vectors does not contain the positive quadrant of commodity space. In particular, to express $\begin{pmatrix} 1 \\ 0 \end{pmatrix}$ as a linear combination of the net output vectors requires a negative amount of process 2. Contrast this situation to a 2×2 productive Leontief linear model, in which case the net output vectors are always aligned as in Figure 2. In the Leontief case every non-negative commodity bundle is expressible as a non-negative linear combination of the processes, and hence labor values are never negative. This point was made originally by Steedman [63], and has generated a small literature

Because the additive model of labor valuation fails in the case of joint production, other approaches have been proposed. Morishima [35–36], proposed to define the labor value of a commodity bundle f as the least amount of labor required to produce f as a net product. Thus, solve the linear program

$$\min \quad Lx$$

$$Bx \geqslant Ax + f$$

$$x \geqslant 0$$

and define labor value of f as the solution. For instance, the labor value of $\begin{pmatrix} 1 \\ 0 \end{pmatrix}$ in the technology above is $1/3$ according to this definition. The justification for this definition is that it preserves the validity of the so-called Fundamental Marxian Theorem (see Section 3). The major criticism of the definition is that it might calculate the labor value of a commodity by using a process which is not in fact used in the economy. That is, the solution Lx^* to the above program might entail $x_j^* > 0$ when process j is not even profitable at equilibrium prices. This point will be explained more precisely below (in Section 6). Further criticisms of the Morishima generalization of labor value are provided by Flaschel [24] and Roemer [50], Chapter 5.

It is possible to generalize the Morishima definition of labor value to production sets which are general convex sets (Roemer [47, 49]). The apparent attractiveness, from a classical Marxian point of view, of the Morishima approach is that it defines labor values independently of prices. Although doctrinally faithful, this is the weakness of the approach: for the position that labor valuation can be independent of prices in a complex production system cannot be sustained, as we shall see. For that reason, other definitions of labor value are price-dependent, and hence demand dependent (see Flaschel [24], Roemer [50]).

2. PRICES

2.1 Equal profit rate prices (prices of production)

Suppose there are $\mathcal{N}$ agents, each of whom can operate the Leontief technology (A, L). Agent v is characterized, for the moment, by the vector of endowments ω^v of produced commodities which he owns. Each agent owns one unit of labor power. Suppose production takes one period of time, and today's prices are $(p^0, 1)$ where p^0 is the n-vector of commodity prices and the wage is normalized at unity. Suppose, for the moment, there is no capital market, and so investment must be financed out of current holdings of finance capital. Suppose material inputs must be paid for at the beginning of the production period, and wages are paid at the end of the period, from sales revenue. Each agent wants to maximize profits. If each agent expects commodity prices p to rule at the end of the period, when goods are sold, then he will choose a vector of activity levels x to

$$\max \left[px - (p^0 Ax + Lx) \right]$$

subject to   (P2.1)

$$p^0 Ax \leqslant p^0 \omega^v \tag{2.1}$$

$$x \geqslant 0$$

The objective of this program is expected profits and the constraint is agent v's capital constraint, which expresses the limitations on his investment choices due to his holdings of finance capital.

It is clear from inspection (or from examining the dual program to (P2.1)) that the only activities which an agent will operate are those generating the maximal profit rate, where the profit rate of sector j is:

$$\pi_j(p, p^0) = \frac{p_j - (p^0 A_{.j} + L_j)}{p^0 A_{.j}} \tag{2.2a}$$

The dual program to (P2.1) is:

choose π to

$$\min \pi p^0 \omega^v$$

s.t.

$$\pi p^0 A \geqslant p - (p^0 A + L) \tag{D2.1}$$

$$\pi \geqslant 0$$

where π is the (scalar) dual variable associated with constraint (2.1) of (P2.1). The dual constraint can be written

$$p \leqslant (1 + \pi) p^0 A + L \tag{2.2b}$$

from which it is clear that π is to be interpreted as the profit rate on capital invested. By complementary slackness, only those activities will be operated which generate the profit rate π. π_j is the rate at which capital invested in sector j expands, and to maximize profits, only sectors which expand capital at the maximal rate are used. If we are interested in equilibrium prices p which will permit all sectors to operate, then all sectors must enjoy the maximal profit rate, and from (2.2) prices will be of the form:

$$p = (1 + \pi)p^0 A + L \qquad (2.3)$$

where π is the maximal and uniform profit rate. If in addition we are interested in stationary prices, then equilibrium prices obey, for some π:

$$p = (1 + \pi)pA + L \qquad (2.4)$$

What assumption might motivate the claim that all sectors should be operated? If the technology (A, L) is indecomposable, then every sector must be operable in order to produce any non-negative non-zero vector of net output. Hence if we want a condition which will assure that the indecomposable economy can avoid running down the stock of any produced commodity, we should require all sectors to operate by profit-maximizing agents. An equilibrium which permits growth of all stocks in this sense has been called a *reproducible solution* (Roemer [49], Chapter 1) and it is assured by (2.4).

Given a Leontief system (A, L), does there exist a non-negative p and non-negative π satisfying (2.4)? If A is productive, the Frobenius–Perron theorem assures this. Attempting to solve (2.4) for p gives:

$$p = L(I - (1 + \pi)A)^{-1} \qquad (2.5)$$

The Frobenius–Perron theorem (see, for example, Roemer [49], p. 110, or Schwartz [59] or Debreu and Herstein [14]) says that a productive matrix A has an eigenvalue $\bar{\rho}$ greater than one and for any $\rho < \bar{\rho}$, the matrix $(I - \rho A)$ is non-negatively invertible. Hence for any value of π in the interval

$$0 \leqslant \pi < \bar{\rho} - 1 \qquad (2.6)$$

Eq. (2.5) is solvable for a non-negative price vector p. Note when $\pi = 0$, $p = \Lambda$.

We have derived *equal-profit-rate* prices from the assumption of profit-maximizing behavior and the requirement that all sectors operate. Under these assumptions, Eq. (2.4) is a necessary condition for equilibrium. This approach is to be contrasted with the dynamic one, which claims that prices converge to the prices of (2.4), because when profit rates differ between sectors, capital will flow from the low profit rate sector to the high profit rate sector; this in turn will increase the supply in the profitable sector, causing prices and profit rate to fall. It is not obvious, however, that this dynamic process will lead to convergence to equal profit rate prices, just as tâtonnement does not in general lead to convergence in the general equilibrium model (Arrow and Hahn [2], Chapter 12). Thus the claim made here is the weaker stationary one, that at equilibrium, prices will be of the equal profit rate variety.†

Thus far, we have a feasible interval of profit rates given by (2.6). Marxist analysis has generally picked out one profit rate from this interval by positing the existence of a real-wage or subsistence bundle. Suppose agents will not sell labor power unless they can buy with one day's wages a column vector of commodities b. Perhaps there is a subsistence sector in which a worker can produce the vector b with a day's work, so b represents his opportunity cost for working in the capitalist sector. If the supply of labor is elastic at this real wage—perhaps the economy is capital-limited, so all capital can be operated by workers willing to sell labor power at real wage b—then prices p will satisfy:

$$pb = 1 \tag{2.7}$$

recalling the wage is unity. Substituting (2.7) into (2.4):

$$p = p((1 + \pi)A + bL) \tag{2.8}$$

The matrix $M = A + bL$ is called the augmented input coeffi-

---

† Dumenil and Levy [16] propose a model where prices initially yield different profit rates to firms who are monopolistic competitors of a sort, and competition eventually leads to an equilibrium where profit rates are equal. This occurs, however, in a series of three stages which can be conceived of as different stages of competition. First, competition forces all firms producing the same good to charge the same price (the 'law of one price'). Second, the *average* profit rate in each 'industry' is equalized. Thirdly, firms using inefficient techniques are weeded out, and hence the profit rates of all firms become equal.

cient matrix (Morishima [35]). The second term bL is the matrix of labor-feeding coefficients. (Thus the input of commodity i into the worker who operates sector j at unit level is b_iL_j.) If M is a productive matrix then it possesses a real eigenvalue greater than one; therefore for some unique positive value of π, the matrix $((1 + \pi)A + bL)$ has an eigenvalue of unity, which is associated with the non-negative eigenvector of prices satisfying (2.8). (A review of the various facts about eigenvalues of non-negative matrices is in Debreu and Herstein [14].) Hence each subsistence bundle b for which the matrix $A + bL$ is productive determines a profit rate and vector of prices.

From (2.5), p can be viewed as a function of π. By differentiating (2.5) with respect to π, notice that as π increases all components of p increase. Since the wage is normalized at unity, a rising profit rate corresponds to a falling real wage. The specification of the subsistence bundle b is simply one way of picking out a point on this *wage-profit frontier*. In principle, the equilibrium profit rate could be solved by closing the system in other ways, by putting the model in a general equilibrium context.

A second simple way of closing the system is to assume there is a capital market and an exogenously given interest rate r. Agents can now borrow and lend finance capital at interest rate r. The profit-maximizing program (P2.1) becomes

$$\text{choose } (x, K) \text{ to max } (px - (pAx + Lx) - rK)$$

$$\text{s.t.} \qquad\qquad\qquad\qquad\qquad\qquad\qquad \text{(P2.2)}$$

$$pAx \leqslant p\omega^v + K$$

$$x \geqslant 0$$

In (P2.2), agent v can borrow capital in amount K (or lend if K is negative). It can be easily seen that solutions to (P2.2) for each capitalist exist which permit the capital market to clear only when $\pi = r$. For if $r < \pi$, then all agents will wish to borrow an infinite amount of capital as they can thereby make infinite profits; and if $r > \pi$ then all agents wish to lend capital but nobody wishes to borrow. Hence an equilibrium in the capital market requires

$$p = (1 + r)pA + L \qquad\qquad (2.9)$$

This observation allows us to note that what neoclassical economists call the interest rate, Marxist economists call the profit rate. In a neoclassical linear model, profits are zero in equilibrium, while in the Marxist model the profit rate is positive. This is because neoclassical analysis considers interest payments on capital to be a cost, while Marxist analysis counts interest as profit. In the model under discussion rents do not exist, which both schools would call profits.

A comment on the timing of wage payments is in order. In the model above, wages are paid at the end of the production period. If wages were paid out of capital at the beginning of the period we would write, instead of (P2.1):

$$\text{choose } x \text{ to max } (px - (pAx + Lx))$$

$$\text{s.t.}$$

$$pAx + Lx \leqslant p\omega^v \qquad \text{(P2.3)}$$

$$x \geqslant 0$$

In (P2.3), investment plus wages must be financed out of finance capital $p\omega^v$. Indeed (P2.3) is not quite accurate because v might also sell some of his labor power, adding his wages (which he now receives at the period's beginning to his capital $p\omega^v$). So in (P2.3) it is assumed, for simplicity of exposition that agent v does not work himself. The sectoral profit rates associated with the prepayment of wages are:

$$\pi_j = \frac{p_j - (pA_{.j} + L_j)}{pA_{.j} + L_j}$$

and so equal-profit-rate prices are defined by:

$$p = (1 + \pi)(pA + L) \qquad (2.10)$$

Many authors use (2.10) instead of (2.4) as the price equation; there are no important analytical differences between the two models, although the algebra differs slightly. For the sake of consistency I will assume wages are paid at the end of the period. For further discussion of the timing of wage payments, see Broome [9].

2.2 The origin of profits: a simple model

To highlight the origin of positive profits in the Marxian model, consider a simple economy which consists of many producers capable of producing one good, corn.

Each producer requires a certain amount of corn in a week to survive—say, one bushel. There are two techniques available for producing corn, and everyone has knowledge of both of them. The first technique is labor intensive (LI); it requires no seed corn as input, but a lot of direct labor. Indeed, it requires six days of labor to produce one bushel of corn using the LI technique. There is also a capital intensive technique (CI) which uses some seed corn (capital) as input. (Neither technique requires land; alternatively, land is in abundance.) Using the CI technique, one bushel of corn can be produced using only three days' labor; that labor also includes the time required to reproduce the seed corn employed. Thus, three days is the labor embodied in one bushel of seed corn produced net, using the CI technique. In Marxian language, socially necessary labor time is three days per week, since in that time the producer can produce his subsistence and replace the capital used up in so doing. (Actually, we will see in a moment that socially necessary labor time may be a bit more complicated.)

The problem is that not everyone can operate the CI technique, because it requires possession of seed corn. A producer will starve unless he eats every week. So a producer with no stock of seed corn cannot operate the CI technique; he does not have time in the week to produce, using the LI technique, both his subsistence needs and a stock of seed corn to operate the CI technique next week.

Suppose, now, there is a limited stock of seed corn. By "limited" I mean there is not enough to employ the whole population in the CI technique. There is, perhaps, enough seed corn to employ half the producers in the CI technique. But the stock of seed is not distributed equally among the population; it is all owned by several people. What will happen in a competitive economy? Assume initially that all the propertyless producers operate the LI technique, and work six days a week. (They do not desire to work the seventh day to accumulate some seed corn, or they are too tired to do so.) The few owners of the seed corn cannot possibly use it all by working it by themselves with their own labor, so they offer to hire others to work up some of it for them. They agree to pay, each week, wages in corn equal to the subsistence needs of the employed worker. The variable they set, which calibrates the real wage, is the number of days in the week the employee must supply as labor to earn his subsistence. If the work week is set at less than six days, the asset holders will be flooded with proletarians offering to sell their labor, because the alternative for a proletarian is to work six days a week using the LI technique. But there is not sufficient seed corn to employ all the propertyless producers; and so the asset holders will competitively set the length of the work week at six days. Six days is the equilibrium length of the work week in this example. (We assume no special disamenities from working in the CI technique compared to the LI technique. If there are such, the work week in the CI technique will equilibrate at something less than six days.)

Notice that for each worker employed, the asset holder receives, net, two bushels of corn (six days' work on the CI technique) and he only pays out one bushel as a wage. Thus, he realizes as many bushels of corn as profit as he employs workers, which number is determined by the size of his capital stock. Each worker is working longer than socially necessary labor time (he produces a surplus over his subsistence needs), but this outcome is not the consequence of any coercion or cheating. It is the competitive outcome of individual optimization facing the given property constraints. It is important to notice that for this example to work, there must be an industrial reserve army—that is, more producers available than seed corn to employ them. For if, instead, seed corn were in excess relative to the labor supply, then the work week in the CI technique would be bid down to three days. Owners of seed corn would compete for workers, rather than the other way around.

What happens if the seed corn, still in short supply, is equally distributed among all the producers? Assume there is just enough to allow half the population to reproduce themselves using the CI technique. Then everyone will work exactly $4\frac{1}{2}$ days a week, assuming no surplus is produced. This can be arranged in various ways. The simplest way is for each producer to work $1\frac{1}{2}$ days a week on the CI technique using up and replacing his seed corn stock, and producing half a bushel of subsistence corn, and to work 3 days a week on the LI technique, producing the other half bushel. Alternatively, the same result can be arranged using either a labor market or a credit market. Using a labor market, some producers will offer to hire others at a real wage of half a bushel of corn for 3 days' labor, in the CI technique. It is easily checked that some producers can spend $4\frac{1}{2}$ days working in the CI technique, earning one bushel of corn, and others will spend $4\frac{1}{2}$ days working in the LI technique, earning a total of one bushel, three-fourths of it from their output in the LI sector and one-fourth of it as profit from the workers they hire on their capital in the CI technique. In this case, one must conceive of socially necessary labor time as $4\frac{1}{2}$ days per week, not 3 days per week as originally claimed, because society must work, on average, $4\frac{1}{2}$ days to reproduce itself, given the scarcity of capital. There is no exploitation in the egalitarian society, since everyone works socially necessary labor time.

Return to the first example, where the propertyless agents work 6 days, in which they are therefore supplying $1\frac{1}{2}$ days a week of surplus labor, from the social point of view, or 3 days a week of surplus labor from the individual employer's point of view. Society has divided itself into three classes, the capitalists who hire labor, the proletarians who sell it, and the peasants who work in the LI sector. Surplus value is expropriated from the proletarians by the capitalists. The proletarians work longer than is socially necessary, and this is so precisely because of their lack of access to productive assets. Indeed, the following are requirements for these results to hold:

1. a class of propertyless producers, in relative abundance to the supply of capital which can employ them;
2. the existence of an inferior technology which can keep the unemployed industrial reserve army alive, so they continue to exert their downward pressure on the real wage next week;
3. the necessity of time in production, so the propertyless ones cannot instantaneously synthesize seed corn, and, in fact,

have no time to accumulate capital on their own, after earning their subsistence needs.

(In modern capitalism, (2) can, alternatively, take the form of state payments to the unemployed, or it can be the agricultural periphery from which workers are drawn to the capitalist sector.)

That the propertyless proletarians (and the peasants) work longer than is socially necessary is called exploitation. The neoclassical replies to this accusation are various, and include the following. First, the model is not complete. Perhaps there is a good reason that some have seed corn assets and others none; perhaps the asset holders worked very hard in the past, and starved themselves, to accumulate their seed stock. Thus the differentiation of the population into asset holders and propertyless, before the model starts, is a consequence of differential rates of time preference on consumption, and not something that, therefore, should lead to results called exploitative. A second reply is that the model is incompletely specified in other ways: perhaps there are some special skills which make it possible to operate the CI technology, which only a few people have. The propertyless ones could not operate CI on their own even with the seed stock. (Perhaps anyone could accumulate seed stock, but only the "capitalists" do, since the other do not know how to use it anyway.) The proper interpretation, then, is that the proletarians are trading their "surplus" labor for the exercise of skills by the capitalist, without which CI could not be used. (We can even change the model slightly so that even the proletarians are strictly better off working for the capitalist than they would be enduring the idiocy of rural life using LI, yet "surplus" labor still passes to the capitalist.) Thus, it is not correct to view the extra work time provided as a surplus, because it is, from the proletarian's viewpoint, a fair trade for the skill of the capitalist. Another scarce skill the capitalist might possess, which the proletarian does not, is a risk-taking propensity. The "surplus" labor provided by the proletarian is then viewed as his insurance premium against the alternative of having to become a capitalist and take those risks himself.

An evaluation of the arguments will not be made here, but will be taken up in later sections (Sections 8, 9). The Marxian contention is that no good justification exists for the differential ownership of the means of production. The purpose of this example is to highlight the three enumerated causes of positive profits. The story changes with the admission of differential preferences, skills, and risk. Note that although time in production is essential for positive profits, that does not imply profits should be considered to be a return to waiting. In the present model, it is differential access to productive capital, not differential rates of time preference, which gives rise to profits. Whether differential capital stocks at the beginning of the period are due to differential rates of time preference in the past is another question.

3. EXPLOITATION AND PROFITS

3.1 Fundamental Marxian theorem

As the model of Section 2.2 defined, an agent is *exploited* when the labor embodied in the goods he purchases with his revenues is less than the labor he expended in production. An *exploiter* is an agent who can purchase goods embodying more labor than he expended. Let x be the aggregate gross activity levels of the economy (A, L). Then

$$Lx = \Lambda(I - A)x \qquad (3.1)$$

The left hand side of (3.1) is total employment and the right hand side is the labor value of net product. The net product is divided among agents according to ownership rules of some sort; he who receives goods embodying more labor than he expended is an exploiter, and he who receives goods embodying less labor than he expended is exploited. Let l^ν be the labor expended by agent ν and f^ν be the goods from the net product which ν owns. According to (3.1), $\sum l^\nu = \sum \Lambda f^\nu$; exploiters are ones for whom $l^\nu < \Lambda f^\nu$, and the exploited are ones for whom $l^\nu > \Lambda f^\nu$. We will have cause to refine this definition presently.

The simplest model of exploitation is the subsistence model, where it is assumed (Section 2.1) that an agent either owns no means of production and provides one unit of labor power for a real wage of b, or owns means of production and hires workers. The Fundamental Marxian Theorem (FMT), a title coined by Morishima [35] states that the profit rate is positive if and only if workers are exploited.

Definition For a technology (A, L) and subsistence vector b, *socially necessary labor time* is Λb. The rate of exploitation is $e = \dfrac{1 - \Lambda b}{\Lambda b}$. The rate of exploitation is the ratio of 'surplus' labor time to necessary labor time, where the worker provides one unit of labor.

A version of the FMT is:

Theorem 3.1   Let $\{A, L; b\}$ be a technology and subsistence wage. Let A be indecomposable. Let the rate of exploitation be $e = (1 - \Lambda b)/\Lambda b$. Then $\pi > 0$ if and only if $e > 0$.

Proof:
From (2.8), $p = p((1 + \pi)A + bL)$. Hence there is a right-hand column eigenvector x for the matrix $((1 + \pi)A + bL)$ satisfying

$$x = ((1 + \pi)A + bL)x \qquad (3.2)$$

By the indecomposability of A, the value vector Λ is strictly positive. Pre-multiplying (3.2) by Λ gives

$$\Lambda x = \Lambda A x + (\Lambda b)Lx + \pi \Lambda A x$$

or

$$\Lambda x = (\Lambda A + L)x - (1 - \Lambda b)Lx + \pi \Lambda A x \qquad (3.3)$$

Recalling that $\Lambda = \Lambda A + L$, (3.3) can be re-written

$$(1 - \Lambda b)Lx = \pi \Lambda A x$$

from which it follows that $\pi > 0$ if and only if $e > 0$, since $1 - \Lambda b = \dfrac{e}{e + 1}$.

Many generalizations and discussions of the FMT exist in the literature. (See, for example, Fujimori [25], Krause [27], Medio [33], Morishima [36], Roemer [49], Steedman [64]) The generalization to joint production models by Morishima [36] was significant because it demonstrated a version of the theorem when a unique vector of labor values does not exist, in the sense discussed in Section 1. Roemer [47] generalized the theorem to a production model which is a convex cone. The key assumption for guaranteeing that positive profits imply exploitation I called *independence of production*: it states that given two vectors of commodities $w \leqslant z$, there should be a way of producing w as a net product using strictly less labor than any way of producing z as a net product requires. If and only if this independence fails, then it is possible to construct a model with positive profits and no exploitation (Roemer [49], pp. 64–70). These generalizations use Morishima's labor-minimizing definition of labor value (see Section 1.2).

The reason for such interest in the FMT is that it purports to demonstrate that the exploitation of labor is the cause of profits. There is, however, a problematic inference: it does not follow from the necessity and sufficiency of labor exploitation for profits that exploitation of labor *causes* or *explains* profits. For it can be shown that every commodity can be viewed as exploited in a system with positive profits—and hence one might just as well infer that the exploitation of oil or steel is the source of profits.

3.2 The generalized commodity exploitation theorem

Consider the augmented input coefficient matrix $M = A + bL$. From Eq. (2.8), it follows that the positivity of the profit rate is equivalent to M being a productive matrix. The economic intuition is clear: if and only if M is productive, it is possible to produce some net output after feeding labor. That net output constitutes profits in physical terms. In proving the FMT, we essentially demonstrated that productiveness of M is also equivalent to the exploitation of labor, to the inequality $\Lambda b < 1$. Hence, the equivalence of labor exploitation and profits. It can, however, be demonstrated that the productiveness of M is equivalent to the exploitation of any commodity, and so the profitability of the system cannot be 'explained' by labor's exploitation. This observation has been made in various ways by many authors, including

Verga [71], Bowles and Gintis [4], Wolff [75], Roemer [50], and Samuelson [58]. (See also Roemer [53] for a related discussion.)

We shall compute embodied values using commodity 1 (say, steel) as the value numeraire. Display the technology in this way:

$$
\begin{array}{c|cccc}
a_{11} & a_{12} & \cdots & a_{1n} & b_1 \\
\hline
a_{21} & a_{22} & \cdots & a_{2n} & b_2 \\
\vdots & \vdots & & \vdots & \vdots \\
a_{n1} & a_{n2} & & a_{nn} & b_n \\
L_1 & L_2 & \cdots & L_n & 0
\end{array}
$$

The jth column of this array lists the inputs of all $(n+1)$ commodities used as inputs into production of the jth good—and this statement is true also for $j = n + 1$, namely, the commodity labor power. The ith row lists the inputs of ith good into the various processes—and this statement is true also for $i = n + 1$, namely, the input of labor. Notice there is, by convention, no input of labor into the production of labor power. In reality, there is such an input but it is performed in the household and not through the market, so it is not recorded in this tableau. (It is assumed that the worker does not hire others to do his chores.)

Let $\mu = (\mu_1, \mu_2, \ldots, \mu_n)$ be the vector of steel values of non-labor commodities. μ_{n+1} is the steel value of labor power. Then the usual conception of embodied value implies the following definitional relations:

$$\mu_j = a_{1j} + \sum_2^n \mu_i a_{ij} + \mu_{n+1} L_j \text{ for } j = 1, n \qquad (3.1)$$

$$\mu_{n+1} = b_1 + \sum_2^n \mu_i b_i. \qquad (3.2)$$

Substitute from (3.2) into (3.1) to eliminate μ_{n+1}:

$$\mu_j = (a_{1j} + b_1 L_j) + \sum_{i=2}^n \mu_i (a_{ij} + b_i L_j)$$

or

$$\mu_j = \sum_{i=1}^{n} \mu_i(a_{ij} + b_i L_j) + (1 - \mu_1)(a_{1j} + b_1 L_j), \text{ for } j = 1, n$$

or

$$\mu = \mu M + (1 - \mu_1) M_1. \tag{3.3}$$

where $M = A + bL$ and M_1. is the first row of M.

We wish to show that $\mu_1 < 1$ if and only if M is productive: that is the statement that the steel value of steel is less than one, and hence that steel is exploited.

If M is productive, Eq. (3.3) can be solved:

$$\mu = (1 - \mu_1) M_1.(I - M)^{-1} \tag{3.4}$$

What solutions μ_1 are possible to (3.4)? If $\mu_1 = 1$, then according to (3.4) $\mu = 0$ which contradicts the assumption that $\mu_1 = 1$. Hence $\mu_1 \neq 1$, and (3.4) is equivalent to:

$$\mu/(1 - \mu_1) = M_1.(I - M)^{-1} \tag{3.5}$$

If M is productive, then $(I - M)^{-1} \geqslant 0$, and so $\mu/(1 - \mu_1) \geqslant 0$. This implies $\mu_1 < 1$. (For $\mu_1 > 1$ would imply $\mu_1/(1 - \mu_1) < 0$.) Hence $\mu_1 < 1$, and a solution $\mu \geqslant 0$ exists to (3.5).

Conversely, if a nonnegative vector μ exists solving (3.3), with $\mu_1 < 1$, then $\mu \leqslant \mu M$, and hence M is productive.

Marx [32] had thought that in the exploitation of labor he had located the secret of capitalist expansion. According to him, there exists one special commodity which is capable of putting more into production than it takes out and that is labor power. He expressed this fact by saying the value of labor is greater than the value of labor power. In the present notation, the value of a unit of labor is one, and the value of a unit of labor power is Λb. But every commodity has this property in a productive system: there is less than one unit of steel embodied in one unit of 'steel power.' Hence profitability of capitalism is not explained by the exploitation of labor unless some other reason can be provided to choose labor as the value numeraire instead of steel.

There has been a tradition in Marxism to argue that exploitation is not primarily of normative interest; the positive explanation of profits that it provides justifies its study. The generalized commodity exploitation theorem shows this is false. If the exploitation of labor is interesting, it is not because labor's exploitation uniquely explains profits, but rather because labor is unique in some other way among commodities. Any relevant uniqueness of labor is most likely of a normative rather than positive variety; if labor exploitation is important, it must be because in some sense it is unfair while the exploitation of steel is not. Such an approach will be developed below. For the moment, it suffices to remark that such unfairness has nothing to do with the purported positive explanation of profits.

3.3 The falling rate of profit

Marx believed that the type of technical change which profit-maximizing capitalists would be compelled to introduce would lead the equilibrium profit rate to fall. For him, this was a dialectical aspect of capitalism: that individual profit-maximization would be collectively irrational for capitalists. Elster [20] characterizes Marxian dialectics as the contradiction between individual rationality and sub-optimality (or collective irrationality), an idea which has now become common place in social science. The falling rate of profit theory, and the theory of capitalist crisis more generally, is a prime example of the phenomenon. Most students of the question, however, believe Marx's theory is wrong.

Marx believed that profits come from the exploitation of living labor. As the technology becomes increasingly capital-intensive, there is less living labor to exploit, and so profits must eventually fall. The argument, when formalized, fails because increasingly efficient technologies raise the rate of exploitation by decreasing the amount of socially necessary labor time, the time embodied in the workers' wage goods. Using the price Eq. (2.8), it can be shown that a profit-increasing technical charge will increase the equilibrium profit rate if the real wage remains fixed.

Let the technology be $(A, L; b)$ with prices p and profit rate π:

$$p = p((1 + \pi)A + bL) \tag{2.9}$$

Suppose in sector j a technological innovation (A_j^*, L_j^*) appears.

Then capitalists will adopt the innovation if at current prices it reduces costs:

$$pA_j^* + L_j^* < pA_{.j} + L_j \qquad (3.6)$$

Such an innovation is called *viable*. For a viable innovation it follows that:

$$p_j > (1 + \pi)pA_j^* + L_j^* \qquad (3.7)$$

Let $(\hat{A}, \hat{L})$ be the technology in which (A_j^*, L_j^*) has replaced $(A_{.j}, L_j)$. Then from (2.9) and (3.7):

$$p \geqslant p((1 + \pi)\hat{A} + b\hat{L}) \qquad (3.8)$$

From (3.8), the eigenvalue of the matrix $((1 + \pi)\hat{A} + b\hat{L})$ is less than one, and by the Frobenius theorem there exists a non-negative vector $\hat{p}$ and a number $\hat{\pi} > \pi$ such that:

$$\hat{p} = \hat{p}((1 + \hat{\pi})\hat{A} + b\hat{L}) \qquad (3.9)$$

$(\hat{p}, \hat{\pi})$ are the prices and profit rate associated with the new technique $(\hat{A}, \hat{L})$, and we have remarked that $\hat{\pi} > \pi$. Thus capitalistically viable innovations increase the rate of profit, contra Marx.

The original argument along these lines was provided by Okishio [42]; it was later generalized by Roemer [46]. Samuelson [57] observed the same result. The same agrument holds when fixed capital is introduced (Roemer [49]). The key assumption is that the real wage remains fixed; if the real wage increases along with the technical innovation then the profit rate can, of course, fall (see Roemer [49]). Various writers have tried to reconstruct the falling rate of profit result by introducing imperfections of various sorts into the model. Alberro and Persky [1] argue that if capitalists systematically overestimate the economic lifetime of new technology, because they underestimate the rate at which more cost-effective technologies will develop, then the rate of profit can fall. Shaikh [62] argues that capitalists are forced by competition to ignore the interest costs on fixed capital when evaluating whether to introduce a new technique. If they do, then the rate of profit can fall, but it is difficult to justify Shaikh's assumption about capitalist behavior (see Steedman [65], Roemer [49]). Laibman

[28] argues for a disequilibrium approach in which the profit rate falls. Webber [72] argues that cost-reducing innovations increase the supply of goods; since workers are the consumers who must purchase the goods, real wages must eventually rise to clear the goods market and the rate of profit, he argues, will thus fall. Taking into account the problem of realizing profits will modify the partial equilibrium argument of this section. An overview of the debate is provided by Van Parijs [69]. In the von Neumann model, it can be shown that a strict increase in the rate of profit following innovation is equivalent to the uniqueness of the equilibrium price vector (Roemer [48]).

It must be reiterated these arguments do not show the rate of profit does not fall in capitalist economies, simply that such a result cannot be concluded without a theory relating the changes in the real wage to technological change, and the effect of technical change on supply and demand. Empirical studies have failed to demonstrate any secular falling rate of profit (see Weisskopf [74]).

3.4 Abstract, concrete and skilled labor

Thus far, it has been assumed that labor expended in all activities is homogeneous, of equal skill level. Labor value is thus the concrete labor time embedded in a commodity. Classical Marxism claims a distinction between concrete labor and abstract labor. Abstract labor was claimed to be the essence of all concrete labor; thus, while concrete labor takes different forms in different productive activities, the labor value of a commodity should be computed using *abstract* labor. Some writers have criticized the definition of labor value of Section 1.1, 1.2 because it is based on concrete labor (for example, Benetti, Berthomieu, Cartelier [3]). Indeed, one attack against the 'revisionist' position of recent years that labor values do not exist logically prior to equilibrium prices is that such arguments consider *concrete* labor values rather than abstract labor values. If labor value were conceived of as sufficiently abstract, the claim goes, its dependence on price would vanish. One problem with these criticisms is that abstract labor is not analytically defined, and hence propositions concerning abstract labor appear to be non-falsifiable, that is, appropriately 'abstract.'

Steedman [66] has shown that however one chooses to define the abstract labor involved in producing a commodity, the abstract labor embodied in a commodity must be proportional to the wage the concrete labor in that activity is paid, if certain crucial Marxian contentions are to be maintained. Thus abstract labor cannot be defined until equilibrium prices (wages) are known. For instance, if there are multiple equilibria with different relative wage rates, then the 'abstract labor' embodied in commodities changes from one equilibrium to another. Consequently, abstract labor, whatever it is, does not exist logically prior to prices. Steedman's argument, which is summarized in this section, applies as well to skilled labor.

Let Λ be the $m \times n$ matrix whose ijth component λ_{ij} is the direct and indirect concrete labor of type i embodied in commodity j. Let L be the $m \times n$ matrix of direct concrete labors; thus the jth column of L lists the amounts of the m types of concrete labor used to produce a unit of good j. Then

$$\Lambda = L(I - A)^{-1} \tag{3.10}$$

Let a be a row vector in R^m_+ of conversion ratios between concrete and abstract labor where a_j is the number of units of abstract labor in one unit of concrete labor of type j. Let the vector of wages for the m types of concrete labor be $w = (w_1, \ldots, w_m)$.

Theorem 3.2   If profits are zero, then exploitation of every worker is zero if and only if the amount of abstract labor in a unit of concrete labor is proportional to its wage: that is, there exists a constant k such that $a = kw$.

Proof:
Let p be the price vector for goods. Profits are zero so $p = pA + wL$, so $wL(I - A)^{-1} = w\Lambda = p$. Suppose the column vector of concrete labor worked by worker v is l^v, and suppose each worker v spends his entire wages on a vector of goods f^v.

Then

$$wl^v = pf^v = w\Lambda f^v \tag{3.11}$$

$a\Lambda f^v$ is the amount of abstract labor embodied in f^v and al^v is the amount of abstract labor performed by v. Thus surplus abstract labor s^v performed by worker v is zero, and hence his exploitation in terms of abstract labor is zero, if and only if

$$s^v = al^v - a\Lambda f^v = 0 \qquad (3.12)$$

Note, that for any constant k

$$(a - kw) \cdot (l^v - \Lambda f^v) = al^v - a\Lambda f^v - [kwl^v - kw\Lambda f^v]$$

$$= al^v - a\Lambda f^v$$

$$= s^v$$

$$= 0 \qquad (3.13)$$

where the term in square brackets vanishes by (3.11). From (3.11), the vector $(l^v - \Lambda f^v)$ is constrained to be in the hyperplane orthogonal to w, $w \cdot (l^v - \Lambda f^v) = 0$. Within this hyperplane, l^v and f^v can be chosen 'essentially' arbitrarily (that is, l^v and f^v can be chosen by different workers in such a way that the vectors $(l^v - \Lambda f^v)$ span the hyperplane). Thus the orthogonality of $(a - kw)$ and all the vectors $(l^v - \Lambda f^v)$, required by (3.13), is guaranteed if and only if $a - kw$ is a multiple of w:

$$a - kw = k_1 w \qquad (3.14)$$

and so $a = (k + k_1)w$.

The inference from the theorem is that if we wish to verify the contention that zero profits imply the absence of exploitation for every worker then there is no choice but to define the conversion ratios between abstract and concrete labors as the respective wages of concrete labors. Thus abstract labor has no meaning before market equilibrium exists, so long as one admits that abstract labor and concrete labor are commensurate in the sense that *some* conversion ratio between them exists.

Steedman generalizes this argument to the case with positive profits. In this case, the price equation can be written

$$p = w\Lambda + \Pi \qquad (3.15)$$

where Π is the vector of unit profits. Now the amount of abstract surplus labor performed by the vth worker is $s^v = al^v - a\Lambda f^v$.

Suppose a is not proportional to w; then whenever we write $a = kw + b$, the vector b is not a multiple of w. Then

$$s^v = (kw + b)(l^v - \Lambda f^v)$$
$$= k(wl^v - w\Lambda f^v) + b(l^v - \Lambda f^v)$$
$$= k(wl^v - pf^v + \Pi f^v) + b(l^v - \Lambda f^v)$$
$$= k\Pi f^v + b(l^v - \Lambda f^v) \tag{3.16}$$

If a were proportional to w then b could be taken to be the zero vector and s^v would depend only on the final consumption f^v. In particular if two workers consumed the same vector then the amount of surplus abstract labor they performed would be the same, regardless of the concrete labor they engaged in. However, when a is not proportional to w then the residual vector b is not proportional to w and s^v depends on l^v. Thus the amount of surplus labor performed would depend not only on final consumption, as it should, but on what concrete labors the worker chose. Steedman argues that advocates of the abstract labor approach maintain that all workers who consume the same bundle (and hence earn the same total wages) should be equally exploited, independently of the concrete labors they engaged in. This contention is verifiable only if $a = kw$.

This section has argued that if rates of exploitation calculated in terms of abstract labor, whatever abstract labor is, obey certain rules then the conversion ratios between abstract and concrete labor are given by the wage rates of concrete labor. If one views concrete labors as labors of different skill, and if one believes that the 'Fundamental Marxian Theorem' should be true for a model with different skills (that is, zero profits implies zero exploitation of each worker) then *Theorem* 3.2 implies that the abstract labor value of a unit of skilled labor must be proportional to its wage.

4. THE TRANSFORMATION PROBLEM

The relationship between the vector of labor values Λ and equilibrium prices p has been a longstanding issue in Marxian economics. In *Capital*, Volume I Marx assumed that prices were proportional to labor values, and on this basis he derived the exploitation of labor. As we have shown in Section 3, the exploitation of labor in a productive system can be derived without any assumption concerning the proportionality of prices and labor values. In general, as will be shown below, the vectors p and Λ are not proportional.

The 'labor theory of value' is usually taken to mean the statement that labor value determines price. At some level Marx appeared to believe in a labor theory of value, which he inherited from Adam Smith and David Ricardo, although Ricardo (like Marx) realized that prices and labor values are in fact not proportional (Stigler [67]). Still, the question remained, could labor values be shown to determine prices in some sense? Are labor values logically prior to prices? In Section 6.2 we show that in general this cannot be claimed.

While Marx realized that prices were not proportional to values (*Capital*, Volume III) he viewed the deviation of prices from values as masking the true social relations between people. The true social relation, for Marx, involved the performance of labor and distribution of the products of labor; when exchange ratios of commodities do not accurately reflect the labor embodied in those commodities, then market relations cast a veil over the underlying labor relations. The most dramatic example of the veil cast by prices is in exchange of labor power for the wage. The worker exchanges a day's labor for a wage which he then uses to purchase his consumption bundle. That bundle embodies social labor of many workers, and because the worker is exploited, the hours embodied in his consumption bundle are fewer than the hours he worked to earn the wage. But because of the social division of labor and the intervention of prices and money, the worker does not perceive the exchange of his labor for the consumption bundle as an unequal one. Both his labor power and the bundle command the same price, assuming there is no worker saving. In this way the price system is said to mystify the underlying social relations of the distribution of labor.

The usefulness of this view depends, however, on the usefulness of the theory of labor exploitation, not on the relationship of values to prices. The interest of the theory of exploitation is independent of the relationship of values and prices, and so the interest in the 'transformation' of values to prices is an anachronism. Various transformation procedures showing how equilibrium prices can be computed as the result of an iterative process beginning with labor values as the first approximation have been proposed, but it is difficult to see what the purpose of such an exercise is (Morishima [35], Shaikh [61]). Such 'determination' of prices from values appears to be entirely formal and lacking in interesting economic content.

The well-known result on the proportionality of labor values to prices follows. Define the *organic composition* of the jth sector as

$$\gamma_j = \frac{\Lambda A._j}{L_j} \tag{4.1}$$

γ_j is the ratio of dead to living labor embodied in commodity j. All sectors have the same organic compositions if and only if the vectors ΛA and L are proportional.

Theorem 4.1   Let $p = (1 + \pi)pA + L$ and $\pi > 0$. Then p is proportional to Λ if and only if all organic compositions are equal.

Proof:
Let all organic compositions be equal, so $\Lambda A = \gamma L$, for a scalar γ. Since $\Lambda = \Lambda A + L$, Λ is proportional to ΛA and to L; so there exists a scalar α such that

$$\Lambda = (1 + \pi)\Lambda A + \alpha L \tag{4.2}$$

From (2.9), $p = (1 + \pi)pA + L$. Therefore

$$\Lambda[I - (1 + \pi)A] = \alpha p[I - (1 + \pi)A] \tag{4.3}$$

Applying $[I - (1 + \pi)A]^{-1}$, which exists to (4.3) yields the required proportionality.

Conversely, let $\Lambda = \alpha p$. By the definition (1.6) of Λ,

$$\alpha p = \alpha pA + L = \alpha pM + (1 - \alpha)L$$

and so

$$p = pM + \frac{1 - \alpha}{\alpha}L \tag{4.4}$$

But

$$p = (1 + \pi)pA + pbL = pM + \pi pA$$

and so $\pi pA = \dfrac{1 - \alpha}{\alpha} L$. Hence pA is proportional to L and so ΛA is

proportional to L.

Because prices are not in general proportional to labor values, relative magnitudes of economic variables will differ according as they are measured in prices or in labor values. For instance, although technical change will cause the price rate of profit to rise (Section 3.3), it can cause the rate of profit measured in labor values to fall. There is, however, no particular significance to this. Another consequence of the 'transformation problem' is that to a given rate of profit can correspond an interval of rates of exploitation, depending on what the consumption bundle of workers is. 'Pathologies' of this sort can occur: two workers can be paid money wages w_1 and w_2 with $w_1 > w_2$, and both work the same number of hours, but the first worker is exploited more than the second. This is due to the non-proportionality of prices and labor values (see Roemer [49], Chapter 8). In these cases it is the price accounts which are important, not the value accounts. In the last example, we would be ill-advised to say the first worker is worse off than the second because he can afford and prefers a more expensive consumption bundle which happens to embody less labor than the second worker's consumption.

In Section 6, we will discuss why labor values cannot be conceived of as logically prior to prices.

5. SIMPLE COMMODITY PRODUCTION

Theorem 4.1 showed that if the rate of profit is positive then, with the exception of a singular technology, equilibrium prices are not proportional to labor values. In Section 2.2, it was pointed out that exploitation has its origin in the scarcity of capital and in its unequal distribution. Marx imagined a pre-capitalist economy where all capital is commonly owned and in this case we will show equilibrium prices are proportional to labor values. Because of this, one can view the 'transformation' of labor values into the prices of Section 4 as a quasi-historical process accompanying some fictitious history of the transition in property forms from communalism or primitive communism to private ownership economies. Morishima and Catephores [37], for example, speak of the transformation problem in this historical sense. It is, however, not generally believed that primitive communism ever existed, and there is no anthropological evidence that labor value pricing has ever been practiced. It is therefore more appropriate to conceive of 'simple commodity production' and 'primitive communism' as thought experiments which demonstrate the correlation between labor-value pricing and non-exploitative regimes.

5.1 Simple commodity production with communal property

Imagine a society of producers $v = 1, \ldots, N$ each of whom can operate the Leontief technology (A, L), where A is an indecomposable matrix. Each producer will work only for himself—there will be no hiring or selling of labor. All inputs which are needed can be borrowed without interest from a common stock, but must be replaced at the end of the production period. Producers may differ in their consumption needs: thus producer v requires a consumption vector b^v. Each producer will produce goods and then trade with others for his needs, replenishing the common capital stock at the period's end. This is a depiction of an exchange economy without a labor market and without private ownership of the means of production.

Suppose the price vector at which the n goods exchange is p. Agent v wishes to produce goods whose exchange value at these prices will be sufficient to purchase his consumption bundle b^v and to replenish the stocks he borrowed to operate his chosen activities. If he chooses to operate an activity vector x^v, then his gross revenue must be

$$px^v \geq pAx^v + pb^v$$

where the two terms on the right-hand side are his investment costs and his consumption cost. We assume that subject to meeting his costs, the producer wishes to minimize the labor he expends. His program is:

$$\text{Choose } x^v \text{ to min } Lx^v \left.\vphantom{\begin{matrix}a\\b\end{matrix}}\right\} \qquad \text{(P5.1)}$$
$$\text{s.t. } p(I-A)x^v \geq pb^v$$

If $\hat{x}^v$ is an optimal solution for agent v to (P5.1), then the total net product is $(I-A)(\sum \hat{x}^v)$. We say:

Definition 5.1   The price vector p is a *communal simple commodity production* (*SCP*) *equilibrium* if there is an optimal solution $\hat{x}^v$ for each v such that $(I-A)(\sum \hat{x}^v) \geq \sum b^v$.

If the inequality in *Definition* 5.1 is met, then total gross production when all producers optimize is sufficient to replace all inputs used and to meet all consumption needs. Thus, each producer can trade at prices p the gross output x^v he produces for the b^v he requires and the investment goods Ax^v he used and must replace.

Theorem 5.1   Let A be indecomposable. Then any communal SCP equilibrium p is proportional to the labor value vector Λ. We may therefore normalize prices by setting $p = \Lambda$.

Proof:
Consider the dual program to producer v's program (P5.1):

$$\text{choose } \gamma^v \varepsilon \, R_+ \text{ to max } \gamma^v p b^v \left.\vphantom{\begin{matrix}a\\b\end{matrix}}\right\} \qquad \text{(P5.2)}$$
$$\text{s.t. } \gamma^v p(I-A) \leqq L$$

Since A is indecomposable, $(I-A)^{-1}$ is strictly positive. If for some v the constraint in (P5.2) is an equation then applying $(I-A)^{-1}$ to both of its sides we have

$$\gamma^v p = \Lambda$$

where γ^v is the solution to (P5.2), and the theorem is proved. So p can only fail to be proportional to Λ^v if:

$$\forall v \; \gamma^v p(I-A) \leqslant L \qquad (5.3)$$

in which case, by the positiveness of $(I-A)^{-1}$, applying $(I-A)^{-1}$ to (5.3):

$$\forall v \; \gamma^v p < \Lambda \qquad (5.4)$$

By the duality theorem of linear programming, it would then follow that

$$\forall v \; L \hat{x}^v = \gamma^v p b^v < \Lambda b^v \tag{5.5}$$

where $\hat{x}^v$ is any optimal solution for v to (P5.1). Consequently,

$$L\left(\sum_1^N \hat{x}^v\right) < \Lambda\left(\sum b^v\right) \tag{5.6}$$

But since p is a communal SCP equilibrium, there are optimal solutions $\hat{x}^v$ for each v such that

$$(I - A)\left(\sum \hat{x}^v\right) \geqq \sum b^v \tag{5.7}$$

Pre-multiplying inequality (5.7) by Λ gives

$$L\left(\sum x^v\right) \geqq \Lambda\left(\sum b^v\right) \tag{5.8}$$

which contradicts (5.6). This contradiction establishes the theorem.

We furthermore observe, from the proof, that

$$\forall v \; \gamma^v p = \Lambda$$

and so by linear programming:

$$(\forall v) \; \gamma^v p b^v = \Lambda b^v = L x^v$$

and so the labor expended by each producer at equilibrium is precisely the amount of labor embodied in the goods he consumes. Thus exploitation is absent in the SCP economy, a result which is not surprising given the absence of private property in the means of production. Furthermore we may observe that this economy is a subsistence one in the sense that no surplus will be produced: at equilibrium, $(I - A)\left(\sum \hat{x}^v\right) = \left(\sum b^v\right)$. For suppose, on the contrary, that:

$$(I - A)\left(\sum \hat{x}^v\right) \geqslant \sum b^v \tag{5.9}$$

Since p is proportional to Λ which is a positive vector (since $(I - A)^{-1} > 0$) it follows from (5.9) that

$$p(I - A)\left(\sum \hat{x}^v\right) > p\left(\sum b^v\right)$$

and so for some v:

$$p(I - A)\hat{x}^v > pb^v \tag{5.10}$$

But if (5.10) holds, $\hat{x}^v$ is not a solution to v's program (P5.1), for he could feasibly reduce all positive components of $\hat{x}^v$, thus reducing the labor he is expending. Hence the SCP economy is a stationary subsistence economy without exploitation.

The model of this section formalizes the notion that if all agents have knowledge of the technology and property is communal then prices are proportional to labor values. In the present model, however, there is no reason for agents to specialize: each agent could operate activities $x^v = (I - A)^{-1} b^v$, producing as net output precisely what he consumes, and trade need not take place at all. To derive the result of division of labor yet preserve the non-exploitative nature of the equilibrium, we would need to postulate, for example, the existence of set-up costs in operating different activities. Thus, suppose if an agent operates r different activities then his set-up costs (in terms of time) are $(r - 1)\tau$, where τ is interpreted as the time used in changing from one activity to the next. Then producer v's program becomes:

choose x^v to min $(Lx^v + (r^v - 1)\tau)$

$$p(I - A)x^v \geqslant pb^v$$

where r^v is the number of positive components of x^v. It is clear that each producer will now optimize by operating just one activity, and the rest of *Theorem* 5.1 goes through as before. Thus we have an egalitarian society with labor-value pricing and a complete social division of labor.

5.2 Simple commodity production with private property

Let us call an equilibrium *non-exploitative* when it supports an allocation in which there is no exploitation, that is, in which each agent expends in production precisely the amount of labor which is embodied in the net product he receives. In Section 5.1, we observed all equilibria in the communal SCP economy are non-exploitative and equilibrium prices are always equal to labor values. In this section we allow private ownership of capital. There may then be exploitation; but the association between non-exploitative equilibria and labor-value pricing remains.

As in Section 5.1, each producer can operate the indecomposable technology (A, L). Producer v now owns a vector ω^v of (capital) goods from which he must finance production. At prices p the value of his finance capital is $p\omega^v$ and he is constrained to choose an activity vector x^v the investment for which (Ax^v) he can advance:

$$pAx^v \leqslant p\omega^v$$

As in Section 5.1, there is neither a labor market nor a market for borrowing finance capital. As before, agent v desires to minimize labor expended subject to producing exchange value sufficient to replace used stocks and to purchase consumption requirements b^v. Thus an aggregate activity vector x must satisfy

$$(I - A)x \geqq \sum b^v \qquad (5.11)$$

and so aggregate stocks ω must be at least:

$$\omega \geqq Ax \geqq A(I - A)^{-1}\left(\sum b^v\right) \qquad (5.12)$$

Inequality (5.12) is a necessary condition for the viability of the economy which has been described. The program of producer v, facing prices p is now:

choose x^v to min Lx^v

$$\text{s.t. } p(I - A)x^v \geqslant pb^v \quad (5.13)$$
$$pAx^v \leqslant p\omega^v \quad (5.14)$$
$$x^v \geqslant 0$$

(P5.3)

As in Section 5.1, a *private ownership SCP equilibrium* is a price vector at which all producers optimize and aggregate production x satisfies inequality (5.11).

Note that program (P5.3) could equivalently be written as a utility maximizing program for agent v who receives utility from goods consumed and disutility from labor performed, thus:

$$\text{choose } b^v, x^v \text{ to max } u^v(b^v, Lx^v)$$

$$\text{s.t.}$$

$$p(I - A)x^v \geqslant pb^v$$

$$pAx^v \leqslant p\omega^v \qquad\qquad \text{(P5.3')}$$

$$x^v \geqslant 0$$

$$b^v \geqslant 0$$

The constraints, as before, express the requirement that the agent not run down his finance capital and that he finance production from current finance capital. Since there is disutility from work, (P5.3) is simply a reduced form of (P5.3'). At the optimal choice b^v, agent v can be viewed as choosing activities x^v which minimize labor expended. Hence the model of a private ownership simple commodity production economy can be viewed in the traditional utility maximizing way, with constraints that are not entirely traditional. The same follows for the communal SCP economy of Section 5.1.

Theorem 5.2 Let aggregate capital stocks ω satisfy $\omega \geqslant A(I - A)^{-1}(\sum b^v)$. Let A be indecomposable. Let p be a private ownership SCP equilibrium. Then p is non-exploitative if and only if p is proportional to Λ.

First, we establish:

Lemma 5.3 Let p be any price vector and v a producer who has an optimal solution $\hat{x}^v$ to (P5.3) at which $pA\hat{x}^v < p\omega^v$ and $\hat{x}^v > 0$. Then p is proportional to Λ.

Proof:
Since constraint (5.14) is not binding for v, (P5.3) can be written for him as:

$$\min Lx^v$$

$$\text{s.t. } p(I - A)x^v \geqslant pb^v$$

$$x^v \geqslant 0.$$

The dual program is

$$\text{choose } \gamma^v \text{ to max } \gamma^v p b^v$$

$$\text{s.t. } \gamma^v p (I - A) \leqslant L$$

$$\gamma^v \geqslant 0.$$

Since $\hat{x}^v > 0$ is a solution, complementary slackness implies

$$\gamma^v p (I - A) = L$$

and so

$$\gamma^v p = \Lambda$$

establishing the required proportionality.

Lemma 5.4   Let A be indecomposable, p a private ownership SCP equilibrium. Then $p > 0$.

Proof:
By indecomposability, since for the aggregate activity vector x, $x \geqq (I - A)^{-1} (\sum b^v)$, it follows that $x > 0$. Suppose that for some commodity j:

$$p_j - pA_{.j} < 0. \tag{5.15}$$

Inspection of (P5.3) shows no producer will produce commodity j, as it would cost him revenue to do so. Hence (5.15) cannot hold, since all commodities are produced $(x > 0)$. Hence $p - pA \geqq 0$. If $p - pA = p(I - A) = 0$ then $p = 0$ since $(I - A)$ is invertible. So $p(I - A) \geqslant 0$. The positivity of $(I - A)^{-1}$ now implies $p > 0$.

Proof of Theorem 5.2
$\Leftarrow$ Let p be proportional to Λ. Then a producer's program can be written

$$\min Lx^v$$

$$\text{s.t.}$$

$$Lx^v \geqslant \Lambda b^v$$

$$\Lambda Ax^v \leqslant \Lambda \omega^v$$

$$x^v \geqslant 0$$

But the first constraint must hold with equality, for otherwise all positive components of x^v could be feasibly reduced, thus reducing the objective. Hence p is non-exploitative.

$\Rightarrow$ Let $(p; \hat{x}^1, \ldots, \hat{x}^N)$ be a non-exploitative equilibrium allocation, so $L\hat{x} = \Lambda b^v$ for all v. Let $\hat{x} = \sum \hat{x}^v$. We have $(I - A)\hat{x} = \sum b^v$, for if $(I - A)\hat{x} \geqslant \sum b^v$, then

$$p(I - A)\hat{x} > p(\sum b^v)$$

by the positivity of p (*Lemma* 5.4) and hence for some v:

$$p(I - A)\hat{x}^v > pb^v$$

which means $\hat{x}^v$ is not an optimal solution for v. Hence

$$A\hat{x} = A(I - A)^{-1}(\sum b^v)$$

and so the assumption on ω in the hypothesis of the theorem implies

$$\omega > A\hat{x}. \tag{5.16}$$

(Note that hypothesis eliminates only the singular case $\omega = A(I - A)^{-1}(\sum b^v)$.) Since $p > 0$, (5.16) implies

$$p\omega > pA\hat{x}. \tag{5.17}$$

Define $\bar{x}^v = (I - A)^{-1}b^v$. Note

$$\sum \bar{x}^v = (I - A)^{-1}(\sum b^v) = \hat{x} \tag{5.18}$$

Therefore, since $\omega = \sum \omega^v$, it follows from (5.17) and (5.18) that:

$$\exists \mu \text{ for which } pA\bar{x}^\mu < p\omega^\mu \tag{5.19}$$

Note also from the definition of $\bar{x}^v$ that

$$\forall v \; p(I - A)\bar{x}^v = pb^v \text{ and } L\bar{x}^v = \Lambda b^v \tag{5.20}$$

From the two equations of (5.20) and from (5.19) it follows that $\bar{x}^\mu$ is a feasible and optimal solution to (P5.3) for agent μ. By the definition of $\bar{x}^\mu$ and by the indecomposability of A, $\bar{x}^\mu > 0$. Hence $\bar{x}^\mu$ fulfills the hypotheses of *Lemma* 5.3; it follows that p is proportional to Λ.

Theorem 5.1 showed that in a simple commodity production economy without private property, equilibrium prices are equal to labor values. Communal economies are non-exploitative and so prices always correspond to labor values in these non-exploitative economies. *Theorem* 5.2 extends this relationship to private ownership economies: the non-exploitative equilibria of a private ownership SCP economy are precisely the ones whose prices are equal to labor values. Thus labor-value pricing is associated with the absence of exploitation, at least in SCP economics. Because of this the 'transformation' of values into equilibrium prices (where there is a positive rate of profit and prices are not proportional to labor values) can be viewed, metaphorically at least, as accompanying the transformation of society from a non-exploitative one to an exploitative one. Thus the 'transformation' has an ethical and a quasi-historical aspect. It does not follow, however, that labor values provide any trenchant insight into the formation of equilibrium prices in a capitalist (exploitative) economy.

5.3 Exploitation in simple commodity production

It is worth drawing attention to the observation that in a private ownership simple commodity production economy, exploitation can exist at equilibrium. (Indeed *Theorem* 5.2 says this will happen whenever equilibrium prices are not proportional to labor values, which in general will be the case. It is not difficult to construct examples.) Noteworthy is the existence of exploitation in the absence of either a labor or capital market. *Agents are exploited* (or are exploiters) *entirely through the trade of produced goods, not through the trade of labor power.*

Thus the existence of a labor market can be viewed as incidental, from a logical point of view, to the issue of exploitation. Indeed when a labor market does exist, then agents who optimize by selling labor power will be exploited (see Section 6). But even in the absence of a labor market exploitation can exist. If one had to locate one cause of exploitation, it would not be the existence of labor markets but private ownership of the means of production. As will be shown in Section 6, exploiters turn out to be those who have a high capital-labor ratio at equilibrium, and the exploited are those with a low capital-labor ratio. (This result is true as well for the model of Section 5.2, but it will not be verified here as it is shown for a slightly different model below.)

The model of this section of trade without a labor market can be viewed as a model of international trade where each agent is a country and there is no flow of labor or capital across borders. 'Exploitation' in this case is a version of what has been called 'unequal exchange' in the Marxian literature. (For a survey of the unequal exchange literature, see Evans [22].) A country is 'exploited' if the labor expended by its labor force is greater than the labor embodied in the goods for which the country trades its net national product. For further extensions of this model to international trade, see Roemer [54].

The point of Sections 5.2, 5.3 is important for evaluating the ethical importance of the concept of exploitation. Exploitation, defined as the unequal exchange of live labor for labor embodied in goods, can exist with or without a labor market. Without a labor market, every agent can work for himself on his own capital, and goods will be traded at some set of prices. Agents will be 'exploited' in this process if their capital-labor ratio is low. Thus defenders of the exploitation concept must locate the injustice in this transaction, independently of the existence of a labor market. The issue of *exploitation* (unequal exchange of labor) must be separated from *domination* (the relation between the boss and the worker at the point of production), for the two are not synonymous. This question will be studied below.

6. CLASSES

6.1 Class formation and the class-wealth correspondence

In Marxism, class is not defined by wealth or status, but by how agents relate to the sale or purchase of labor power. The three main classes are the bourgeoisie who hire labor, the proletarians who sell their labor, and the self-employed. In this section, we shall derive class position of agents from their optimizing behavior. Class position will be chosen by the agent as a consequence of his preferences and initial endowment. This will provide microfoundations for the class stratification of society.

We continue to assume (although only for simplicity) that the technology is the Leontief system (A, L). There are N agents; the vth agent has an endowment vector of produced goods ω^v and a utility function u^v. Assume every agent has one unit of labor (although it could be assumed they have different endowments of labor). Assume that there is a labor market but no capital market; this assumption is relaxed in Section 7. Instead of positing the existence of firms, as in the Arrow–Debreu model, assume that each agent can operate the technique (A, L). (Indeed, since there are constant returns to scale, there would in any case not be any neoclassical profits to distribute to shareholders.)

The agent must decide how much to work for himself, how much labor to hire, and how much labor to sell. Let

x^v be the vector of activities v operates himself

on his own account

y^v be the vector of activities v hires labor to operate

z^v be the amount of labor v sells to others

Facing the price-wage vector $(p, 1)$, agent v will earn revenues

$$\Pi^v = p(I - A)x^v + (p - (pA + L))y^v + z^v$$

Agent v faces two constraints: he must finance the investment for the activity vector $(x^v + y^v)$ from his finance capital, which has value $p\omega^v$. Secondly, he has a labor constraint. At the given prices, we can view v's preferences as a function of revenues and labor performed. Thus his utility maximizing program can be written:

choose x^v, y^v, z^v to maximize $u^v(\Pi^v, l^v)$

such that

$$\Pi^v = p(I - A)x^v + (p - (pA + L))y^v + z^v \qquad (P6.1)$$

$$pAx^v + pAy^v \leqslant p\omega^v \qquad (6.1)$$

$$Lx^v + z^v = l^v$$

$$l^v \leqslant 1$$

Notice that v must advance the material costs for production out of capital (inequality (6.1)); by assumption the wage costs to his hired labor are paid at the end of the period out of revenues.

We will assume that the prices $(p, 1)$ are equilibrium prices of some more complete general equilibrium model; (P6.1) is the reduced form of the individual's problem. In particular, the markets for goods and labor clear at these prices. It is easily seen that no agent will operate, either on his own account or with hired labor, an activity making less than the maximal profit rate. Therefore, assuming all activities operate at equilibrium, we have as before a uniform profit rate π and

$$p = (1 + \pi)pA + L$$

It is assumed that u^v is increasing in Π and decreasing in l.

An agent's *class position* is defined by the vector (x^v, y^v, z^v) which he chooses. Schematically, this vector can be abbreviated as a list of three symbols " + " or "0". For instance the class position $(0, +, 0)$ means the agent sets $x^v = 0, y^v \neq 0, z^v = 0$, and so he only hires labor, and is a member of the bourgeoisie. Altogether there are seven possible class positions, thus defined (since $(0, 0, 0)$ can be ruled out as not occurring—everyone must earn some revenue, let us assume). We shall show every agent is a member of one of five classes:

$(0, +, 0)$	bourgeoisie
$(+, +, 0)$	small bourgeoisie
$(+, 0, 0)$	self-employed
$(+, 0, +)$	mixed proletarian
$(0, 0, +)$	proletariat

(Thus the class positions $(0, +, +)$ and $(+, +, +)$ are always redundant. An agent will always have at least one optimal solution placing him in one of the above named classes.)

Lemma 6.1   (1) Every agent with positive wealth has an optimal solution to (P5.1) placing him in class position $(0, +, +)$. An agent with zero wealth has solutions only of form $(0, 0, +)$. (2) at the optimum, $\Pi^v = \pi p \omega^v + l^v$.

Proof:

Let (x^v, y^v, z^v) be a solution for v to (P5.1). Define

$$\bar{x}^v = 0, \quad \bar{y}^v = x^v + y^v, \quad \bar{z}^v = z^v + Lx^v.$$

Check in (P6.1) that $(\bar{x}^v, \bar{y}^v, \bar{z}^v)$ is feasible for v, and achieves the same revenue Π^v. This demonstrates the first claim. That agents with no wealth have solutions only of form $(0, 0, +)$ follows from the capital constraint (6.1), since they must set $x^v = y^v = 0$.

Hence every agent has a solution generating revenue $(p - (pA + L))\bar{y}^v + \bar{z}^v$, where $\bar{x}^v = 0$. Since u^v is increasing in Π^v, v will engage all his capital, assuming $\pi > 0$. Hence $pA\bar{y}^v = p\omega^v$. Thus $(p - (pA + L))\bar{y}^v = \dfrac{p - (pA + L)}{pA} pA\bar{y}^v = \pi p\omega^v$ and since $z^v = l^v$ it follows that $\Pi^v = \pi p\omega^v + l^v$.

From *Lemma* 6.1 it follows that any solution (x^v, y^v, z^v) in which v fully utilizes his finance capital and supplies l^v labor will be an optimal solution, since all such solutions will earn him revenues $\pi p\omega^v + l^v$. From this observation we can characterize class position with respect to the five listed classes with respect to the ratio W^v/l^v, the agent's 'capital-labor ratio,' where $W^v \equiv p\omega^v$. For example, v will have a solution of the form $(+, 0, 0)$ precisely when

$$\left(\frac{pA}{L}\right)_{\min} \leqslant \frac{W^v}{l^v} \leqslant \left(\frac{pA}{L}\right)_{\max} \tag{6.2}$$

for when and only when† (6.2) holds there is a non-negative

---

†This is a consequence of an algebraic fact. Suppose

$$\sum a_i x_i = K, \quad \sum b_i x_i = L.$$

Then

$$\frac{\sum a_i x_i}{\sum b_i x_i} = \frac{\sum \dfrac{a_i}{b_i} b_i x_i}{\sum b_i x_i} = \sum \left(\frac{a_i}{b_i}\right) \frac{b_i x_i}{\sum b_i x_i} = \frac{K}{L}$$

Thus $\dfrac{K}{L}$ is a weighted average of the ratios $\left(\dfrac{a_i}{b_i}\right)$, since the weights $\dfrac{b_i x_i}{\sum b_i x_i}$ add to

1. Hence $\left(\dfrac{a_i}{b_i}\right)_{\min} \leqslant \dfrac{K}{L} \leqslant \left(\dfrac{a_i}{b_i}\right)_{\max}$.

vector x^v such that

$$pAx^v = W^v$$

$$Lx^v = l^v$$

$\left(\left(\dfrac{pA}{L}\right)_{\min}\right.$ is the minimum of the component ratios $\dfrac{pA_j}{L_j}$, and $\left(\dfrac{pA}{L}\right)_{\max}$ is the maximum component ratio.$\left.\right)$ If $\dfrac{W^v}{l^v} > \left(\dfrac{pA}{L}\right)_{\max}$,

then

$$x^v \geqslant 0, \quad Lx^v = l^v \text{ implies } pAx^v < W^v.$$

Thus in this case v cannot possibly fully utilize his capital with the labor he is willing to supply, and so he must hire others. Therefore

$$\infty > \frac{W^v}{l^v} > \left(\frac{pA}{L}\right)_{\max} \text{ implies } \begin{array}{l} v \, \varepsilon(+, +, 0) \text{ and} \\ v \, \notin (+, 0, 0). \end{array}$$

With similar reasoning we prove the remaining parts of:

Lemma 6.2   Let $\pi > 0$. Then

$$v \, \varepsilon(0, +, 0) \Leftrightarrow W^v/l^v = \infty \qquad (\text{i.e., } l^v = 0)$$

$$v \, \varepsilon(+, +, 0)\backslash(+, 0, 0) \Leftrightarrow \infty > \frac{W^v}{l^v} > \left(\frac{pA}{L}\right)_{\max}$$

$$v \, \varepsilon(+, 0, 0) \Leftrightarrow \left(\frac{pA}{L}\right)_{\min} \leqslant W^v/l^v \leqslant \left(\frac{pA}{L}\right)_{\max}$$

$$v \, \varepsilon(+, 0, +)\backslash(+, 0, 0) \Leftrightarrow 0 < W^v/l^v < \left(\frac{pA}{L}\right)_{\min}$$

$$v \, \varepsilon(0, 0, +) \Leftrightarrow 0 = W^v/l^v \qquad (\text{i.e., } W^v = 0)$$

Here, the notation '$v \, \varepsilon(+, +, 0)\backslash(+, 0, 0)$' means '$v$ is a member of class $(+, +, 0)$ but not of class $(+, 0, 0)$.' Thus, there is a partition of society into five (disjoint) classes, and class membership ascends with the agent's wealth-labor ratio.

Suppose agents do not have any desire for leisure. Then all agents will supply $l^v = 1$, and according to *Lemma* 6.2, class membership is monotonically related to wealth. Indeed, the relationship between wealth and class position is the classical one discussed in Marxian literature: with the proletariat having 'nothing to lose but their chains,' the self-employed in the middle and the bourgeoisie at the top of the wealth pyramid. (Strictly speaking, if everyone supplies some labor, there is no pure bourgeoisie, since membership in $(0, +, 0)$ is characterized by $l^v = 0$.)

What about the correspondence between *wealth* and class position? The monotonic correspondence between wealth and class is maintained as long as labor supplied by agents does not increase too rapidly with wealth. Viewing labor supplied as a cross-sectional function of wealth $l(W)$, then the wealth-labor index is $\gamma(W) = W/l(W)$ and class position will be monotonically related to wealth as long as $\gamma(W)$ increases in W, by *Lemma* 6.2. Assuming for the moment we have a continuum of agents and that $\gamma(W)$ is differentiable, compute that

$$\frac{d\gamma}{dW} > 0 \Leftrightarrow \frac{dl}{dW} \cdot \frac{W}{l} < 1 \tag{6.3}$$

Summarizing,

Theorem 6.3   (Class-Wealth Correspondence) If labor supplied cross-sectionally by agents increases inelastically with their wealths at equilibrium prices, then class position is monotonically related to wealth in the 'proper' way, with the proletariat at the bottom and the bourgeoisie at the top of the wealth pyramid.

The elasticity condition (6.3) is probably historically reasonable; indeed, it is often believed that labor supplied decreases with wealth. Indeed, for two preference profiles that might be considered to be polar opposites, the inelasticity condition holds: when all agents have no preference for leisure (6.3) holds since all agents work one unit of labor, and when all agents have an 'infinite' preference for leisure in that they desire to work only long enough to produce some subsistence requirement (assumed to be the same for all) net of reproducing their capital stock, the elasticity of labor with respect to wealth is negative. These two cases are studied Roemer [50], Parts I and II.

The Class-Wealth Correspondence informs us that if labor is supplied inelastically with respect to wealth, in the sense of the inequality (6.3), then we can identify the act of hiring labor with being wealthy and the act of selling labor with being relatively poor. Hence class position and wealth are good proxies for each other. From a logical as opposed to empirical viewpoint, this correlation does not hold, since there may be intervals of wealth in which an increase in wealth calls forth a greater fractional increase in labor supplied. In such a case, we could observe the relatively poor agent hiring the relatively richer one.

It is important to underscore that *Theorem 6.3* shows that the relationship between wealth and class position—that the wealthy are the labor hirers and the poor are the labor sellers—does not always hold. Thus the classical Marxian correlation, although empirically a good one, is not a logical one. This point is an important one for fundamental understanding of the usefulness of the exploitation concept, and it is pursued in Section 8.2.

6.2 Class formation and domination

In the model of Section 6.1, expending labor is assumed to involve a disutility, but there is no additional disutility involved in working for others contrasted with working on one's own account. The additional disutility which is a consequence of working for another can be said to be due to domination of the worker by the employer. The domination disutility can be modelled by assuming agents have utility functions of the form $u^v(\Pi^v, l_o^v, l_s^v)$ where l_o^v is labor performed on one's own account (self-employment) and l_s^v is labor sold, performed on an employer's account. We assume

$$\frac{\partial u^v}{\partial l_o} > \frac{\partial u^v}{\partial l_s} \tag{6.4}$$

which guarantees that the agent would always prefer to shift labor performed for another to labor performed on a self-employed basis. The analysis of Section 6.1 can be repeated under assumption (6.4). In this case, no agent ever optimizes by choosing a class position $(0, +, +)$ or $(+, +, +)$: no agent will simultaneously hire and sell labor, as he could increase his utility by quitting his employer, firing some of his hired labor and doing their work himself. Hence with domination, the five class positions of *Lemma 6.2* are the *only* class positions that will be observed, while in the absence of domination, an agent will in general have optimal solutions of the forms $(+, +, +)$ and $(0, +, +)$ as well as a solution of one of the five classes in the partition (see *Lemma* 6.1).

A *dominator* is one who optimizes by hiring labor and a *dominated* agent is one who must sell labor to optimize. Thus the dominators are bourgeoisie and small bourgeoisie. *Theorem* 6.3, when the *domination effect* (6.4) is postulated, becomes:

Theorem 6.4 (Wealth-Domination Correspondence) If labor supplied cross-sectionally by agents at equilibrium prices is inelastic with respect to wealth, then dominators are all agents who are wealthier than some $\bar{W}$ and dominated agents are all those who are less wealthy than some $\underline{W}$.

Theorem 6.4 follows directly from *Theorem* 6.3: for with the inelasticity condition, class position (and hence domination status) is monotonic in wealth. Self-employed agents are neither dominating nor dominated; they are the agents with wealths in the interval $[\underline{W}, \bar{W}]$.

7. THE CLASS EXPLOITATION CORRESPONDENCE

In Section 3, exploitation was defined for an economy where all workers consume the same bundle of consumption goods b. Surplus labor was defined as labor worked in excess of 'socially necessary labor time' Λb. In the present section, we propose an extension of the definition of exploitation to the model of Section 5, where agents can consume the bundle of their choice. We then demonstrate the relationship between exploitation and class.

7.1 The Leontief model

At equilibrium prices p which sustain a profit rate π in the model of Section 5, an agent v earns revenues $\Pi^v = \pi W^v + l^v$ where $W^v = p\omega^v$. An agent is *exploited* if there is no bundle of goods he can purchase with his revenues which embodies as much labor as he worked. This is the natural extension of the classical subsistence-related concept of exploitation. The most effective way for an agent to purchase embodied labor time in goods is to spend all his revenue on the good with the maximum labor value-price ratio.

Thus agent v is exploited if and only if:

$$\left(\frac{\Lambda}{p}\right)_{\max} (\pi W^v + l^v) < l^v \tag{7.1}$$

In like manner, we will say an agent v is an *exploiter* if, no matter how v spends his revenues on goods, he cannot help but buy back more embodied labor time than he expended. This occurs precisely when:

$$\left(\frac{\Lambda}{p}\right)_{\min} (\pi W^v + l^v) > l^v \tag{7.2}$$

From (7.1) and (7.2), compute that:

$$\left.\begin{array}{c} v \text{ is exploited if and only if } \dfrac{W^v}{l^v} < \dfrac{1 - \left(\dfrac{\Lambda}{p}\right)_{\max}}{\pi\left(\dfrac{\Lambda}{p}\right)_{\max}} \\[3em] v \text{ is an exploiter if and only if } \dfrac{W^v}{l^v} > \dfrac{1 - \left(\dfrac{\Lambda}{p}\right)_{\min}}{\pi\left(\dfrac{\Lambda}{p}\right)_{\min}} \end{array}\right\} \tag{7.3}$$

If W^v/l^v lies in between the two numbers appearing on the right hand side of the inequalities in (7.3) then v is neither exploited nor exploiting, as he is able to purchase a bundle of goods embodying precisely as much labor as he expended as production. Thus as long as

$$\left(\frac{\Lambda}{p}\right)_{\min} < \left(\frac{\Lambda}{p}\right)_{\max}$$

which occurs whenever the organic compositions are not identical across sectors (*Theorem* 4.1) there is a *gray area* of agents who are neither exploited nor exploiting. The existence of gray area of agents is the manifestation of 'the transformation problem' in this model.

Inequalities (7.3) provide an indexation of agents' exploitation status by the wealth-labor ratios W^v/l^v, and *Lemma* 6.2 provides an indexation of class membership by the same ratio. By comparing the two characterizations we can conclude:

Theorem 7.1 (Class Exploitation Correspondence Principle) Let $\pi > 0$. Every agent who optimizes by hiring labor power (in the top two class positions of *Lemma* 6.2) is an exploiter; every agent who optimizes by selling labor is exploited (the bottom two classes of *Lemma* 6.2).

Proof:
By comparing the inequalities of *Lemma* 6.2 with inequalities (7.3), it suffices to prove:

$$\left(\frac{pA}{L}\right)_{\max} \geq \frac{1 - \left(\frac{\Lambda}{p}\right)_{\min}}{\pi \left(\frac{\Lambda}{p}\right)_{\min}} \tag{7.4a}$$

and

$$\left(\frac{pA}{L}\right)_{\min} \leq \frac{1 - \left(\frac{\Lambda}{p}\right)_{\max}}{\pi \left(\frac{\Lambda}{p}\right)_{\max}} \tag{7.4b}$$

We prove (7.4a). Suppose it were false. Then

$$\forall j \; \frac{pA_{.j}}{L_j} < \frac{1 - \left(\frac{\Lambda}{p}\right)_{\min}}{\pi \left(\frac{\Lambda}{p}\right)_{\min}}$$

and so the following vector inequality holds:

$$\left(\frac{\Lambda}{p}\right)_{\min} \pi p A < L - \left(\frac{\Lambda}{p}\right)_{\min} L \tag{7.5}$$

By the price Eq. (2.9) this can be written

$$\left(\frac{\Lambda}{p}\right)_{\min} [p(I - A) - L] < L - \left(\frac{\Lambda}{p}\right)_{\min} L$$

or

$$\left(\frac{\Lambda}{p}\right)_{\min} p(I - A) < L \tag{7.6}$$

Post-multiplying (7.6) by the non-negative matrix $(I-A)^{-1}$ yields:

$$\left(\frac{\Lambda}{p}\right)_{\min} p < L(I-A)^{-1} = \Lambda \qquad (7.7)$$

But (7.7) is a contradiction, since for at least one component j, $\left(\frac{\Lambda}{p}\right)_{\min} p_j = \Lambda_j$. Hence (7.4a) is verified. In like manner, (7.4b) can be verified.

The Class Exploitation Correspondence Principle (CECP) proves a relationship between class and exploitation which in classical Marxism was simply postulated. As such, it provides microfoundations for the claim that capitalists (those who hire labor) exploit proletarians (those who sell labor). Note the CECP is true whether or not the elasticity condition of *Theorem* 6.3 attains. Thus class and exploitation are always associated as the theorem claims—although neither exploitation nor class will be 'properly' correlated with wealth unless the inelasticity condition on labor supply holds.

It should be remarked that the converse of *Theorem* 7.1 does not hold. There can be exploiters (or exploited agents) who are not labor hirers (or labor sellers). The proof shows the gray area of agents lies entirely within the class of self-employed $(+, 0, 0)$— but it does not strictly coincide with it. Only when prices are proportional to values do the gray area and the class $(+, 0, 0)$ coincide, in which case they both collapse to a single point on the W^{ν}/l^{ν} line.

If we adopt the domination model of Section 6.2 then the CECP states that any dominator is an exploiter and every dominated agent is exploited: but again the converse does not hold. There are, in general, exploited and exploiting agents who are neutral with respect to domination.

7.2 The CECP with general technology

The extension of the CECP to a model with more general technology than the Leontief model is of interest because it contains a lesson concerning the classical Marxian question of the logical priority of labor values or prices.

Consider the model of exploitation and class, but allow the

technology to be of the von Neumann type. Indeed, the results of this section are true, more generally, when the technology is a convex cone (see Roemer [50], Chapter 5)). To define exploitation it is first necessary to define embodied labor time; we might use the definition proposed by Morishima and discussed in Section 1.2, where the labor value of a vector of goods f is defined as the solution of the program:

$$\min Lx$$

$$\text{s.t. } Bx \geqslant Ax + f \tag{P7.1}$$

$$x \geqslant 0$$

where $(B, A; L)$ is the von Neumann technology. With labor value so defined, an agent can be classified as exploited (or exploiting) if he is not able to purchase goods embodying as much labor as he expended, as in Section 7.1. The analog to *Lemma* 6.2 remains true for the more general technology. With the Morishima definition of labor value, however, *the CECP is in general false.*

There is an alternative definition which preserves the validity of the CECP. To produce a net output vector f, instead of scanning the entire production set for ways of producing f, limit the scan to those processes which achieve the maximal profit rate *at equilibrium prices.* In the von Neumann model, equilibrium prices satisfy:

$$pB \leqslant (1 + \pi)pA + L \tag{7.8}$$

for some maximal profit rate π; only those processes will be operated for which

$$pB._j = (1 + \pi)pA._j + L_j \tag{7.9}$$

Consider the alternative definition of the labor embodied in f as the solution of the program:

$$\min Lx$$

s.t.

$$Bx \geqslant Ax + f \tag{P7.2}$$

$$pBx = (1 + \pi)pAx + Lx$$

$$x \geqslant 0$$

The equality constraint in (P7.2) assures that the only eligible processes for producing f are those which attain the maximal profit rate π.

Under the definition of labor value given by (P7.2) the CECP is true for general technology. (The proof is provided in Roemer [50], Chapter 5.) The theorem tells us that if we wish to preserve the relationship between exploitation and class, then we must adopt a definition of labor valuation in which embodied labor time *depends upon equilibrium prices*. We cannot define labor value, by (P7.2), until equilibrium prices are known. This appears to settle the issue of the logical priority of prices versus values, and the verdict is not favorable to the doctrinaire position of many interpreters of classical Marxism.

Indeed, consider an economy which supports multiple equilibria, which can certainly occur. Then the data of the model (preferences u^v, technology $(B, A; L)$ and endowments ω^v) are not sufficient to define labor values. For the economy can support different price equilibria, and in general the labor values of commodities depend, according to (P7.2), on prices as well as the given data.

There is one claim of classical Marxism which is strengthened by the price-dependent definition of labor value. Socially necessary labor time, according to (P7.2), is defined as the labor which must be expended to produce commodities using processes that capitalists would use (that is, profit maximizing processes), not simply technological feasible processes (as (P7.1) implies). Thus the 'correct' definition of labor value views it as associated with capitalist production in particular, not commodity production in general. Indeed the non-equivalence of the two definitions is a consequence of the fact that labor-minimizing processes of production are not necessarily profit-maximizing ones, that is, efficient ones. Furthermore, as demand or the distribution of endowments change, but the technology remains fixed, equilibrium prices will change, and so embodied labor times will change. Embodied labor time must be conceived of as a general equilibrium concept: it depends on tastes and endowments as well as on technology, and indeed on equilibrium prices.

7.3 The isomorphism between labor and capital markets

In the models thusfar there is a labor market but no capital market. In this section a capital market is introduced in place of a labor market, and it is shown that in the absence of domination effects (Section 6.2) the capital market economy is isomorphic to the labor market economy with respect to properties of exploitation and class. Finally, an economy with both labor and credit markets will have no new characteristics.

Let us imagine the economy of Section 7.1–7.2 existing on Labor Market Island. On a neighboring island, there is identical replication of the agents who appear on Labor Market Island, but on Capital Market Island there is no labor market; instead agents lend or borrow finance capital at an interest rate r. Equilibrium prices consist of a price vector p of commodity prices and an interest rate r which permit all markets to clear when agents optimize. As before each agent maximizes utility subject to his capital constraint where he can now borrow or lend capital—but no labor hiring exists. Then the program of agent v is to:

$$\text{maximize } u^v(\Pi^v, l^v)$$

$$\text{subject to}$$

$$\Pi^v = p(I - A)x^v + (p - (1 + r)pA)z^v + ry^v \qquad (\text{P7.3})$$

$$pAx^v + y^v \leqslant p\omega^v$$

$$Lx^v + Lz^v = l^v$$

$$l^v \leqslant 1$$

where x^v is an n-vector

z^v is an n-vector

y^v is a scalar

x^v is the vector of activities which v operates using his own finance capital, z^v is the vector of activities he operates using borrowed capital, and y^v is the amount of capital he lends to others. The capital constraint in (P7.3) expresses the fact that one's funds must be sufficient to finance production and lending activity.

The analysis of (P7.3) is analogous to that of Section 6.1. We define capital market classes which describe how an agent relates to the borrowing and lending of capital when he optimizes. Write solutions to (P7.3) as vectors (x^v, y^v, z^v) and then the five relevant class positions become:

1. $(0, +, 0)$ pure lender
2. $(+, +, 0)$ lender plus own financing
3. $(+, 0, 0)$ solely own financing
4. $(+, 0, +)$ borrower plus own financing
5. $(0, 0, +)$ pure borrower

As in *Lemma* 6.1, we have:

Lemma 7.1   (1) Every agent has an optimal solution to (P7.3) of the form $(0, +, +)$. (2) Maximum revenue for v is $\Pi^v = rp\omega^v + l^v$, with an appropriate normalization of prices p.

Proof:
Let (x^v, y^v, z^v) be an optimal solution to (P7.3) and define a new solution $(\bar{x}^v, \bar{y}^v, \bar{z}^v)$ by

$$\bar{x}^v = 0$$

$$\bar{y}^v = y^v + pAx^v$$

$$\bar{z}^v = x^v + z^v$$

In $(\bar{x}^v, \bar{y}^v, \bar{z}^v)$ agent v lends out all his capital and works entirely on borrowed capital. Check that

$$L\bar{x}^v + L\bar{z}^v = Lx^v + Lz^v$$

$$pA\bar{x}^v + \bar{y}^v = pAx^v + y^v$$

and so the new solution is feasible for (P7.3). Moreover check that $\bar{\Pi}^v = \Pi^v$ and $\bar{l}^v = l^v$ and so the new solution is optimal, which demonstrates the first claim.

Calculate that revenues for the new solution are

$$\bar{\Pi}^v = (p - (1 + r)pA)(x^v + z^v) + rp\omega^v$$

where we use the observation that v will lend out all his capital in the solution so long as $r > 0$. Define the *implicit wage* in sector j as w_j where

$$w_j L_j = p_j - (1 + r)pA._j \tag{7.10}$$

and then revenues can be written

$$\Pi^v = \sum w_j L_j (x_j^v + z_j^v) + rp\omega^v \qquad (7.11)$$

Notice from (P7.3) that if $w_j > w_i$ then the agent will not operate sector i, since according to the revenue function (7.11) he would generate more revenue for the same labor expenditure by operating sector j. Therefore, assuming all sectors in the Leontief technology are operating at equilibrium, we have $w_j = w_i$ for all i and j, and so there is a uniform implicit wage. Normalize prices p by setting the uniform implicit wage equal to unity, and according to (7.11):

$$\bar{\Pi}^v = rW^v + l^v \qquad (7.12)$$

Note that revenue formula (7.12) is identical to the revenue formula (*Lemma* 6.1) of Labor Market Island, with the interest rate replaced by the profit rate. This observation allows us to prove:

Theorem 7.2 (Isomorphism theorem) Let (p, π) be an equilibrium on Labor Market Island. Then (p, r) with $r = \pi$ is an equilibrium on Capital Market Island. The equilibria are isomorphic with respect to class and exploitation properties of the agents: every agent on Capital Market Island is in the 'same' class position as his replicated twin on Labor Market Island and works precisely as long as his twin, and twins have identical wealths.

Proof:
Let (x^v, y^v, z^v) be an optimal solution for v on Labor Market Island at equilibrium prices (p, π). We construct a solution on Capital Market Island for his twin, who will be called $\bar{v}$. On Capital Market Island let $\bar{x}^{\bar{v}} = x^v$; let $\bar{v}$ operate on borrowed funds precisely the activities that his twin v operated for his employers on Labor Market Island (so that $z^v = L\bar{z}^{\bar{v}}$); and let $\bar{v}$ lend out capital precisely equal to the capital that v advanced on Labor Market Island to hire workers with (so $pAy^v = \bar{y}^{\bar{v}}$). If every agent behaves this way, then we have simply mimicked the labor hiring/labor selling activity on Labor Market Island with lending/borrowing activity on Capital Market Island. Instead of selling labor power (on Labor Market Island) an agent on Capital

Market Island borrows capital and operates activities on that capital which his twin operated as a wage laborer. It is easily checked that (P7.3) is feasible and optimal for the proposed solution if and only if (P6.1) was optimal on Labor Market Island. Furthermore, the activities operated on the two islands are identical, and so if the solutions are globally feasible and market clearing on Labor Market Island, that remains the case on Capital Market Island. Since labor selling transforms itself into borrowing of capital and labor hiring into lending of capital, the class isomorphism of twins is demonstrated. The exploitation isomorphism follows since each pair of twins has identical wealths $p\omega^v$ and work identical hours l^v, and so the exploitation inequalities (7.3) hold identically on the two islands.

It follows from the Isomorphism Theorem that the Class Exploitation Correspondence Principle holds on Capital Market Island: agents who must borrow to optimize are exploited and agents who must lend to optimize are exploiters. Clearly the isomorphism theorem can be proved as well in the other direction: any equilibrium (p, r) on Capital Market Island can be transformed into an identical equilibrium on Labor Market Island. To do this, we use what was shown in *Lemma 7.1*, that there is a uniform implicit wage in an equilibrium on Capital Market Island, and that becomes the wage in the equilibrium to be constructed on Labor Market Island. Moreover if both labor and capital markets exist on a third island, then it is easily seen that in equilibrium $r = \pi$, for if the interest rate were greater than the profit rate from hiring labor, all agents would wish to arbitrage by selling labor (at a high real wage associated with the low profit rate) and lending capital at the high interest rate. There would, however, be no borrowers and no hirers and so neither labor nor capital market would clear. Thus at equilibrium $r = \pi$ and one of the two markets is redundant in the sense that the equilibrium can be arranged using either market without the other. Therefore nothing new happens with the introduction of both markets in one economy.

The Isomorphism Theorem is a verification of the Wicksell-Samuelson theme that it does not matter whether labor hires capital (as on Capital Market Island) or whether capital hires labor (as on Labor Market Island). In both cases, those with a higher capital-labor ratio are the exploited. What the model does not explain is why in actual capitalism labor markets are sometimes used while other times capital markets are. Factors which are important in determining this institutional choice are not specified in the model: these might include economies of scale, issues relating to information and risk, and the different social relations which hold with the two types of market institution. If economies of scale, for example, are present, that might dictate in favor of labor markets. Were a capital market to be used, many producers would have to cooperate to borrow capital to take advantage of the scale economies. Marxists have also maintained that labor markets have been used in capitalism in order to control the working class and maintain capitalists' monopoly of knowledge of the production process (see, for example, Braverman [6], Marglin [31], Edwards [18]). Issues relating to the institutions associated with the labor process are discussed in another monograph in this series

An important inference follows from the Isomorphism Theorem: exploitation is a phenomenon associated primarily with differential ownership of the means of production, not primarily with the institution of the labor market. The class and exploitation properties of 'labor market capitalism' can be precisely replicated in 'credit market capitalism,' where no labor market exists. Thus the labor market is not the institutional culprit in the genesis of exploitation: if one culprit has to be singled out, it is private and differential ownership of the means of production. Given differential ownership, there are a variety of institutions all of which will skin the cat in the same manner.

If labor markets (and the institution of selling labor power) are to be a focus of Marxian concern, that concern must be one of domination and not exploitation, for the Isomorphism Theorem shows that exploitation is not characteristically a labor market phenomenon. As Section 6.2 has argued, however, labor markets may lead to a characteristic form of domination. The *class structure* generated by labor markets, although it is isomorphic to the class structure of the credit market economy, may have an entirely different set of repercussions with respect to consciousness of class members, because of the methods of domination employed in the workplace. Of course, forms of domination have existed historically in credit market economies (such as sharecropping economies); it is not implied here that domination as such can only be realized with labor markets.

Marxian exploitation has now been studied in a precise analytical fashion. In the next section we attempt to study the foundations of the concept: why is exploitation an informative concept, from a normative or positive point of view?

8. WHY BE INTERESTED IN EXPLOITATION?

Two kinds of reason have been advanced for being interested in exploitation, defined as the unequal exchange of live, direct labor for labor embodied in goods. As we will now be investigating the motivation behind the concept, it is imperative to keep in mind the *technical* definition of exploitation which has been employed throughout this monograph: an agent is exploited if the social labor embodied in goods which he can purchase with his revenues is less than the amount of labor he expended in production. It is an open question to what extent technical exploitation is a measure of an injustice, or 'ethical exploitation.' For terminological purposes, I choose to use exploitation in its technical sense.

Exploitation of man by man has been claimed to be of interest for *positive* and *normative* reasons. The chief positive reason advanced is that exploitation explains accumulation. Marx thought he had located, in the exploitation of labor, the place where value was created in the process of production. In competitive markets, every good exchanges for its fair price, its competitive price, including the exchange of labor power for the wage. How, then, could a surplus systematically emerge? Marx thought that in labor power he located the one commodity capable of producing more value than it was worth, and hence the capitalist who purchased labor power for its competitive wage was the owner of that unique commodity which could produce more value (in terms of labor) than it had to be paid (in terms of labor). The formal summary of this insight is what has been studied in this monograph as the Fundamental Marxian Theorem: profits exist if and only if labor is exploited at the going wage. But it was pointed out in Section 3.2 (the Generalized Commodity Exploitation Theorem) that labor is not unique in this regard: any commodity is exploited in a productive system if it is chosen as the value numeraire. Marx was simply wrong in proposing exploitation of labor as the explanation of accumulation and profits. Equally, the exploitation of steel or coal or corn explains profits. There must be some other reason for an interest in exploitation.

Perhaps, however, there is a reason to single out labor as the exploited commodity, on positive grounds alone, in that the wage of labor is set by class struggle, rather than by supply and demand. This, however, was not Marx's position, although it is the position of many contemporary Marxists and neo-Ricardians. (Neo-Ricardians, in particular, emphasize the arbitrariness of the wage, by discussing the wage rate-profit rate frontier. Once the wage is settled, the profit rate is settled, and conversely.) Marx had a supply and demand theory of the wage: the supply price of labor was given by the cost of the subsistence basket the worker had to consume, and this was determined by an 'historical and moral element,' and was not seen to be an object of class struggle. Indeed, in his pamphlet *Wages, Price and Profit* it is quite clear that Marx thought the wage was determined outside the control of workers (see Roemer [49], Chapter 7).

The other problem with claiming exploitation theory is primarily interesting as a positive theory of accumulation is that no distinction would be made between exploitation under capitalism and under socialism. So long as a surplus above present consumption is produced, workers must be exploited in the technical sense. If workers under socialism receive wages which permit them to buy back only part of the net product, then they are exploited in the technical sense: but most Marxists would shun this evaluation. Hence there must be more motivating an interest in the exploitation concept than its association with growth and accumulation.

The second kind of reason for an interest in exploitation is normative. Exploitation is interesting, it is claimed, because it indicates a certain injustice is occurring. That injustice may be defined in various ways. I will list three possible injustices: workers are in a dominated position, by virtue of their subordinate relation to capitalists at the point of production; workers are unjustly treated by virtue of their lack of ownership of the means of production, because of unequal distribution; workers are unjustly treated because their labor is expropriated by others. It can be claimed that exploitation is a measure of these kinds of injustice, and hence a prior commitment against these three injustices motivates an interest in exploitation, as their statistic. The technical apparatus that has been developed in the first 7 sections permits some discussion of the association of exploitation with these three types of injustice.

8.1 Exploitation and domination

Domination at the point of production of workers by capitalists or their agents is an aspect of capitalism which Marxists have attacked; and the need to dominate workers has given rise to a theory of the development of technology which is an important contribution of Marxian sociology (see, for example, Braverman [6]). But the issue here is: can an interest in exploitation be justified by an interest in domination? Is exploitation considered a bad thing because domination is bad? Various arguments indicate that this is not the case.

First, exploitation can exist in the absence of domination. Two cases have been pointed out: in Section 7.3, the Isomorphism Theorem demonstrated that producers can be exploited by the use of credit markets, even when no labor market exists, and presumably no domination exists, as each producer works for himself on borrowed finance. Marxists are generally opposed to the exploitation that exists in instances of credit market economies (such as share-cropping, or agricultural credit markets) even though domination may be absent. Secondly, as was observed in Section 5.3, exploitation as unequal exchange can exist even when there are no credit or labor markets, but only exchange of produced goods. Clearly there is no domination in this case— except perhaps, the domination of maintaining property relations, which is an altogether different phenomenon. (For a discussion of the distinction between these two kinds of domination, see Roemer [51, 56]. For a further discussion of the issues of domination and exploitation, and for an opposing view, see Wright [77], and Bowles and Gintis [5]).

Secondly, even when domination and exploitation both exist,

as in the economy with labor market of Section 6, the class-exploitation theorem states that if an agent hires labor he is an exploiter and if he sells labor he is exploited. If hiring is associated with dominating, then all dominating agents exploit and all dominated agents are exploited, but not conversely: there will in general exist agents who are neither dominating nor dominated but are exploiting or exploited (those in the petty bourgeoisie). Hence exploitation is not a good statistic for domination. It is, moreover, not a good statistic because it is the dominating which is observable, not the exploiting (which has to be calculated by a complicated algebraic procedure, given knowledge of the technology). Thus it would be peculiar to justify an interest in exploitation on grounds that it is a proxy for domination, since, first, it is a poor proxy, and second, it is a proxy which is more difficult to observe than the phenomenon it is intended to indicate.

Thirdly, I would argue that exploitation is a phenomenon which exists with perfect competition and perfect markets, where all contracts are enforceable and perfectly delineable. Marx's project was to discuss exploitation under these pristine conditions. But domination of workers is necessary because of imperfections in the technology for writing and enforcing contracts. Capitalists do not dominate workers at the point of production because they are malevolent, but because of the impossibility of writing a perfectly delineated, costlessly enforceable contract for labor. Thus domination exists because of an 'imperfection' in transactions, while exploitation exists even under perfect conditions. Imagine as a thought-experiment a world with perfectly delineable labor contracts: labor would still be exploited (assuming inequality in the ownership of the means of production) but there would be no domination. Marxists would, I think, be still opposed to such a world on grounds of exploitation, absent domination.

8.2 Exploitation as expropriation

Just because there is an unequal exchange of labor does not imply that the exploited one is having his labor expropriated by someone else in society. An expropriation takes place only if something that is rightfully his is taken from him without due compensation. If exploitation comes about because of unequal distribution of the means of production, then the unequal exchange of labor between agents cannot be deemed an expropriation unless it is first decided that the unequal distribution of capital was unjust. If it is decided that the distribution of capital is just, then it is difficult to argue that the transfers of labor arising from voluntary exchange of those in possession of that capital comprise an expropriation. The verdict of expropriation, therefore, follows only from a verdict that the underlying distribution of capital which gave rise to the pattern of labor transfers was unjust. Hence the expropriation justification for an interest in exploitation must be founded upon the underlying issue of whether the distribution of means of production was just. For further discussion, see Cohen [10].

8.3 Exploitation as unequal distribution of the means of production

The strongest justification for exploitation is that it is the consequence of unequal and unjust distribution of the means of production. As we have seen in the simple example of Section 2.2, exploitation emerges with the unequal distribution of the capital stock, when labor is abundant relative to capital. I think the most powerful justification for an interest in exploitation theory is that exploitation is a proxy for the (unjust) flows which are a consequence of an unjust initial distribution of assets. If an unequal initial distribution of assets is deemed to be unjust, then the flows under market arrangements which come from them give rise to exploitation of labor, and *usually* the rich exploit the poor. Thus the true reason to be interested in exploitation is not that we are concerned with labor flows, but that we are concerned with the underlying inequality of the means of production, or finance capital.

There are two important caveats. First, although the underlying distribution of finance capital may be unequal, it may not be unjust. For various reasons, the inequality in distribution of capital may be just, having been arrived at by a process which is just. This is, in essence, the libertarian argument of Nozick [41] and others, which will be alluded to below, and has been alluded to in Section 2.2. For instance, it may be maintained that inequality in the distribution of assets today is a consequence of differential hard work or skill in the past, and people have a right to the return on their differential labor or skill. Marxists, for the most part, have maintained that the original distribution of capital came about through plunder of various sorts, not through differentially hard work, and hence the exploitation arising from that original distribution is indeed unjust. (This was, indeed, Marx's history of the original accumulation of capital in England, in *Capital*, Volume I, Part VIII.) But from a theoretical point of view, and from the point of view of modern socialism where markets and accumulation are permitted, a more articulated discussion is necessary of the conditions under which an unequal distribution of capital among agents is just—and hence the exploitative flows coming from it, although characterized by the unequal exchange of labor—are not unjust.

The second caveat is a technical one, which is evident from *Theorem* 6.3. It is possible that with certain preferences, *the poor may exploit the rich*. Indeed, according to *Theorem* 6.3, exploitation is not necessarily monotonically related to wealth unless the wealth-elasticity of labor supply is less than one. A concrete example of the pathology, where the poor agent exploits the rich agent, follows.

Imagine two technologies for producing corn:

(capital intensive) 1 day labor + 1 corn capital → 1 corn, net output

(labor intensive) 3 days labor → 1 corn.

There are two agents, Karl and Adam. Initial distribution of capital: Karl owns 1 corn and Adam owns 3 corn. Suppose Adam's and Karl's preferences for pairs of (Corn, Labor) include the following:

$$\text{Adam:} \ (3\ 1/3,\ 4) \succ (3,\ 3)$$
$$\text{Karl:} \quad (\ 2/3,\ 0) \succ (1,\ 1)$$

The first line reads: Adam prefers to consume 3 1/3 corn and work 4 days than to consume 3 corn and work 3 days. Now if Karl works up his corn stock using the capital intensive technology he can produce 1 corn net with 1 day labor, thus availing himself of the corn-labor bundle (1, 1). Similarly, if Adam works up his capital on the capital intensive technique, he can have the bundle (3, 3). But this is not Pareto optimal. Suppose instead Karl hires Adam at the wage rate of 1/3 corn per day to work up his 1 corn capital. Then Adam, who already has worked up his own capital in 3 days works an extra day for Karl, and gets 3 1/3 corn total for 4 days labor, while Karl works not at all, and gets 2/3 corn net profit, which he consumes, from Adam's labor. Hence by this exchange of labor for the corn wage Adam and Karl have achieved the bundles (3 1/3, 4) and (2/3, 0), respectively. Hence they will enter into this agreement, preferring it to the autarchic arrangement. Now in the new agreement Karl obviously exploits Adam in the Marxian sense, since he lives off Adam's labor. (Note, incidentally, the wage of 1/3 corn per day is the competitive wage that would be set given the alternative technology which is available to Adam, whereby he can produce 1/3 corn per day. I am not worried here about bargaining between Adam and Karl, but assume the competitive wage which would emerge with a large economy of Adams and Karls.) *But* Karl is the poor one and Adam is the rich one. Hence, the exploitation of Adam by Karl cannot be condemned on the grounds that it follows from the unjust unequal distribution of the means of production: for normally, one would assume the injustice under discussion is the injustice of Karl having too little of the capital stock.

It is noteworthy that Adam and Karl need not have *different preferences*: that is, the two orderings of bundle pairs on which this example is based can be embedded in *one* consistent, convex set of indifference curves. Hence, we cannot blame the pathology of the poor exploiting the rich on their having different preferences: but only on the preference ordering exhibiting wealth-elastic labor supply. That is the essential underlying characteristic of the pathology, as is brought out by *Theorem 6.3*.

Hence, if we admit the possibility of these kinds of preferences, then exploitation ceases to be a good proxy for the underlying inequality in the distribution of the means of production. We are forced to ask: is it exploitation, the unequal exchange of labor, which is of interest, or the underlying inequality in the distribution of the capital stock? I think the real ethical interest for which exploitation is a proxy, and not a perfect one, is inequality in productive assets. This leads to the proposal that exploitation be conceived of more generally than as the unequal exchange of labor: that it be conceived of as the unjust nature of the flows that result from an unjust distribution of initial assets. Usually, the direction of the injustice in the flows is well measured by exploitation (that is, the wealthy exploit the poor); but, as I have shown, this is not always the case. And when the correlation fails, it is the underlying distribution of assets which is interesting, not the labor flows.

8.4 Exploitation and preference

We have seen, in Section 8.2, that when preferences of agents are taken seriously, then the traditional measure of Marxian exploitation can fail to be ethically interesting. Exploitation no longer necessarily measures what it is supposed to measure. It is, therefore, more appropriate to replace the classical definition with another one (which will be discussed in Section 9, below) which does not make reference to labor flows, but is stated in terms of property relations alone. Another example of taking preferences seriously will be provided here, which is essentially the neoclassical critique of Marxian exploitation theory, based on different preferences of the two agents.

Suppose Karl and Adam, who have available to them the technologies of Section 8.3, start off with equal endowments of capital: they each have 1/2 corn capital. Karl wishes to work only long enough to produce one corn net each period, to eat; while Adam has a lower rate of time preference, and wishes to save in the first period so that he may work less in later periods. In week 1, Karl works 1/2 day in the capital intensive technology, producing 1/2 corn net, and then works 1 1/2 days in the labor intensive technology to produce the other 1/2 corn he requires. Thus he works 2 days in the first week, consumes 1 corn, and starts week 2 off with 1/2 corn capital, as in week 1. Adam, however, works up his 1/2 corn in the capital intensive technology, then works 4 1/2 days in the labor intensive technology, producing a total of 2 corn net, of which he eats 1. He starts off week 2 with 1 1/2 corn. In week 2, he hires Karl to work up his 1 1/2 corn in 1 1/2 days; Karl produces 1 1/2 corn net in so doing. Adam pays him the competitive wage of 1/3 corn per day, or 1/2 corn for his 1 1/2 days labor. Karl works up his own capital stock, as in week 1, in 1/2 day and gets 1/2 corn from that. Adam gets 1 corn net profit from Karl's labor, consumes it, and does not work himself. Thus in week 2 each of them consumes 1 corn, but Karl works 2 days and Adam works zero days. They begin week 3 with the same endowments as at the beginning of week 2, and so this arrangement can continue forever, of Karl working 2 days each period, and Adam living off Karl's labor. (Or, one might argue Karl is in part living off Adam's labor from the first period.) So exploitation emerges but from an initial distribution of corn capital which was equal. The eventual inequality in the distribution of capital which leads to exploitation is a consequence of the differential preferences of the two agents for present consumption versus leisure. Adam has a lower rate of time preference, and thereby comes to exploit Karl.

The Marxist theory of exploitation cannot reach a verdict on this situation. There is not enough information provided to decide whether the distribution of corn assets which comes about is just or not. Suppose, for example, that Adam has a low rate of time preference because he came from a rich and privileged family in which saving was the norm and the culture; while Karl has a high rate of time discount because he came from a poor background where he was taught to consume and not to save, indeed where that was the rational policy. Then the preferences of the two agents are a product of their past unequal opportunities, or differential wealths, and there might be grounds for saying Adam is taking unfair advantage of Karl, is exploiting him. In this case one might support intervention forbidding the exploitation of Karl by Adam, or some redistribution through taxation, either of the initial assets or the income. But if, on the other hand, we decide that the preferences of Karl and Adam are formed under conditions of equal opportunity, and autonomously, and furthermore that each has a right to the genetic make-up he is born with which, in part, gives rise to his preferences, then there would be no grounds for condemning the result of exploitation, for what Nozick calls 'capitalist acts among consenting adults' (Nozick [41]).

The general lesson is that to reach a verdict about the ethical interest of exploitation in subtle cases one must go beyond the labor accounts which exploitation calculates: one must investigate the conditions under which preferences were formed, indeed, one must have some theory of endogenous preference formation. Preferences must be taken seriously. It is perhaps ironical, that although exploitation is proposed as a non-welfarist theory of ethics, as it makes calculations in terms of labor and not in terms of utility, it nevertheless must eventually take preferences seriously in reaching a verdict as to the significance of the exploitation accounting it makes.

9. EXPLOITATION AS INEQUALITY OF ASSETS

In Section 8, it was claimed that exploitation, calculated by comparing labor expended to labor embodied in goods purchased, derives its interest from the correlation of exploitation with wealth, with the value of initial assets. Class position is a proxy for exploitation status, and because of the Class-Exploitation Correspondence (Section 7), class is correlated to wealth, assuming the appropriate wealth elasticity of labor supply. But exploitation is not always a good correlate of wealth, due to the possible wealth-elasticity of labor supply: and it is therefore desirable to provide a definition of exploitation directly in terms of property relations, which does not calculate surplus-value accounts. The essential idea is that an agent is exploited if he does not own or have access to the share of society's capital assets to which he is entitled. Deciding on that entitlement is a difficult question, as the examples in the previous section have shown, since one must have a prior definition of what sort of asset-generating activity entitles one to the proceeds. Is one entitled to accumulated capital due to one's special skill, or to one's attitude towards risk-taking, or to one's attitude towards savings? Or must each generation begin with an egalitarian distribution of society's capital stock? Precisely what allocations would reflect a fair entitlement in society's productive assets is pursued more formally in Section 10.

9.1 A property relations approach to exploitation

The first approximation, which does not treat the questions just posed in a sufficiently subtle manner, is to define an agent as exploited at an allocation in an economy if he would be better off if the initial distribution of alienable, productive assets in the economy had been an equal division one. Imagine a capitalist economy in which agents begin with vectors of alienable assets, and other endowments (personal ones, such as skills), and preferences. Compare the equilibrium allocation to the allocation that would have come about had the original endowments of alienable productive assets been equal, and divide the society into exploited and exploiters according as the agent is better or worse off, respectively, in the equal division counterfactual than he is at the current equilibrium. This definition is not precise, because no method has been specified for defining what the allocation is in the counterfactual situation: is it a new competitive equilibrium, arrived at from equal division endowments, or is it a point in the core of the equal division economy? Each definition has its associated problems. The problem with using the competitive allocation as the benchmark is that there may be multiple equilibria, and an agent's position in the counterfactual world may not, therefore, be well-defined in comparison to his position in the actual economy. The approach of using the core to define non-exploitative allocations is appealing because it avoids the problem of prices. Thus, we would say exploitation exists at an allocation if that allocation is not in the core of the economy where initial endowments are re-defined to be an equal division endowment of the alienable goods. A coalition is said to be exploited if at the allocation it is a blocking coalition, and it is an exploiting coalition if it is the complement of a blocking coalition. This idea is developed at length in Roemer [50, 52].

There are several advantages to this definition of exploitation and several disadvantages. The chief advantage is exploitation is now directly defined in terms of a counterfactual which specifies egalitarian distribution of the alienable means of production. The definition thus goes to the heart of the issue which was located in Section 8, and avoids the circuitous route of calculating embodied labor accounts. Thus, the definition will yield intuitively better outcomes when agents' preferences are of the perverse variety which render the unequal labor exchange definition of exploitation superfluous. Moreover, an advantage of the property relations definition is that it does not depend on the special assumptions which are necessary to define embodied labor value. Thus, there may be primary factors other than labor, there may be joint production, and there may be heterogeneous labor. All these phenomena make the notion of embodied labor value problematical: but the conception of a counterfactual egalitarian distribution of alienable assets is conceptually simple. There are, however, disadvantages to the core approach. For example, it is coalitions which are defined as exploited, not individuals. If there are increasing returns to scale, then no individual may be exploited according to the core definition: for if any individual is given his per capita share of the alienable assets, there may be little or nothing he can do with them by himself. Thus, even if in the original economy he has no capital, he may be much better off than if he is given his per capita share and has to 'withdraw' in a coalition of one. So the core definition will produce a class of exploited coalitions and a class of exploiting coalitions, but it is not obvious, in general, how to decide what individuals are exploited. (This problem, however, is a fairly subtle one, in the sense that the usual Marxian definition of embodied labor value is constructed with a constant returns technology. With constant returns in production, the core definition works quite well in capturing which individuals are exploited.) Another problem with the core approach is that exploitation now becomes a property of agents or coalitions, rather than a relationship between agents. Elster [19] has pointed out some examples in which the core definition fails to give a good intuitive account of 'exploitation' because of this. The same, however, can be said of the unequal exchange definition of exploitation, in which an agent is said to be exploited not because of his relation to other people, but because of a discrepancy between the labor value of what he consumes and the labor he expends. These issues are pursued further in Roemer [55], and various refinements are proposed which render the core definition more accurate in capturing our intuitive notion that agents are exploited by virtue of the consequences of having less than their equal share of society's assets in alienable means of production.

9.2 An historical materialist taxonomy of exploitation

In the counterfactual which captures Marxian exploitation, only one kind of asset is equalized: alienable productive assets, or finance capital. We could define other kinds of exploitation based on equalizing, in a counterfactual manner, other kinds of asset. Consider feudalism, where agents also own shares of other people, or rights to their labor. Under feudalism, one might say there are two important kinds of asset: assets in other people (feudal property), and assets in alienable means of production (capitalist property). There are, in addition, personal assets, such as skills, which may or may not be owned by others (depending on whether the feudal lord has an entitlement to 3 days of the serf's unskilled labor, or 3 days of his special skills). *Feudal exploitation* can be thought of as that inequality that arises due to the unequal distribution of property in people: that some people own a property right in the labor of others, and those rights are unequally distributed. To capture feudal exploitation, we can define a counterfactual in which feudal property rights are abolished, and so everyone owns an equal share in the labor of others (namely, a zero share). Capitalist property is not abolished. A coalition of agents is feudally exploited if it would be better off in the counterfactual with an equal division of feudal property than it is in the feudal equilibrium; and feudal exploiters are analogously defined.

The bourgeois revolution annihilates feudal exploitation, as it annihilates feudal property. However, even under feudalism, a feudal ideologue would claim that serfs were not feudally exploited: he would claim that serfs benefited from feudalism, due to the public goods of military organization and manorial goods provided and organized by the feudal lord. This is, indeed, the argument of North and Thomas [39]—that feudalism comprised an implicit contract between lord and serfs, entered into because of the mutual advantages. Brenner [7] argues forcefully against this interpretation of feudalism. The Marxist view is that feudalism constituted an expropriation of serf labor, it was not to the advantage of the serfs, and they would have been better off with the annihilation of feudal property rights. Hence they were feudally exploited.

In like manner, Marxists argue that workers under capitalism are *capitalistically exploited*, where the appropriate counterfactual is the core of the game where capitalist property (alienable productive property) is equally divided. But just as the feudal ideologue could argue that serfs were not feudally exploited, so the capitalist ideologue can argue that workers under capitalism are not capitalistically exploited: that if the capital stock were divided up evenly among everyone, workers would be worse off than they are under capitalism. They would be worse off, it is claimed, because capital is really a return to inalienable, personal assets embedded in capitalists (skill, risk-taking ability, etc.), and the workers who withdraw (as the test of the equal division core requires) with their per capita share of the capital, but their own (meagre) skills will be worse off than they are in capitalist society with a small share of the capital, but with access, through trade, to the skills of capitalists.

This disagreement between the capitalist ideologue and the Marxist on the question of capitalist exploitation is an important one, and a subtle one. A less subtle disagreement also exists, which is founded upon a confusion between feudal and capitalist exploitation. Critics of the Marxian concept of exploitation often ask: How can the workers be exploited if they gain from trade? Surely, under capitalism, workers do gain from trade with capitalists, or else they would not voluntarily sell their labor power. But this merely says workers under capitalism are not *feudally* exploited—that is, they would not be better off to withdraw with their current capital assets and their own skills.

Indeed, the competitive equilibrium of a capitalist economy is in the core of the feudal game—that is, no coalition of agents can do better for its members by withdrawing with its own capital and personal assets. But the test for capitalist exploitation is different: it compares the present allocation not to the private property core, the core of the feudal game, but to the core of the game which divides equally the endowment of alienable assets.

We can define a third kind of exploitation, based on private property in the third kind of property, personal assets (to be thought of as skills). In the transition from capitalism to socialism, private ownership in alienable means of production is abolished: in principle, every agent has equal opportunities in respect of society's capital stock. (For the distinction between equal opportunities and equal ownership, see Section 10.) But agents maintain their private ownership of personal assets, assuming differential wages to differential labor are the norm, as they are, in principle, in socialist society. Thus the transition to socialism abolishes capitalist exploitation: but inequalities remain due to unequal division of personal (inalienable) assets. One might call such inequality socialist exploitation, and set up a counterfactual wherein every agent owns an equal share in everyone else's labor and skills; one would then say an agent is *socialistically exploited* if the socialist equilibrium allocation is not in the core of this equal-division-of-personal-assets game, and he is a blocking coalition. More vaguely, an agent is socialistically exploited if he would be better off with an equal endowment of society's pool of skills than he is, under socialism, with his own skills. The unskilled are socialistically exploited by the skilled.

There are certain parallels and regularities to be noted in this transition from feudalism to capitalism to socialism, which is, of course, the historical evolution claimed by the theory of historical materialism. At each stage, society nationalizes or socializes a kind of property: an ideology emerges which associates exploitation or injustice with the private ownership of a particular kind of asset. Thus in the passage from feudalism to capitalism, feudal property becomes illegal, feudal exploitation disappears. Agents are allowed to own capitalist property but they are not allowed to 'feudalize' the returns from that property, that is, to buy serfs, even with voluntary contracts. Feudal acts between consenting adults are forbidden, to paraphrase Robert Nozick. Similarly, in the passage from capitalism to socialism, capitalist property becomes illegal, capitalist exploitation is abolished; agents are allowed to own and benefit from their socialist property (skill) but they cannot capitalize the returns from that property, they cannot buy alienable means of production. Doubtless this gives rise to certain inefficiencies, at least in the short-run, but it may give rise to long-run dynamic efficiency, just as most historians agree that the abolition of feudal contracts in capitalism gave rise to dynamic efficiency.

Of course, the actual history of socialist societies is more variegated, just as the actual history of capitalist societies is more complex than has been idealized here. The issues are more carefully investigated in another monograph in this series, and in the book by Nove [40].

In summary, historical materialism claims that property rights evolve in a certain way. The assets which are deemed appropriately held in private hands become progressively fewer as history develops. First, slave and feudal property rights are abolished, then capitalist property rights, and finally socialist property rights are abolished. (In 'communism,' no one has a property right in his own skills or talents.) It is not claimed that property rights of various kinds are abolished *because* they come to be viewed as unjust or exploitative. Indeed, historical materialism claims that property rights are abolished because they hinder the further development of technology, for efficiency reasons. But class struggle is based on underlying notions of injustice or exploitation, associated with certain kinds of private property ownership. There issues are discussed in the monograph in this series on historical materialism.

For further discussion and application of ideas in this section, see Van Parijs [70], Wright [78], Elster [20], Roemer [50, 52, 55].

9.3 An application to class consciousness

In recent work, Erik Wright [78] has used a similar taxonomy of types of exploitation to predict class consciousness, with good results. Wright views people as being owners of various assets: capitalist assets, skill assets, and organizational assets. (Organizational assets are defined by degree of control in the organization, the number of subordinates one has, and so on.) Associated with each type of asset is a kind of exploitation. A particular agent might be exploited with respect to one of these categories of asset and an exploiter with respect to another. For instance, an unskilled supervisor who owns no capital would be an exploiter with regard to organization assets, but exploited with regard to capitalist and skill assets. Wright asks how well class consciousness (for which he has independent measures) correlates with exploitation, and finds that it correlates well with an aggregate measure of the three kinds of exploitation. He also has investigated some Eastern European economies, and has shown that organizational assets are much more important for class consciousness there than in the United States, where the predominant form of exploitation and consciousness is associated with capitalist assets.

The following two tables (from Wright [78]) summarize some of his results. In both tables, wage laborers are divided into nine categories based on whether they possess a lot ($+$), an average amount (0), or very little ($-$) of skill assets and organization assets. For example, a highly skilled worker with no supervisory duties would be in the bottom left-hand cell ($+$, $-$). Observe from Table 1 that income in both Sweden and the United States correlates well with the degree of exploitation: as one moves to the right or down the 3×3 matrix describing the 'class location' of wage laborers, income decreases monotonically (with two exceptions). In Table 2, class consciousness is tabulated by class location. Pro-working class consciousness increases monotonically in both Sweden and the United States as possession of either organization assets or skill assets decreases.

Furthermore, when Wright controls for income and a range of other mediating variables, the relationship between class location and consciousness is retained, suggesting that this is indeed an effect of the material interests linked to exploitation relations. What is more, although the overall level of ideological polarization is greater in Sweden than in the United States, the basic pattern linking class structure to class consciousness is similar in

TABLE I

Mean annual individual incomes by class location in Sweden and the United States

Owners		Assets in the means of production Nonowners (wage laborers)			
1 Bourgeoisie US: $52,621 SW: $28,333	4 Expert manager US: $28,665 SW: $29,952	7 Semi-cred. manager US: $20,701 SW: $20,820	10 Uncred. manager US: $12,276 SW: $15,475	+	
2 Small employers US: $24,828 SW: $17,237	5 Expert supervisors US: $23,057 SW: $18,859	8 Semi-cred. supervisor US: $18,023 SW: $19,711	11 Uncred. supervisor US: $13,045 SW: $15,411	>0	Organization assets
3 Petty bourgeoisie US: $14,496 SW: $13,503	6 Expert nonmanager US: $15,251 SW: $14,890	9 Semi-cred. workers US: $16,034 SW: $14,879	12 Proletarian US: $11,161 SW: $11,876	−	
	+	>0 Skill assets	−		

United States: N = 1282
Sweden: N = 1049
Entries in cells are the means for gross annual individual income from all sources before taxes. The Swedish incomes were converted to dollars at the 1980 exchange rate.

both countries, even though these two countries are at opposite extremes among advanced capitalist countries with regard to state efforts at income redistribution. This suggests that the underlying class structure of the two societies defines a common terrain of interests upon which various kinds of political forces act.

9.4 Summary: the central idea of exploitation

Exploitation, fundamentally, is not an idea about transfer of labor but about the unequal distribution of property. In many historical cases, the transfer of labor was a good statistic for the underlying inequality in property ownership: but as has been shown, that need not be the case. It is theoretically possible for the poor to exploit the rich according to the Marxian definition. If one recognizes preferences as important, then this theoretical possibility cannot be ignored. The labor theory of exploitation

TABLE II
Class consciousness by location in the class structure

I. The United States

Owners	Assets in the means of production			
		Nonowners (wage laborers)		
1 Bourgeoisie −1.31	4 Expert manager −1.46	7 Semi-cred. manager −0.34	10 Uncred. manager −0.29	+
2 Small employers −0.87	5 Expert supervisors −0.78	8 Semi-cred. supervisor −0.24	11 Uncred. supervisor +0.54	>0 Organi- zation assets
3 Petty bourgeoisie −0.09	6 Expert nonmanager −0.09	9 Semi-cred. workers +0.78	12 Proletarian +0.78	−
	+ 	>0 Skill assets	−	

II. Sweden

Owners	Assets in the means of production			
		Nonowners (wage laborers)		
1 Bourgeoisie −2.00	4 Expert manager −0.70	7 Semi-cred. manager +1.03	10 Uncred. manager +1.81	+
2 Small employers −0.98	5 Expert supervisors +0.07	8 Semi-cred. supervisor +0.74	11 Uncred. supervisor +1.98	>0 Organi- zation assets
3 Petty bourgeoisie +0.46	6 Expert nonmanager +1.29	9 Semi-cred. workers +2.81	12 Proletarian +2.60	−
	+ 	>0 Skill assets	−	

Entries in the table are means on the working class consciousness scale. The values on the scale range from +6 (pro-working class on every item) to −6 (pro-capitalist on every item).

just does not work as an analytically convincing theory of distributive injustice, and must be replaced by the property relations approach, which says a group or person is exploited if he does not have access to his fair share (which so far I have taken to be his per capita share) of the alienable productive assets of society. This definition immediately solves the classical problems of heterogeneity of labor which plague classical Marxian economics, since labor value is now seen to be a fetish to the true concerns of exploitation theory. But other problems come about, in the precise specification of the counterfactual against which one evaluates that a particular allocation is exploitative, or in which a particular coalition or person is exploited. For further discussion, see Elster [20].

The property relations approach to exploitation immediately shifts the burden of interesting argument from the labor theory of value to the legitimacy of capitalist property relations, which is where the argument should be. As Cohen [11] has written "...the labour theory of value is a terrible incubus on progressive reflection about exploitation. Instead of desperately shifting about for some or other way of defending the labour theory, Marxists and quasi-Marxists should direct themselves to the crucial question which is whether or not private ownership of capital is morally legitimate."

10. EQUALITY OF OPPORTUNITY IN ALIENABLE ASSETS

Marxian exploitation, then, is a form of distributive injustice. Stripped of its unnecessary connection to labor value—and, indeed, its generally false connection to labor value as the example of Section 8 showed—it is the consequence of an unjustly unequal distribution of property in the alienable means of production. The next step must be to ask: when is an initial unequal distribution of alienable productive assets unjust? Marxists have argued that historically capitalist accumulation occurred through plunder, and was therefore unjust, and hence the proletarianization of masses of people and their consequent exploitation was unjust exploitation. Neoclassical economists, while not explicitly denying this history, have as their model the accumulation of assets as returns to personal traits and talents of various kinds, and since they view people as the proper owners of their talents, the consequent distribution of alienable property is not unjust.

The Marxist recipe has not been to recommend a different distribution of the capital stock in order to alleviate the injustice of the capitalist distribution, but to socialize capital, to eliminate the institution of private property in the means of production altogether. Public ownership would seem to be unnecessary, given the second theorem of welfare economics, that any efficient distribution can be achieved by some initial distribution of resources. Of course, the recommendation to socialize capital may be justified if the usual conditions do not hold. With non-convexities of various sorts and an incomplete set of markets, the case for planning and public ownership of capital may be strengthened. Moreover, a traditional claim of Marxists has been that preferences of the economic agents are not exogenous, but are themselves formed in response to the environment, and even in response to the allocation mechanism. Thus the preferences which people learn to have with a market allocation mechanism may lead to welfare levels, measured according to some absolute standard, which are inferior to the welfare levels that would be achieved if people had the preferences which would be induced by an allocation mechanism based on public ownership of capital.

These kinds of criticism of market allocations based on private ownership of the means of production require, in some sense, a change of the rules of the game. Changing those rules is beyond the scope of the present survey. It is perhaps more challenging to ask: Suppose we accept the rules of the game (that markets are complete, Arrow-Debreu equilibria exist and are efficient, and that preferences are autonomously formed and should be respected as the final indicator of the agents' welfare); what allocations of social output and labor would implement a conception of 'equal opportunities in respect to access to society's alienable assets?' If such equal opportunities are a requirement for the annihilation of exploitation, in the Marxian sense, how could they be achieved? Will an equal per capita division of the capital stock, as suggested in previous sections, be appropriate?

The question can be pursued by asking what sort of distributional rule would reflect equal opportunities with regard to alienable assets, and at the same time would respect 'self-ownership', the requirement that people be allowed to retain private opportunities with respect to their own skills and talents. This pair of principles is not necessarily the final goal of a Marxian ethic—which asks for distribution according to needs—but it reflects the abolition of capitalist exploitation only, those inequalities due to differential opportunities in respect to alienable assets. Contemporary theorists of capitalism, such as Robert Nozick [63] have supplied one answer to this question, but it is not necessarily the only one, or the correct one. G. A. Cohen [12, 13] has challenged the Nozickian justification of private property, and has argued that other conceptions than the Nozick-Locke one of what constitutes equal opportunities in respect of alienable assets, or the external world, must be considered.

In this section, a model is outlined to suggest how one might approach this problem. The project is suggested by the Cohen papers referred to, although there are departures from his approach in this formal incarnation. Imagine there is a world with an external, or alienable resource 'land' which is publicly owned by its inhabitants, who also possess personal resources of skills and labor. Suppose, for simplicity of exposition, there are two people. These two possess, in general, different degrees of skill, called s^1 and s^2. Land and labor are used to produce corn according to the production function $f(W, L)$ where W and L are the inputs of land and labor. The skill levels s^i of the agents measure the labor they can supply in efficiency units. Thus if agent i expends L^i days of labor and agent j expends L^j days of labor on amount W of land, total production of corn will be $f(W, s^1L^1 + s^2L^2)$. Each agent has the same utility function for corn and leisure $u(C, l)$. These are the only two goods. Suppose there is a public resource of $\bar{W}$ amount of land and each agent has 1 unit of leisure which can be converted into labor. All corn must be produced. An *environment* is now completely specified: it is a collection $\varepsilon = (\bar{W}; u(C, l); f(W, L); s^1, s^2)$. Given an environment ε, the problem is to decide what allocations of corn and leisure to the two agents will respect *both* their equal opportunities in respect to the land (the public external resource) and their private opportunities in respect to their skills.

An *allocation* is a list $\{(C^1, 1 - L^1), (C^2, 1 - L^2)\}$ which assigns corn and leisure (or labor) to the two agents. Let the set of feasible allocations for the environment ε be called $\Omega(\varepsilon)$. We desire a *mechanism* which, for any given environment ε, will prescribe an allocation in $\Omega(\varepsilon)$ which respects the two principles stipulated. Such a mechanism is a mapping from the space of environments to their sets of feasible allocations.

$$F: \varepsilon \rightarrow \Omega(\varepsilon)$$

Let us write $F^i(\varepsilon) = (C^i, 1 - L^i)$ for the assignment of corn and labor to individual i under the mechanism F.

I suggest that such a mechanism should satisfy the following axioms. In the following, ε and ε' represent two environments, where $\varepsilon = (\bar{W}; u; f; s^1; s^2)$ and $\varepsilon' = (\bar{W}'; u'; f'; s^{1'}; s^{2'})$.

(1) (Unrestricted Domain) F is defined on a domain of environments ε where u can be any concave utility function, f can be any constant-returns-to-scale production function, and $\bar{W}$, s^1, s^2 can be any non-negative numbers.

(2) (Pareto optimality) $F(\varepsilon)$ is a Pareto optimal allocation in $\Omega(\varepsilon)$.

(3) (land monotonicity) Let ε' and ε differ only in that $\bar{W}' > \bar{W}$. Then $u(F^i(\varepsilon')) \geqslant u(F^i(\varepsilon))$ for $i = 1, 2$.

(4) (incentive compatibility in skill) Let ε' and ε differ only in that $s^{1'} > s^1$. Then $u(F^1(\varepsilon')) \geqslant u(F^1(\varepsilon))$. (Same postulate for s^2.)

(4′) (no negative skill externalities) Let ε' and ε differ only in that $s^{1'} > s^1$. Then $u(F^2(\varepsilon')) \geqslant u(F^2(\varepsilon))$.

(5) (technological monotonicity) Let ε' and ε differ only in that $f'(W, L) \geqslant f(W, L)$, $\forall (W, L)$. Then $u(F^i(\varepsilon')) \geqslant u(F^i(\varepsilon))$ for $i = 1, 2$.

(6) (self-ownership) of skill) In ε, suppose $s^i \geqslant s^j$. Then $u(F^i(\varepsilon)) \geqslant u(F^j(\varepsilon))$.

(7) (continuity) F is a continuous function, in the appropriate topology, in all its arguments.

Call an F that satisfies Axioms (1)–(7) *acceptable*.

Axiom (1) says the mechanism F must be a general rule that can work for 'all' environments. Axiom (2) is easily justified (although for technical reasons one might wish to weaken the axiom to require only weak Pareto optimality). Axioms (3) and (5) embody the principle of 'equal opportunities in external resources.' As the external resource $\bar{W}$ or the technical knowledge f increases or improves, neither agent should be hurt. Whatever equal opportunities in external resources means, one can claim it means *at least* what axioms (3) and (5) require. Axioms (4) and (6) embody self-ownership of skill. Axiom (4) says that as an agent's skill increases, his welfare must not decrease: this is an incentive compatibility axiom since if it fails there would be cases in which an agent would be penalized for revealing his true skill. Axiom (6) is also a self-ownership axiom, as it says that the more skilled person gets at least as much utility as the less skilled. One cannot but benefit from being skillful. Note that Axiom (6) injects interpersonal comparability of utility. In particular, it implies *symmetry*, that if $s^1 = s^2$ then $u(F^1(\varepsilon)) = u(F^2(\varepsilon))$. Equally skilled agents are treated equally in respect to welfare. Axiom (7) is strong, and I think it would be an error to view it as merely technical. It can be justified by saying that the mechanism should not change its prescription much due to small measurement errors.

Axiom (4′) is perhaps the most objectionable axiom, from the point of view of the two fundamental principles. It says that one agent's welfare shall not decrease as the other agent's skill increases. It might be viewed as saying that both agents have some property rights in each other's skills, and if it is so viewed, it clearly violates the self-ownership principle. On the other hand, if it is verbally translated as requiring that Mr. 2's welfare should not be invaded by an increase in Mr. 1's skill, it seems like a tenable requirement against negative externalities, perhaps justifiable in terms of 2's self-ownership and equal rights in the external world.

At least what this axiomization does is show that it is not easy to be precise in formulating the requirements of the two fundamental principles. Questions of interpretation abound. One can even question whether Axioms (3) and (5) are too strong as requirements for public ownership of the external resources. I am not committed to this particular axiomatization, but present it as an example of an approach to the question at hand.

The project is now to ask what allocation mechanisms F satisfy these axioms. It can be demonstrated that on an unrestricted domain of economies, the mechanism 'equal division competitive equilibrium' (ED-CE), where the land $\bar{W}$ is divided equally between the two agents who then trade and produce to a competitive equilibrium, is not acceptable. It can be the case that under ED-CE, as Mr. 1's skill increases, Mr. 2's welfare falls, so Axiom (4') is violated.

There is one mechanism that does satisfy these axioms on a broad, though perhaps not entirely unrestricted, class of economies: the mechanism which assigns the Pareto optimal allocation which equalizes utilities of the two agents. (There are some caveats: there must be an equal-utility allocation which is Pareto optimal; otherwise one could weaken Axiom (2) to weak Pareto optimality.) Perhaps on a suitably unrestricted domain of economies, this is the only acceptable mechanism. If this were so, it would mean that even respecting self-ownership in the way that Axioms (4) and (6) require, there would be no acceptable private appropriation of returns to skill. The guarantees of public ownership of the external world (Axioms (3) and (5)) combined with the necessity for a general constitution with insurance against measurement error (Axioms (1) and (7)) and stipulation against 'invasion' (Axiom (4')) would nullify any advantage to owning one's skill.

If there are other mechanisms than welfare egalitarianism which satisfy the above axioms, it will nevertheless be true that public ownership of the external world will force considerably more equality than one might have thought, in conjunction with self-ownership. (In particular, as noted above, equal division competitive equilibrium is not in general acceptable.)

Thus, even the limited and 'conservative' goal of requiring equal opportunities in respect to external, alienable resources but making no *explicit* adjustments for unequal skills and talents may mandate an allocation not likely to be achievable with even a very clean capitalism—and, certainly, one not achievable by an equal division, private property, distribution of the external resources among the agents.

In summary, the model of this section attempts to motivate why, even if markets are perfect and preferences are autonomous in the sense discussed, a mechanism which provides equal opportunities to agents in so far as alienable assets are concerned may be considerably more egalitarian in outcomes than a syndicalist solution would achieve. Syndicalism, here, is a perhaps inappropriate abbreviation for a market economy based on equal division of the external resources among the population.

11. A FURTHER STEP

In Section 10, it was argued that the elimination of capitalist exploitation might require significant incursions against the institution of private property, not simply its redistribution. It was, at the least, claimed that the appropriate negation of 'unequal opportunities in access to the means of production' is not necessarily 'equal distribution and private ownership of the means of production.' But the program of Section 10 was itself conservative in the sense that attempts were made (perhaps in the final analysis to no avail) to respect self-ownership of skills. One can now take the further step of asking whether this should be the case. What one might call the 'radical' program maintains that skills and many other traits of individuals should be socialized, in the sense that the product of them should not belong to the agents in whom they reside. One can distinguish between the ownership and possession of an asset. A factory may be possessed by the workers and managers; likewise, a talent may be possessed by an individual and owned by many others. In both cases, there are incentive problems when the owner of the asset tries to get the possessor to do something with it. It is beyond the scope of this monograph to discuss the extension of the jurisdiction of resources to include inalienable ones such as talent; but that is the clear question which is indicated by the path which has been taken to this point in the analysis.

For this reason, the Marxian theory of exploitation, I believe, merges now with a much broader class of egalitarian theories of distributive justice, which concern themselves with the problem of distributing social resources in such a way as to equalize something. Other members of this class of theories are those of Rawls [45], who wishes to equalize, so far as incentive effects allow, certain goods which he calls *primary*; the theory of Dworkin [17], in which he discusses equality of *resources*, including talents and handicaps; the theory of Sen [60], in which he calls for the equalisation, so far as is feasible, of *basic capabilities*. Exploitation theory is an equality-of-resource theory of justice, where the resources in question are limited to a certain class of alienable productive assets. The relevance of this class of resources is, specifically, to the capitalist era. In the feudal era, as I wrote in Section 9, other assets (property in persons) were relevant as well, and in post-capitalist societies, other assets will again become important (talents, skills, and so on).

With respect to class, the questions are in large part sociological and historical. To what extent are classes, as defined in Section 6, important historical actors? Class consciousness, presumably, is a kind of endogenous preference formation, where members of the same class learn to think in a similar way about their situation, and to take collective action on that basis. Are classes more important than non-class collectivities in history, such as religious or national collectivities? (See, for instance, Elster [21] for a discussion.) Wright [78] has shown that the theory of expoitation outlined in Section 9 predicts degrees of class consciousness quite well. Is there a general conception of class, as a group of people who relate to property in a certain way, which will remain useful as the property forms of society change? How useful are generalized conceptions of exploitation and class for analysis of historical change?

University of California, Davis

REFERENCES

1. Alberro, J., and J. Persky, 1981, "The dynamics of fixed capital, revaluation and scrapping," *Review of Radical Political Economics* **13**, 32–37.
2. Arrow, K., and F. Hahn, 1971, *General Competitive Analysis*, San Francisco: Holden Day.
3. Benetti, C., C. Berthomieu and J. Cartelier, 1975, *Economie classique, economie vulgaire*, Paris: Maspero.

4. Bowles, S., and H. Gintis, 1981, "Structure and practice in the labor theory of value," *Review of Radical Political Economics* **12**, 1–26.
5. Bowles, S., and H. Gintis, 1983, "The power of capital: on the inadequacy of the conception of the capitalist economy as 'private'," *The Philosophical Forum* **14**, Spring-Summer, 225–245.
6. Braverman, H., 1974, *Labor and Monopoly Capital*, New York: Monthly Review Press.
7. Brenner, R., 1977, "The origins of capitalist development: a critique of neo-Smithian Marxism," *New Left Review* **104**, 25–92.
8. Brody, A., 1970, *Proportions, Prices and Planning*, New York: American Elsevier.
9. Broome, J., 1983, *The Microeconomics of Capitalism*, London: Academic Press.
10. Cohen, G. A., 1979, "The labor theory of value and the concept of exploitation," *Philosophy and Public Affairs* **8**, 338–360.
11. Cohen, G. A., 1983, "More on exploitation and the labor theory of value," *Inquiry* **26**, 309–331.
12. Cohen, G. A., 1984, "Self-ownership, world ownership and equality, part I" All Souls College, Oxford (mimeo).
13. Cohen, G. A., 1984, "Self-ownership, world ownership and equality, part II" All Souls College, Oxford (mimeo).
14. Debreu, G., and I. Herstein, 1953, "Non-negative square matrices," *Econometrica* **21**, 597–607.
15. Desai, M., 1974, *Marxian Economic Theory*, London: Gray-Mills.
16. Dumenil, G., and D. Levy, 1983, "The dynamics of competition: a restoration of the classical analysis," Paris, C.E.P.R.E.M.A.P. (processed).
17. Dworkin, R., 1981, "What is equality? part I: Equality of welfare; part II: Equality of resources," *Philosophy and Public Affairs* **10**, 185–246; 283–345.
18. Edwards, R., 1979, *Contested Terrain*, New York: Basic Books.
19. Elster, J., 1982, "Roemer versus Roemer: a comment," *Politics and Society* **11**, 363–374.
20. Elster, J., 1985, *Making Sense of Marx*, Cambridge: Cambridge University Press.
21. Elster, J., 1986, "Three challenges to class," in J. E. Roemer (ed.) *Analytical Marxism*, Cambridge: Cambridge University Press.
22. Evans, D., 1983, "A critical reassessment of some neo-Marxian trade theories," Institute of Development Studies, Sussex (processed).
23. Flaschel, P., 1983a, *Marx, Sraffa und Leontief: Kritik und Ansatze zu ihrer Synthese*, Frankfurt: Peter Lang.
24. Flaschel, P., 1983b, "Actual labor values in a general model of production," *Econometrica* **51**, 435–454.
25. Fujimori, Y., 1981, *Modern Analysis of Value Theory*, University of Josai Publishing.
26. Hirschman, Albert O., 1981, "Morality and the social sciences: a durable tension," in *Essays in Trespassing*: Cambridge University Press.
27. Krause, U., 1982, *Money and Abstract Labor*, London: New Left Books.
28. Laibman, D., 1981, "Two-sector growth with endogenous technical change: a Marxian simulation model," *Quarterly Journal of Economics*, February, 47–75.
29. Lippi, M., 1979, *Value and Naturalism in Marx*, London: New Left Books.
30. Maarek, G., 1975, *Introduction au Capital de Karl Marx*, Paris: Calmann-Levy.

31. Marglin, S., 1974, "What do bosses do?" *Review of Radical Political Economics* **6**, Summer.

32. Marx, K., 1947, *Capital, Volume I*, New York: International Publishers.

33. Medio, A., 1972, "Profits and surplus value: appearance and reality in capitalist production," in E. K. Hunt and Jesse Schwartz, *A Critique of Economic Theory*, Middlesex: Penguin.

34. Morishima, M., 1969, *Theory of Economic Growth*, Oxford: Oxford University Press.

35. Morishima, M., 1973, *Marx's Economics*, Cambridge: Cambridge University Press.

36. Morishima, M., 1974, "Marx in the light of modern economic theory," *Econometrica* **42**, 611–632.

37. Morishima M., and G. Catephores, 1978, *Value, Exploitation and Growth*, London: McGraw Hill.

38. Morishima, M., and F. Seton, 1961, "Aggregation in Leontief matrices and the labour theory of value," *Econometrica*.

39. North, D., and R. Thomas, 1973, *The Rise of the Western World*, Cambridge: Cambridge University Press.

40. Nove, A., 1983, *The Economics of Feasible Socialism*, London: George Allen and Unwin.

41. Nozick, R., 1974, *Anarchy, State and Utopia*, New York: Basic Books.

42. Okishio, N., 1961, "Technical changes and the rate of profit," *Kobe University Economic Review* **7**, 85–99.

43. Okishio, N., 1963, "A mathematical note on Marxian theorems," *Weltwirtschaftsliches Archiv*.

44. Pasinetti, L., 1977, *Lectures on the Theory of Production*, New York: Columbia University Press.

45. Rawls, J., 1971, *A Theory of Justice*, Cambridge: Belknap.

46. Roemer, J. E., 1977, "Technical change and the 'tendency of the rate of profit to fall'," *Journal of Economic Theory* **16**, December, 403–424.

47. Roemer, J. E., 1980, "A general equilibrium approach to Marxian economics," *Econometrica* **48**, 505–530.

48. Roemer, J. E., 1980, "Innovation, rates of profit, and uniqueness of von Neumann prices," *Journal of Economic Theory* **22**, 451–464.

49. Roemer, J. E., 1981, *Analytical Foundations of Marxian Economic Theory*, New York: Cambridge University Press.

50. Roemer, J. E., 1982, *A General Theory of Exploitation and Class*, Cambridge: Harvard University Press.

51. Roemer, J. E., 1982a, "Reply," *Politics and Society* **11**, 375–394.

52. Roemer, J. E., 1982b, "Exploitation, alternatives and socialism," *Economic Journal* **92**, 87–107.

53. Roemer, J. E., 1983a, "R. P. Wolff's reinterpretation of Marx's labor theory of value: comment," *Philosophy and Public Affairs* **12**, no. 1, 70–83.

54. Roemer, J. E., 1983b, "Unequal exchange, labor migration, and international capital flows: a theoretical synthesis," in Padma Desai (ed.) *Marxism, Central Planning and the Soviet Economy: Essays in Honor of Alexander Erlich*, Cambridge: MIT Press.

55. Roemer, J. E., 1983c, "Property relations versus surplus value in Marxian exploitation," *Philosophy and Public Affairs* **11**, 281–313.

56. Roemer, J. E., 1985, "Should Marxists be interested in exploitation?" *Philosophy and Public Affairs*, **14**, no. 1, 30–65.

57. Samuelson, P., 1972, "A note on 'understanding the Marxian notion of exploitation'," *Journal of Economic Literature* **10**, 50–57.

58. Samuelson, P., 1982, "The normative and positivistic inferiority of Marx's values paradigm," *Southern Economic Journal* **49**, no. 1, 11–18.

59. Schwartz, J., 1961, *Lectures on the Mathematical Model in Analytical Economics*, New York: Gordon and Breach.

60. Sen, A., 1980, "Equality of what?" in S. McMurrin (ed.) *Tanner Lectures on Human Values, I,* Cambridge: Cambridge University Press.

61. Shaikh, A., 1977, "Marx's theory of value and the 'transformation problem'," in Jesse Schwartz (ed.) *The Subtle Anatomy of Capitalism*, Santa Monica: Goodyear.

62. Shaikh, A., 1978, "Political economy and capitalism: notes on Dobb's theory of crisis," *Cambridge Journal of Economics* **2**, 233–251.

63. Steedman, I., 1975, "Positive profits with negative surplus value," *Economic Journal* **85**, March, 114–123.

64. Steedman, Ian, 1977, *Marx after Sraffa*, London: New Left Books.

65. Steedman, I., 1980, "A note on the 'choice of technique' under capitalism," *Cambridge Journal of Economics* **4**, 61–64.

66. Steedman, I., 1983, "Heterogeneous labor, money wages, and Marx's theory," Dept. of Economics, Manchester (processed).

67. Stigler, G., 1958, "Ricardo and the 93% labor theory of value," *American Economic Review* **48**, June, p. 361.

68. Takayama, A., 1974, *Mathematical Economics*, Hinsdale, Ill.: Dryden.

69. Van Parijs, P., 1980, "The falling rate of profit theory of crisis. A rational reconstruction by way of obituary," *Review of Radical Political Economics* **12**, 1–16.

70. Van Parijs, P., 1983, "Nozick and Marxism: socialist responses to the libertarian challenge," *Revue Internationale de Philosophie* **146**, 337–362.

71. Vegara, J., 1979, *Economia Politica y Modelos Multisectorales*, Madrid: Biblioteca Tecnos.

72. Webber, M., 1983, "Technical change and the rate of profit," Dept. of Geography, Mcmaster University (processed).

73. Weeks, J., 1981, *Capital and Exploitation*, Princeton: Princeton University Press.

74. Weisskopf, 1979, "Marxian crisis theory and the rate of profit in the postwar U.S. economy," *Cambridge Journal of Economics* **3**, 341–378.

75. Wolff, R. P., 1981, "A critique and reinterpretation of Marx's labor theory of value," *Philosophy and Public Affairs* **10**, no. 2, 89–120.

76. Wolfsetter, 1977, *Wert, Profitrate und Beschaftigung*, Frankfurt, Campus Verlag.

77. Wright, E. O., 1982, "The status of the political in the concept of class structure," *Politics and Society* **11**, 321–342.

78. Wright, E. O., 1986, "What is middle about the middle class?" in J. E. Roemer (ed.) *Analytical Marxism*, Cambridge: Cambridge University Press.

INDEX

CAPITALIST IMPERIALISM, CRISIS AND THE STATE

JOHN WILLOUGHBY

ROUTLEDGE
ROUTLEDGE
Taylor & Francis Group

Capitalist Imperialism, Crisis and the State

John Willoughby
The American University, USA

A volume in the Marxian Economics section
edited by
John E. Roemer
University of California, Davis, USA

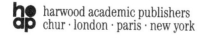

harwood academic publishers
chur · london · paris · new york

©1986 by Harwood Academic Publishers GmbH
Poststrasse 22, 7000 Chur, Switzerland
All rights reserved

Harwood Academic Publishers

P.O. Box 197
London WC2E 9PX
England

58, rue Lhomond
75005 Paris
France

P.O. Box 786
Cooper Station
New York, NY 10276
United States of America

Library of Congress Cataloging-in-Publication Data
Willoughby, John, 1949–
   Capitalist imperialism, crisis, and the state.

   (Fundamentals of pure and applied economics; v. 7. Marxian economics section)
   Includes index.
   1. Imperialism. 2. Capitalism. 3. Marxian economics. I. Title. II. Series:
Fundamentals of pure and applied economics; v. 7. III. Series: Fundamentals of
pure and applied economics. Marxian economics section.
JC359.W54   1986   325′.32   86-14967
ISBN 3-7186-0322-5

Contents

Introduction to the Series

Drawing on a personal network, an economist can still relatively easily stay well informed in the narrow field in which he works, but to keep up with the development of economics as a whole is a much more formidable challenge. Economists are confronted with difficulties associated with the rapid development of their discipline. There is a risk of "balkanisation" in economics, which may not be favorable to its development.

Fundamentals of Pure and Applied Economics has been created to meet this problem. The discipline of economics has been subdivided into sections (listed inside). These sections include short books, each surveying the state of the art in a given area.

Each book starts with the basic elements and goes as far as the most advanced results. Each should be useful to professors needing material for lectures, to graduate students looking for a global view of a particular subject, to professional economists wishing to keep up with the development of their science, and to researchers seeking convenient information on questions that incidentally appear in their work.

Each book is thus a presentation of the state of the art in a particular field rather than a step-by-step analysis of the development of the literature. Each is a high-level presentation but accessible to anyone with a solid background in economics, whether engaged in business, government, international organizations, teaching, or research in related fields.

Three aspects of *Fundamentals of Pure and Applied Economics* should be emphasized:

—First, the project covers the whole field of economics, not only theoretical or mathematical economics.

—Second, the project is open-ended and the number of books is not predetermined. If new interesting areas appear, they will generate additional books.

—Last, all the books making up each section will later be grouped to constitute one or several volumes of an Encyclopedia of Economics.

The editors of the sections are outstanding economists who have selected as authors for the series some of the finest specialists in the world.

J. Lesourne   *H. Sonnenschein*

Capitalist Imperialism, Crisis and the State

Dept. of Economics, The American University, Washington D.C., USA

1. EVALUATING THE EARLY LENINIST THEORY OF IMPERIALISM

Introduction: The central role of Lenin in the development of the Marxist theory of Imperialism

What gives to Lenin's analysis of this new stage of development so much of its importance is that he clearly enunciated the respects in which this new stage modified or transformed certain of the relationships which were characteristic of the earlier pre-imperialist stage. [51, p. 246]

Apart from certain isolated cases, the efforts of Marxists, during the period when Lenin's conception of imperialism corresponded most closely to reality, were directed not so much towards refinement of his conceptual apparatus, as to mechanical and ritualistic repetition of his pronouncements. Lacking a sufficiently precise conceptual structure, they then found themselves unprepared to tackle even such macroscopic anomalies as those which became manifest after the Second World War. Instead of isolating and ordering these, to see... what their effective consequences for the paradigm were, Marxists took the course described above—*displacement of anomalies from the field of analysis into ever increasing ambiguities and imprecisions of language.* [15, p. 19]

The Marxian theory of imperialism inhabits a unique position in Marxian theory: the categories and hypotheses central to what is now the orthodox perspective do not originate with Marx or Engels, but rather were primarily formed during the first two decades of the twentieth century. One might say that this analysis of imperialism by Marxists represents the first systematic attempt to understand a phenomenon never addressed in a sustained way in Marx's major work.[1]

At first, this lack of theoretical direction from the masters proved to be beneficial. Unlike the mechanistic theories of crisis characteristic of the Second International, the radical European theorists were explicitly engaged in an attempt to *apply* Marxism to a series of new events and structural shifts in advanced capitalism. In the case of Luxemburg, this led to a reconsideration of Marx's theory of expanded reproduction [121]. And Hilferding contributed much rich analytic detail to the Marxist conception of the concentration and centralization of capital [89]. Marxian economic theory in general was clarified and deepened as a result of these early "neo-Marxian" efforts.

Unfortunately, this creative adaptation of materialist theory came to a halt by the mid 1920s.[2] Two major events were responsible for this theoretical stagnation. Most fundamentally, the period of revolutionary socialist upheaval following World War I shattered the Marxist theoretical tradition of German Social Democracy. Karl Kautsky, the most prominent socialist theoretician of the pre-World I period, became isolated and was rendered almost irrelevant by the dual movements of Sparticist-inspired upsurge and Social Democratic management of capital's contradictions. And Rosa Luxemburg, the most creative thinker within German Marxism during this period, was assassinated while a leader of the newly-formed German Communist Party.

The second major event responsible for the death of creative Marxian thinking about imperialism was paradoxically the triumph of the Bolshevik Revolution. As the Soviet Union's party leaders began to exert their hegemony over the other national Communist Parties, Lenin's popular pamphlet on imperialism began to emerge

---

[1] V. G. Kiernan makes this clear in his excellent essay "The Marxist Theory of Imperialism and Its Historical Formation." See [104].

[2] One of the signs of Marxism's degeneration is the fate of those whose works which failed to follow the Soviet perspective slavishly. Fritz Sternberg's work *Der Imperialismus* [170] represents an extremely interesting attempt to integrate a labor-aristocracy theory with Luxemburg's original attempt to explain the necessity for capital expansion. Unfortunately, few Marxists even know about Sternberg's effort.

as a holy text.[3] Lenin's work on this subject is crucial in its own right. Many of his formulations remain central to our understanding of the concept today. On the other hand, this rigidification of theory has interrupted and deflected alternative radical attempts to understand more recent developments in the capitalist world economy. A new master, Lenin, emerged, and the peculiar necessity of Marxian thought to rely conservatively and exegetically on one source of wisdom for the development of its theory was reproduced.

A. Lenin's three arguments

If it were necessary to give the briefest possible definition of imperialism, we should have to say that imperialism is the monopoly stage of capitalism. [113, p. 85]

With this pithy statement, Lenin attempted to summarize sharply his view that imperialism is an inherent and inevitable outgrowth of the evolution of advanced capitalism. Monopoly emerges from the ongoing concentration and centralization process; this leads to the fusion of bank and industrial capital; and finally, the formation of these finance capital trusts stimulates, through intensified capital export, increased and intensified competition for monopolistic control over the territories of the world. This chain of reasoning is especially clear in Lenin's additional five-point description of imperialism:

1) The concentration of production and capital has developed to such a high stage that it has created monopolies which play a decisive role in economic life;

---

[3] Thus, Stalin writes:
Is it not true that the question of imperialism, the question of the spasmodic character of the development of imperialism, the question of the victory of socialism in one country, the question of the Soviet form of the state, the question of the role of the Party in the system of the dictatorship of the proletariat, the question of the paths of building socialism—that all these questions were elaborated precisely by Lenin? [169, p. 145]
Despite Lenin's contributions, it is precisely these issues that contemporary Marxism have *not* settled.

2) Bank capital has merged with industrial capital and created an oligarchy of finance capital;

3) The export of capital as distinguished from the export of commodities has acquired exceptional importance;

4) International monopoly capitalist associations have formed to share the world among themselves; and

5) The territorial division of the whole world among the biggest capitalist powers has been completed. [113, p. 86]

Points 1 and 2 refer to the structure of capitalist organization: the creation of monopolies and the rise of a financial oligarchy based simultaneously on industrial enterprises and banks. Point 3 argues that the form of international capital expansion is characterized by the export of money capital rather than increased commodity trade. And finally, points 4 and 5 stress the claim that this age of monopoly culminates in the division of the world among the major capitalist trusts and the nation-states that represent them.

Methodologically, this means that Lenin began at the economic "base" by focussing on the shifting organization of capital engendered by concentration and centralization. He then deduced the new forms of capital expansion which allow for much more extensive movements of capital into "external" territories. And *only then* did he discuss what we would more ordinarily consider to be imperialism: the attempts by dominant classes and "their" nation-states to establish control over external territories. For Lenin these moments of structural evolution, capital expansion and struggles for domination are so tightly and obviously linked to each other that he felt justified in labelling them all as *imperialism*. This is the first important innovation of the Leninist theory: *imperialism* is seen as a stage in the development of capitalism.

To reach a full understanding of Lenin's purpose in developing this theory of imperialism, however, it is necessary to delve further. The Bolshevik leader was not interested only in generally discussing the capitalist domination of the world economy. Rather, *Imperialism* was written to provide a political understanding of the specific results of this era of "monopoly capital" expansion. Beyond the general argument that advanced capitalism must lead to imperialism (and indeed is indistinguishable from imperialism) run two additional claims: that capitalist imperialism is characterized by chronic imperialist warfare, and that it culminates in the parasitic exploitation of backward economic regions by the advanced capitalist social formations. Lenin used these theoretical statements to strengthen his revolutionary socialist politics: only socialist revolution can free the globe from the related perils of misery and war.

In *Imperialism,* the second argument, that war is a central feature of monopoly capitalism, is more heavily stressed. This is hardly surprising, since Lenin wrote this pamphlet during World War I in order to argue against Kautsky's reformist perspective that there is no inevitable connection between capitalism and warfare.[4] To combat the Kautskyist position, Lenin maintained that capital accumulation is inherently uneven—in both a temporal and geographic sense. This implies that one can expect accumulation units in separately located territories to be differentially affected by capitalist growth, and thus booms and slumps can over time erode the competitive position of economic leaders and strengthen those firms positioned in more backward economic environments. From this postulate of an economic law of unevenness, Lenin then argued that no attempt to divide up the world among separate monopoly capitalist combines can ever be stable. Capitalist development will eventually make it advantageous for one firm to attempt to cut back the power of their erstwhile partners. This chronic economic tension will inevitably draft nation-states into the battle for economic territory. Thus, intensified competition among finance capitalist trusts leads to militarism and war among the major capitalist states—not just for resources in external, undeveloped regions, but eventually for territorial control over the capitalist world itself. In this sense, the logical structure of this capitalist rivalry argument is identical to the general claim that advanced capitalism is imperialism. An economic law is put forward (the law of uneven development), the effect of this law on firm behavior is deduced (the inability for any alliance of competitive enterprises to be stable), and the imperialist behavior of states is explained (imperialist rivalry and ultimately war).

---

[4] Kautsky argued for the formation of a trade union-liberal bourgeois alliance that would agitate for peace, while Lenin and Luxemburg campaigned for the mobilization of the proletariat for a revolutionary overthrow of the capitalist order. [193]

The third theme of imperialist parasitism is more difficult to derive from a particular economic law. Nevertheless, given Lenin's method, it is reasonable to attempt the discovery of an economic tendency which can serve as the "ultimate" cause of territorial exploitation. Fundamental to this search is the suggestion in *Imperialism* that the emergence of monopoly capitalism shifts the role that capitalism plays in world history: from being a progressive force of technological dynamism, monopoly negates the laws of competitive capitalism and ushers in a world of technological stagnation and intensified exploitation.[5] This theme appears in *Imperialism's* reference to both the rentier status of England's coupon clippers and the small "aristocracy of labor" that attains some of the benefits (through higher wages) of imperial exploitation. [113, p. 98]

In Lenin's hands, imperialism becomes a stage in capital's expansion, a system of implacable nation-state rivalry, and the routinization of territorial exploitation. None of these hypothesized features need contradict each other. On the other hand, it is important to assess this general neo-Marxist framework of analysis. It could be that particular flaws in theoretical reasoning and empirical analysis have weakened the connections among the complex of factors that Lenin outlined.

B. Early twentieth century theory: The confusion of Lenin's definition

Before proceeding to an assessment of Lenin's (and other early Marxists') detailed hypotheses, it is important to note that Lenin's own tendency to define advanced capitalism as imperialism constitutes a barrier to clear thinking. One could treat this "definition" as

---

[5] This is a more controversial interpretation of Lenin. He does argue that monopoly capitalism is a result of intensified competition. On the other hand, it seems clear that this competition is seen as parasitic rather than leading to progressive technical change. For Lenin, the transition from competitive to monopoly capitalist almost seems to lead to different laws of motion. Lenin writes the following:

As we have seen, the deepest economic foundation of imperialism is monopoly. This is capitalist monopoly; i.e., monopoly which has grown out of capitalism, commodity production and competition, in permanent and insoluble contradiction to this general environment. Nevertheless, like all monopoly, it inevitably engenders a tendency to stagnation and decay. [113, pp. 95–6]

what Arrighi calls a "hypothesized statement of fact"—which may or may not be true [15, pp. 10-1], but all too often advocates of the Leninst theory merely vaguely assert that imperialism is capitalism and therefore since capitalism exists so must imperialism. More sophisticated defenses rest on picking out that aspect of the Leninist theory that seems most valid, while ignoring the rest of the thesis.

Fortunately, there is a growing consensus among Marxian theorists that Lenin's definition must be abandoned if we are to understand the evolution of capitalist imperialism.[6] For this crucial purpose, Lenin's definition is both too general and too specific. It is too general because the definition leads us away from studying the specific phenomena of territorial domination/exploitation and nation-state conflict which most consider central to understanding imperialism today. It is too specific because far too many historically-situated aspects of early twentieth century international capitalism are seen as fundamental to a general theory of capitalist imperialism.

It is appropriate, therefore, to return to a more prosaic definition of imperialism that considers it as *attempted practices of domination over one territory and/or nation by the state and/or ruling elite which "represents" another territory or nation.* A theory of capitalist imperialism, then attempts to explain how the expansion of capital organizes global economic life and thereby contributes to imperial oppression and conflict. In this spirit, a more precise definition of capitalist imperialism (that should be treated carefully as a hypothesized statement of fact) is given by Peter Evans:

... a system of capital accumulation based on the export of capital from advanced countries to less developed regions (or more precisely center capital's acquisition of control over the means of production in those regions) accompanied by the utilization of political and military resources to protect and maintain the means of production over which control has been acquired [57, p. 16].

C. Early twentieth century theories continued: Reductionist flaws in the explanations of capital expansion

Lenin's attempt to explain imperialism through an examination of the laws of capitalist development is not unique. Most of the early radical writers assumed that if it were possible to identify a reason

---

[6] See Anthony Brewer for a clear criticism of Lenin's definition, [32, p. 110].

why capital *must* expand, then it would be self-evident that the state
would support this expansion in an imperialistic way; i.e. introduce
policies that would allow one state to control the political-economic
life of another. Because of this reductionist tradition, the Marxian
theory of imperialism is often considered solely as a radical theory
of capital expansion, which attempts to identify certain contradictions in the accumulation process impelling capital outward.
Modern commentaries on this subject, thus, often revolve around
an attempt to identify the "correct" contradiction—in the apparent
economistic belief that any examination of the political choice of
imperialist policies is unnecessary.[7]

There are two major problems with this approach. Most fundamentally, there is not a clear connection between any particular
contradiction which might cause capital to expand and the form
which imperialism might take. In a sense, the early theorists
demanded too much of themselves: the implicit method assumes
that one could deduce specific political behavior from a given set of
economic contradictions. This claim is highly problematic; a theory
of state behavior is crucial to any theory of imperialist conflict and
oppression.

The second problem, on which the contemporary literature has
tended to concentrate, is that few of the economic theories of
contradiction are persuasive in their own right. Rosa Luxemburg's
approach reveals in an extreme way the problems inherent in the
attempt to discover the "correct" barrier to accumulation. She
argued that capitalism contains within it a fatal flaw: the laws of
competition force each capital to attempt to expand and yet,
according to her, capital cannot survive without invading non-
capitalist areas of production. Because of an inevitable failure in
demand, the intensified outbreak of imperial tension is not due
fundamentally to any change in the organization of capital, but
rather to the desperate scramble for new "external" territories. (See
[121].)

It is now generally recognized that Luxemburg failed to prove
that there must always and necessarily be insufficient demand to
purchase the additional product that any expanding capitalist

---

[7] See in particular Tom Kemp's survey of early radical theories of imperialism
[101].

economy places on the market. Luxemburg had an unreasonably mechanistic model of realization because she misunderstood the elastic properties of credit extension and discounted the possibility of deficit financing by the state in the purchasing of military hardware. This does not mean that Luxemburg made no contribution to the theory of imperialism, but the point here is that her insights are swamped by her own methodology.[8] Luxemburg placed so much emphasis on the "inevitable" realization crisis that we are left with some profound description, but no serious explanation, of capitalist imperialism.

If we evaluated every early twentieth century radical theory of imperialism by the same criterion, (that there can be no effective explanation of imperialism without the correct identification of the cause of capital expansion), we would be forced to reach the same conclusion. *Luxemburg's failure is not unique.* Hobson, for instance, developed an under-consumptionist model of the realization crisis which maintains that the skewed distribution of income brought about by monopolization forces capital to attempt to export its excess product to external territories. This thesis rests on an empirical claim about the inability of the working class to agitate for higher real wages. Ironically, this premise was being contradicted by the formation of the first powerful general unions in Britain just at the time that Hobson was developing his thesis in [92].

The same criticism can be raised against the arguments that capital expansion is caused by chronic raw material shortage or working class militance.[9] There is no inherent reason why capital cannot overcome raw material difficulties through technological innovation, and indeed, the terms of trade between raw materials and industrial products do not exhibit any simple trend which suggests that advanced capitalism is plagued by this form of scarcity.[10] An argument about the determinants of working class

---

[8] One of Luxemburg's major contributions is that she specifically examines the role that debt plays in integrating non-capitalist sectors into the world economy.

[9] Karl Kautsky and Fritz Sternberg are especially associated with the raw material and class conflict theories of imperialism respectively. See [160] and [170].

[10] It could still be maintained that the general relative scarcity of raw materials is not as important as shortfalls in certain key commodities. While it is an important consideration for the capital penetration of any particular region, one cannot build a general theory of capital expansion on this basis.

opposition to the prerogatives of capital (either through wage conflicts or shop-floor struggles over the direction of production) is more complex. But it is clear that we cannot maintain that intense capital-labor conflict is necessarily associated with capital expansion.

Finally, the falling rate of profit thesis, which is important to Hilferding's analysis in *Finance Capital* [88, pp. 239–98], depends on Marx's original analysis of the tendency of the rate of profit to fall and the plausible observation that the new industries of the late nineteenth century and early twentieth century required massive amounts of fixed capital investment. We now know that if Marx's theory is viewed through comparative statics methodology then one cannot argue that capitalist evolution will produce a lower rate of profit unless the real wage also rises. (See [156].) Most early Marxian theorists did not realize this, and thus the explanation of capital export which rests on this "law" is seriously flawed.

Despite these shortcomings, the writings of the early theorists do allow the formulation of a more adequate accounting of capital expansion. In fact, Hilferding, Bukharin and Lenin actually articulated it, even while muddling their perspective with the search for the "fundamental" contradiction. If competition is viewed as constantly threatening the economic viability of any given accumulation unit, then it is clear that firms must always be engaged in a constant search for new ways to reorganize production, new markets and new input sources. This by no means, however, implies that the tendency for capitalism to expand is always expressed in the same way. Capital is constantly undergong social and technical reorganization. As finance capital emerges, the ability of monopoly capitalists to distribute their money capital to various accumulation projects expands. Moreover, this strengthening in the social power of the firm is necessarily coincident with massive developments in transportation, communication and military technologies, which make possible both expanded overseas investments and the launching of ambitious territorial conquests. In other words, the increasingly sophisticated evolution of capitalist technology (the forces of production) combines with new structural features of the giant capitalist enterprise to permit an intensifying foreign expansion of capital.

In the discussion of the simultaneous evolution of capital organization and the forces of production, the early twentieth century theorists emphasized the former, while Marx, writing before the maturation of finance capital, stressed the latter.

> The bourgeoisie, by the rapid improvement of all instruments of production, by the immensely facilitated means of communication draws all, even the most barbarian, nations into civilization. [130, p. 477]

Nevertheless, it is possible to synthesize these differing emphases by noting that:

1) Capital inherently tends to expand because of the social relations of competition basic to its organization;

2) By the late nineteenth century, key developments in the forces of production (and destruction) permitted enterprises to exert more international control over their investment projects;

3) New organizational forms within and among accumulation units emerged to facilitate the exercise of this coercive power.[11]

These arguments were key to the early Marxist account of pre-World War I economic expansion. Nevertheless, it must also be said that the early theorists were reluctant to stay at this descriptive level. Realization crises, raw material shortages, chronic profitability pressures and even working class resistance to capitalist

---

[11] This approach permits a response to one further complaint. It has often been noted that Hilferding's and Lenin's description of finance capital suffers from its heavy emphasis on the development of Germanic investment banks. On superficial empirical grounds, the fusion of industrial and banking capital appears to have little to do with capital export because most foreign investments were organized by the City of London rather than the investment banks. (See [42].) This criticism, however, is not at all fatal to the Marxian understanding of finance capital. A good case can be made that the development of the City of London as the center of capital export is an indiciation of a new expansive power, which was manifested institutionally in Germany and the United States by the development of investment banks, and in Britain by the further maturation of the City of London. As North points out in [139, p. 159] some of the American investment banks were originally branches of English financial houses. A similar story could be told for France and Germany. (See [42, pp. 27 and 32].)

prerogatives are epiphenomena of the contradictions of accumulation, but nearly all radical theorists mistakenly rejected this perspective and attempted instead to identify one of these factors as a "fundamental" contradiction. This reductionist approach continues to breed confusion in Marxist theory today.

D. Did the early radicals understand the significance of capital export?

The findings of the previous section have serious consequences for any analysis of capital export to the Third World. It must be admitted that none of the theories of capital export offered compelling reasons for the *necessity* of the penetration of non-capitalist regions. Hobson's theory of under-consumption, Luxemburg's realization crisis analysis and Hilferding's falling rate of profit hypothesis suggest that capital will flow to "capital-poor" regions, but these precise formulations must be rejected. Even the theories of raw material scarcity or working class militancy do not automatically imply movements of capital outside of the advanced capitalist social formations. New raw materials might more readily be developed in capitalist territories where infrastructural investments are easier to mobilize, and the disruptions involved in the rapid creation of a modern proletariat make it unlikely that cheap labor can always be exploited in pre-capitalist social formations.[12]

This disposal of the arguments which predict the disproportionate flows of capital to "backward" economic regions are confirmed by the data. Money capital did not, by and large, flow to those territories in which capitalist social relations were not consolidated. Instead, much of it travelled to the rapidly expanding capitalist territories of Canada, the United States and Australia [42, p. 27]. The data indicate that the drive of competition which leads to capital expansion results in intensified accumulation within the capitalist territories themselves; it is not possible to maintain that capital will predominantly expand "outside itself."

Such a view is *not* foreign to some of the early theorists. Despite

---

[12] Gerschenkron makes this point especially clearly in [78].

his falling rate of profit thesis, Hilferding in particular emphasized the intensification of competition within the capitalist world, and Lenin stressed that imperialism involves more than competition over peripheral territories (see [89, pp. 301–10; and 113, p. 88].)

But this emphasis on sharpening inter-capitalist competition also missed an important point. Stressing the quantitative shares of capital flows downgrades the social impact of capital export to the periphery. The key role which economic expansion played in creating new capitalist nations in North America and Oceania has already been mentioned. Furtado has noted in [75] that the South American economies experienced a major social transformation as a result of the completion of infrastructural projects that allowed the intensified export of cash crops and mineral raw materials. India's economy did not experience as dramatic a transformation, but economic historians such as Gadgill [76] have stressed that the early twentieth century did witness the accelerated introduction of more advanced machinery and motors into factories. (As Marx had predicted, engineering and repair workshops began to emerge in response to the growing railway system.) It is also in this period that Europeans ceased to be content with maintaining trading posts on the coast of Africa and instead established colonial rule over the total continent. (See [63, pp. 251–383].) Finally and perhaps most significantly, capital export proved crucial to the capitalization projects of the governments and entrepreneurs of the European periphery—particularly Italy and Tsarist Russia. (See [79 and 80].)

In the late 19th and early twentieth centuries, capital did expand its influence everywhere. Despite the occasional theoretical and empirical hyperbole, it is justifiable to accept the neo-Marxist argument that imperialism is partly characterized by the increased flows of trade, finance and productive capital to capital-poor regions. Unfortunately, the recognition of this fact does not guarantee an adequate understanding of its significance. The traditional emphasis on capital flows tends to obscure the political and cultural dimensions of the creation of the capitalist world economy. The transformation of new networks of commodity production and distribution is associated with the simultaneous creation of new state structures and cultural identities. As we shall see, the early Marxist failure to grapple with this process lies at the root of its inadequate accounting of imperialist practices.

E. The crucial issue: Explaining pre-war capitalist imperialism

In order to provide a general framework of analysis, a theory of imperialism must be able to account for historical variety. Unlike other "imperialisms," the domination of other territories by capitalist powers has never been associated with one monolithic process, and this implies that the connection between capital export and imperialism is not at all straightforward. The failure to recognize this heterogeneous experience is the most glaring weakness in the early Marxist theory.

Of the territories external to Europe, for example, there are obvious counter-examples to the claim that capital expansion is always associated with intensified imperialism. To the extent that Britain's capital export assisted the capitalist development of North America, Oceania and South Africa, this weakened Britain's *imperial* influence even as it provided clear economic benefits to a significant sector of British capitalists.[13] For South America, most of Africa and Asia, the neo-Marxian argument is on stronger ground. The case of politically independent South America is complex, but there is a general consensus that Britain in particular established enough political hegemony over the region to determine the economic policies of the nominally independent states as well as to guarantee the security of the substantial British capitalist interests in the region.[14] Finally, there can be little argument that capital penetration in India, Indochina, China and Africa is associated with the intensified imperial control of these regions.

These historical examples strongly indicate that capital export *by itself* did not cause colonialism or other more subtle forms of imperialist domination in the pre-war era. Unfortunately, the Leninist theory in particular fails to grasp this conclusion. Instead, Lenin and Bukharin introduced a monolithic theory of rivalry and

---

[13] Certainly, important segments of British capital benefitted from capital export to the United States. But to the extent that capital export assisted the continental unification of North America, British capital export contributed to the building of a rival imperial pole.

[14] In 1914, British long-term investments in Latin America totaled $756.6 million. This compares with a $754.6 value for the United States and holdings worth $931.3 m in Canada, Australia and New Zealand. (See [63, p. 55].) There are some British historians who deny this assumption of British imperialism in Latin America. For a presentation and criticism of this perspective, see Tony Smith in [168, pp. 23–6].

parasitism that predicts the spread of capitalist colonialism to all sectors of the world economy.

This point can best be seen through a combined appraisal of the early theories of parasitism and rivalry. In *Imperialism*, Lenin maintained that the ability of modern capitalism to exert monopoly control over territories and industries heightens the tendency of capital to prey on rivals' fields of operations rather than attempting to compete through the development of the forces of production. This reliance on state power attains added importance because every capitalist enterprise's future is threatened by the erratic logic of accumulation. The temporally and spatially uneven nature of growth increases with advanced capitalism because capital's expansive power is so much greater. This forces even the largest accumulation units to demand the forceful political backing of "their" nation-state.

Finance capital and trusts have not diminished but increased the differences in the rate of growth of the various parts of the world economy. Once the relations of forces are changed, what other solution to the contradiction can be found *under capitalism* than that of force? (Lenin's emphasis in [113, p. 93].)

The basic problem with this thesis is revealed by the ease with which it can be reversed. Kautsky, for instance, suggested that the dominant characteristic of capital expansion is integration, not disruption, and this perspective led him to predict a unity of rather benign and progressive imperial interests. This rather implausible argument actually leads to a theoretical advance. Kautsky clearly realized that this hypothesis requires one to accept the possibility that the imperialism of the pre-World War I epoch and its associated militarism are *not* inevitable results of capitalist evolution.

The arms race rests on economic *causes* but not on economic *necessity*. Its suspension is in no way an *economic impossibility*. That in itself, however, tells us nothing about the *probability* of the advent of disarmament. Powerful classes have an interest in the arms race. Whether or not their resistance will be overcome is a question of political power. (Kautsky's emphasis in [160, p. 173].)[15]

---

[15] In a sense, Kautsky's approach is similar to Schumpeter's in his famous article "The Sociology of Imperialisms" [163]. For Schumpeter, imperialism only exists because of feudal, militaristic political elements which permit the flourishing of monopolistic interests. There are many anomalies in Schumpeter's theory—the most serious being the quite 'healthy' imperialistic impulse in the non-feudal United States. See [191] for documentation of this point.

This unity-rivalry conflict raises an important methodological point. It is impossible to analyze nation-state conflict without referring to the evolution of the capitalist state. Whether or not uneven development unifies or divides nation-states crucially depends on how they have been historically constructed within a specific international environment.

A closer look at the Marxian theories of the early twentieth century reveals that some of the authors did at times explicitly understand this argument. Hilferding, for instance, explained that the consolidation of the German nation-state in the late nineteenth century must be viewed in the framework of Britain's reigning imperial hegemony. It is in this context that protectionist tensions resulted in the imperialist fusion between finance capital and the rural Prussian aristocracy.

Lenin and Bukharin clearly wished to propose a less territorially-specific argument than Hilferding's. They maintained that there are forces at work which breed imperialism in *all* of the advanced capitalist social formations. Bukharin addressed this issue most directly. He hypothesized that uneven development will lead to militarized state capitalisms in all of the advanced capitalist social formations. Any disruption of the international basis of national accumulation leads to an internal and external mobilization of the nation-state's activities. This tightens the links between the military and capital even further, and moreover, the dependent middle strata are mobilized behind imperialist rhetoric to support even the most dangerous international adventures. The results of this process for the working class are also clear for Bukharin.

> With state capitalism making nearly every line of production important for the state, with nearly all branches of production serving the interests of war, prohibitive legislation is extended to the entire field of economic activities. The workers are deprived of the freedom to move, the right to strike, the right to belong to the so-called "subversive" parties, the right to choose an enterprise, etc. They are transformed into bondsmen attached, not to the land, but to the plant. They become white slaves of the predatory imperialist state, which has absorbed into its body all productive effort [34, pp. 159–60].

This formulation provides the deepest theoretical backing for Lenin's assertion that territorial domination and imperialist wars are inevitable features of advanced capitalism. For Bukharin, the instability of the global economy combined with the imperialistic merging of militarism and finance capital makes any rational calculation of the social costs and benefits of imperialism irrelevant; the prospects for a peaceful and progressive capitalism are minimal.

Despite the gripping power of Bukharin's prognosis, it is not necessarily superior to Kautsky's more prosaic perspective. Both visions are flawed by economic reductionism (with Kautsky emphasizing integration and the Leninists, uneven development). And consequently, both can only be more plausible if they are applied to specific historical environments in which the interaction between nation-state formation and world economic evolution can be observed more precisely.

This last criticism implies that the early Leninist attempts to explain the necessity of capitalist imperialism are incomplete. We cannot deduce capitalist rivalry from the logic of uneven development without additional arguments which connect the evolution of national social formations to the world accumulation process. And this, in turn, means that the roots of metropolitan territorial domination are still obscure. We have neither a general explanation of capitalist imperialism, nor an accounting of its heterogeneous character. This is a fundamental failure. No theory of imperialism can be complete without a compelling explanation of the varying forms of metropolitan capitalist state domination. And this requires an attention to the formation of varying political structures throughout the world economy—an attention which is diverted by the reductionist theories of capital expansion and, in the Leninist case, by the actual definition of imperialism itself.

Despite these harsh criticism, there are two key insights in Lenin's and others' works which are essential to the development of a more adequate Marxist explanation of capitalist imperialism.

1. Despite the tendency to overstress the quantitative intensity of capital flows between the "advanced" and "backward" sectors of the world economy, the early Marxist emphasis on the changing forms of capital expansion is crucially important. Finance capital and the related developments in the technologies of transportation, communication and warfare are fundamental to an analysis of the new dynamic power of capital in the pre-World War I period. For the first time, it was possible for firms to anticipate controlling

production and exchange in every corner of the globe. This is the kernal of truth in Lenin's claim that imperialism is characterized by the territorial division of the world economy among the major capitalist centers.

2. Most pre-war theorists recognized that it is necessary to explore the ways in which the international economy's evolution affects the economic and political reproduction of social relations in the advanced capitalist center. This insight is inadequate, for the social impact of capital penetration on the periphery was often ignored. Nevertheless, Hilferding's account of the industrialist/ Prussian alliance, Luxemburg's description of rising militarism, Lenin's cryptic analysis of the labor aristocracy, and Kautsky's hope for a liberal, professional middle class remain important features of contemporary analyses of imperialist politics.

Moreover, this attempt to link capitalist evolution to political and social structures provides a meeting ground for Marxist and non-Marxist theories of imperialism. Here, Veblen's, Weber's and even Schumpter's attempts to explain the culture of German imperialism can be connected to the early European Marxist stress on the logic of accumulation. A careful synthesis of these strands of thought can only enrich the materialist theory of imperialism.

2. TOWARDS A CONTEMPORARY MARXIAN THEORY OF IMPERIALISM

It is not easy to develop a theory of imperial oppression and conflict. The dynamics of capital expansion and capitalist state formation have both to be connected to the politics of imperialism.[16] Moreover, it is clear that all three processes in some sense mutually determine each other. How do we know where to begin?

Keat and Urry's recently articulated realist methodology of social science provides some guidelines for solving this problem. On the

---

[16] *Capitalist state formation* does not merely refer to the emergence of a political entity that is historically connected to the rise of capitalist social relations. This expression also means the continued development of the capitalist state as the economy and class relations evolve.

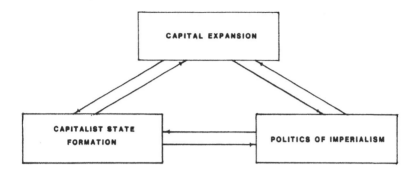

one hand, it is essential for Marxists to construct a theoretical system that is directly connected to the logic of capital accumulation. On the other hand, the problematic reasoning of the early Marxian literature stems from its economic reductionist methodology. The realist school suggests that the study of any social phenomena requires the construction of a theoretical model that, step-by-step, embraces more of the "real" world's dynamics.[17] It is necessary to begin with the abstract laws generated from within the contradictions of the mode of production before proceeding to a consideration of how these laws construct and deconstruct a more complex social formation or set of social formations. This method does *not* imply that the economic "base" must directly regulate all other arenas of social life. Rather, the claim is that the *understanding* of social processes can best begin with a study of the dominant social relations that organize material production and reproduction.[18]

---

[17] For Marx's description of this method, see [129, p. 100].

[18] A justification for this methodological claim can also be found in Russell Keat and John Urry, *Social Theory as Science* [100]. I would make the weaker argument that starting with an investigation of the capitalist mode of production is particularly important for studying the political economic evolution of the present world economy. It may well be that beginning at the economic "base" is inappropriate for studying the evolution of pre-capitalist social formations. In this case the organization of production is inextricably linked to the command over state-controlled "authoritative" resources. See [81].

In the case of imperialism, this approach suggests the following order of presentation.

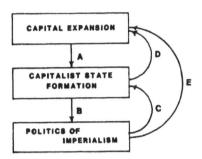

This schematic implies that the early theorists were correct in first studying the global expansion of capital—even if the search for the single contradiction that impels capital outward was misplaced. Analyzing the modalities of economic change in any given era provides the foundation for understanding capital international-ization's political impact.

How do capital expansion and nation-state evolution culminate in a systematic politics of territorial oppression and conflict? Answering this question is the ultimate goal of this investigation. The realist method, however, cautions against moving to this issue immediately, just as it warns against stopping too soon.

A. The internationalization of capital

Describing the internationalization of capital is less easy than would appear at first glance. For Marxists, *capital* is a term which embraces the key dynamic manifestations of the accumulation process—including trade, banking and productive investment and, most importantly, the creation of capitalist class structures.[19] One

---

[19] One common error in Marxist theory is the rhetorical conflation of terms. Thus, it is common to argue that capital *is* a social relation. This makes as much sense as claiming that snow *is* cold temperature. The generalized expansion of capital is predicated on the existence of certain social relations, but capital is not proletariat-bourgeois conflict itself. Rather, this term stands for those resources (human, physical, financial) that are employed in the attempted creation (or capturing) of surplus value.

cannot trace capital export by focussing on one variable. Moreover, following the paths of internationalization requires a regional perspective even though capital itself is a category which most abstractly eschews any geographically-bounded identification. Any empirical approach to this issue is bound to be makeshift. Data limitations, for instance, require the utilization of national categories to examine the logic of uneven development even though nationality should not be introduced at this stage of the analysis. Even more severe empirical constraints require the viewing of the proletarianization process in the Third World from information on the distribution of national populations between urban and rural sectors.

The most straight-forward beginning is to disaggregate the forms of capital expansion. Marx himself suggests that expanded reproduction (the "quantitative" aspect of the valorization process) can be conceived as a series of three interlocking moments: the money capital circuit $\left(M-\genfrac{}{}{0pt}{}{LP}{MP}-P\text{------}C'-M'\right)$; the productive capital circuit $\left(P\text{------}C-M\text{------}\genfrac{}{}{0pt}{}{LP}{MP}\text{------}P'\right)$; and the commodity capital circuit $\left(C-M-\genfrac{}{}{0pt}{}{LP}{MP}\text{------}P\text{------}C'\right)$.[20] Since Rudolf Hilferding's *Finance Capital* [88], this framework has been employed in analyses of the world economy and Christian Palloix, in particular, is known for his contemporary adaptation of this schema. In Palloix's early studies, there is an evolutionary story implicit in his presentations. (See [144].) The growth of the capitalist world economy begins with the internationalization of commodity capital (the growth of international trade), proceeds to the internationalization of money capital (portfolio and banking investments) and concludes with the internationalization of productive capital (direct foreign investment). This stylized history is only plausible if one ignores the inter-war period of the twentieth century (in which trade and lending collapsed) and the 1970s (in

---

[20] Marx developed this terminology and representation in [127, pp. 109–79]. *M* represents money capital; *P*—productive capital; and *C*—commodity capital. *LP* and *MP* stand for *labor power* and *means of production* respectively.

which the growth in the volume of lending clearly outstripped
expansions of the more 'advanced' productive capital circuit).
Because of these anomalies, it is not my purpose to make a linear
historical argument while using these distinctions. Rather, Marx's
reproduction circuits are useful in empirically disentangling the
complex networks of accumulation that presently exist in the world
economy.

*The internationalization of commodity capital: multilateralization
and uneven development within the core*

Most discussions of commercial trends in the global economy since
the close of World War II begin with two important observations:
the relative share of trade in global production has risen substan-
tially for the advanced capitalist nations, while the proportion of
commerce flowing to and from the United States has declined.
Tables I and II provide documentation of both these points.

It appears that this most recent period of unprecedented capitalist
expansion is similar to the one that preceded the outbreak of World
War I. Then, world trade also grew at a faster pace than national
production, and the United States and German capital were
effectively challenging Britain's international commercial hegemony. It would be a mistake, however, to overstate the similarities
between these two periods. Multilateral trade networks between the
European imperial center and the Southern territories were strictly
limited by the spreading reality of colonial control over Africa and
Asia. There was always the imminent possibility (which Lenin in
particular stressed) of breakdown and the subsequent creation of
rival imperial zones. The inter-war period bears somber witness to
this potential. This collapse has not been characteristic of the 1970s.
Despite deep recessions, high inflation and sluggish growth, trade
has both continued to expand more rapidly than domestic production and becomes even more multilaterialized.[21] Uneven development is a powerful reality of the capitalist world economy, but
speculating about the possible manifestations of this contradiction
during periods of crisis requires a more thorough, historically-
sensitive analysis.

---

[21] For a report on trends through the late 1970s, see [192, pp. 195–211].

TABLE I
Exports and imports as percentages of GDP

	Exports			Imports		
	1960–6	1967–73	1974–80	1960–6	1967–73	1974–80
USA	5.1	5.6	8.7	4.4	5.6	9.4
Japan	9.9	10.5	12.9	9.7	9.2	12.6
FRG	18.2	21.1	25.9	16.6	18.4	23.8
France	13.8	15.8	21.2	12.9	15.1	21.6
UK	20.2	22.5	28.8	20.9	22.6	29.2
Italy	14.8	17.8	25.1	14.4	17.0	25.6
Canada	18.9	22.5	28.8	18.9	21.1	25.4
Total	9.7	11.1	15.8	9.1	10.6	15.8

Source: OECD Economic Outlook: Historical Statistics 1960–80 (Paris: OECD, 1982): 63.

The internationalization of productive capital: The intensification of integration and uneven development
Data ambiguities require a skeptical handling of quantitative reports of investment trends. (Trade figures certainly cannot be accepted with complete confidence, but foreign commerce accounting is less subject to error and more regularly available in the reports of

TABLE II
Shares of trade

	Exports as Percentage of OECD Exports		
	1962–6	1967–73	1974–80
USA	20.4	18.2	17.8
Canada	6.1	6.3	5.5
North America	26.5	24.5	23.3
Japan	4.8	7.1	9.8
EEC	51.8	51.7	52.2
	Imports as Percentage of OECD Imports		
	1962–6	1967–73	1974–80
USA	20.7	20.9	18.7
Canada	5.0	5.1	5.4
North America	25.7	26.0	24.1
Japan	5.9	8.1	8.9
EEC	51.1	50.1	51.4

Source: OECD, *National Accounts, 1951–80, vol. I* (Paris: OECD, 1982): 87. Computed from data in 1975 prices and 1975 exchange rates.

TABLE III

	Percentage distribution of US capital exports (flows)						
	1953	1956	1966	1973	1979	1982	1983
Direct foreign investment	101.1	61.7	84.1	34.4	42.8	−2.8‡	17.6§
Portfolio investment	−23.4	9.7	11.4	5.7	8.2	7.4	17.3
Other financial investment†	21.9	28.6	4.5	59.9	49.1	95.4	57.8

Source: Various issues of Survey of Current Business (March 1955, March 1958, March 1975, March 1981, March 1984).

† Other financial investments include short-term and long-term claims by U.S. banks and other private institutions.

‡ 1982 was a peculiar year because of a $8.3 b. inflow in equity and inter-company accounts from the Netherland Antilles. If this is excluded from Direct foreign investment figures, the DFI outflow would have been $6.5 b.

§ The corresponding disinvestment from the Netherland Antilles was "only" $1.8 b. in 1983. The DFI outflow figure would have been $12.4 b. if this inflow had been excluded from the accounts.

international agencies such as the OECD, IMF and UN.) Despite these problems, it is possible to summarize key aspects of productive capital export. Table III, for instance, indicates that direct foreign investment represented the largest type of capital export (not including trade) from the US until the mid-1960s. (In contrast, British capital exports before World War I primarily took the form of money capital portfolio investments.)

As direct foreign investment grew in absolute terms, the focus of US transnational corporate activity shifted away from its traditional locations in Latin America and Canada and towards Europe. This result parallels the increasing concentration of trade within the advanced capitalist world during the 1950s and 1960s. In the 1970s, the trend reversed itself and the Third World became a slightly greater focus of productive capital investment. This result is not surprising. Most theories would predict that foreign investment and trade movements should complement each other.[22]

---

[22] Even Raymond Vernon's early 1970s product cycle hypothesis, which suggests that Direct Foreign Investment *replaces* exports, can be modified to take account of the significant presence of intra-company trade in the modern world economy. See [185, pp. 65–77]. For data on the distribution of foreign investment between advanced capitalist and Third World territories, see [141, p. 54].

TABLE IV

	Geographical position of US direct foreign investment abroad†				
	1953	1956	1966	1973	1979
Canada	32.9	34.6	30.3	25.2	21.3
Europe	14.6	15.8	31.6	37.8	42.3
Other developed	4.1	4.5	6.2	8.3	8.0
Latin America	35.5	32.4	18.8	16.3	19.1
Other developing	9.8	9.0	7.9	6.3	5.7
Developed	51.7	55.0	68.1	71.3	71.6
Developing	45.5	41.4	26.8	22.6	24.8

Source: Obie G. Wichard, "Trends in U.S. Direct Investment Abroad," *Survey of Current Business* **61** (February 1981): 50–1.

† Figures do not add up to 100 because unallocated and international categories are not included.

The process of uneven development is also indicated by foreign investment data. The US is no longer the *only* major home of transnational enterprise. Indeed, the domestic American economy itself has become a major "host" zone for capital export. Rival national corporations clearly possess the technological and marketing abilities to compete with previously dominant US businesses on their own terms. As a result, each national economy has become more interlocked with most others. In the modern period, uneven development is strikingly associated with metropolitan capital inter-penetration—both within the core and periphery.

The internationalization of money capital: the differentiation of the periphery

The post-1945 epoch is not just distinct because of the major importance of direct foreign investment and the related shifts in trading activity. Contemporary capitalism has been maintained and extended by the globalization of the money capital circuit as well. Because of the enormous rise of lending during the 1970s, some analysts have been tempted to suggest that the importance of direct foreign investment is receding. The OECD, for instance, has

TABLE V

	Outward direct investment flows		
	Percentage distribution among predominant industrial capitalist countries†		
	1961–7	1968–73	1974–8
Canada	2.3	4.5	6.2
US	61.1	45.8	29.3
Original EEC‡	22.4	29.2	42.6
UK	8.7	9.1	9.2
Japan	2.4	6.7	13.0
Other Europe &Asia§	2.7	4.4	6.8

See Table VI for notes.

TABLE VI

	Inward direct investment flows		
	Percentage distribution among predominant industrial capitalist countries†		
	1961–7	1968–73	1974–8
Canada	16.1	12.1	3.2
US	2.6	11.4	26.7
Original EEC‡	50.2	47.5	50.4
UK	9.7	7.4	6.1
Japan	2.0	1.7	1.2
Other Europe & Asia§	21.5	19.7	17.8

Source: OECD, *International Investment and Multinational Enterprise: Recent International Direct Investment Trends* (Paris: OECD, 1981).

† The U.K. & U.S. data do not include re-invested profits in order to keep national data comparable. The UK data do *not* include the petroleum sector.

‡ Belgium, France, Germany, Italy, Luxemburg, the Netherlands

§ Australia, Norway, Spain, Sweden

concluded that:

> Multinational firms may be tending increasingly to focus on the provision of technology, marketing arrangements and certain aspects of management as their source of profit, relegating control of the purely financial dimension of international investment to financial organizations and the managerial aspects as well as legal ownership to their host country associates.[23]

This argument is premature. The aggregate rate of direct foreign investment growth has not slackened until recently, and new arenas of accumulation have emerged at the same time that metropolitan capital has withdrawn from others.[24] It is true that metropolitan bank lending has become an increasingly important form of capital export, but this should not be considered competitive with productive capital export. For these reasons, Andreef makes a compelling argument in [13] that international capital's total position in the world economy has never been stronger.

The internationalization of money capital does add a qualitatively new dimension to global capitalism, but not because direct foreign investment has lost its force. Rather, the extension of bank lending is directly associated with the sharp differentiation of the periphery. It is during the 1970s that Third World oil-exporting nations acquired a particular, short-term economic power; that commentators began to note the emergence of "newly industrializing countries" (NICs) in Latin America and East Asia; that categories such as *least developed* and *basic needs* countries acquired currency. If the evolution of the world economy is viewed by tracking changing financial flow patterns, these rhetorical divisions of the Third World become less arbitrary. The rapid expansion of bank capital was almost solely directed to the NICs, and after each of the two oil price shocks of 1974 and 1979, OPEC nations for a short time afterwards actually provided money capital to the world economy. For the rest of the Third World, "official development

---

[23] Cited in [141, pp. 28–9].

[24] This repositioning of metropolitan capital is not just geographic, but also sectoral. Peter Evans has especially stressed the role that evolving market structure plays in regulating the "triple alliance" among Third World states, local capitalists and multinational capital. See [57].

assistance" sponsored by a single industrial nation-state, by a grouping of states (such as the EEC) or by multilateral institutions, has continued to play the major role in integrating these less dynamic territories with the world economy.

TABLE VII

	Percentage shares of total resource flows to different categories of developing countries, 1981				
	NICs	MICs	OPEC	LICs	Total
Total Resource Flows ($86.8)	37.9	31.9	0.9	29.3	100.0
Official Development Assistance ($28.1)	2.8	36.3	1.1	59.8	100.0
Non-concessional ($58.7)	54.7	29.8	0.8	14.7	100.0
Bank Lending	88.9	22.7	−9.9	−1.7	100.0
Export Credits	34.9	29.8	8.5	26.8	100.0
Direct Investment	44.4	27.4	2.1	26.0	100.0
Multilateral	34.5	47.0	0.9	17.6	100.0

Allocated amounts based on preliminary estimates. Totals exclude some bond issues.

Low income countries (LICs) had GNP *per capita* below $600 in 1980.

Middle income countries (MICs) had GNP *per capita* above $600.

Newly industrialized countries (NICs) are Argentina, Brazil, Greece, Hong Kong, S. Korea, Mexico, Portugal, Singapore, Spain, Taiwan, and Yugoslavia.

The OPEC category does not include Indonesia (a LIC) and Nigeria (a MIC).

Source: *World Economic Interdependence and the Evolving North-South Relationship* (Paris: OCED, 1983):67.

The concentration and centralization of capital: finance capital's maturation and the proletarianization of the periphery

The capital circuit approach to studying the internationalization of capital is largely useful in describing the contradictory processes of integration/differentiation that are basic to the accumulation dynamic. This focus on the quantitative logic of expanded reproduction, however, cannot directly illuminate those qualitative shifts in the material organization of economic life that have resulted from post-war economic expansion. For this project, it is necessary to turn to another aspect of Marx's analysis and focus instead on what Marx called the concentration and centralization of capital.

Normally, this term refers to the increase in the average size of accumulation units (concentration) and their merger into large monopoly or finance capitalist enterprises (centralization). Hilferding, for instance, argued that this process changes the nature of inter-capitalist competition because the successful valorization of capital becomes pre-eminently associated with money capital/conglomerate management.[25] In the post-war period, technological breakthroughs have made this early twentieth century thesis even more compelling: it is now possible to control global production and marketing operations from a single managerial center. One key result of the post-war expansion has, thus, been the rise of the transnational corporation; its power is a fundamental aspect of modern capitalism.[26] In other words, a key aspect of the multi-laterialization of international capitalist competition in the post-war period has been the concomitant centralization of corporate power. The networks of capitalism are simultaneously more diffused and more tightly linked; the continuous extension of global competition increasingly requires the hierarchical organization of the firm.

This transformation of both the internal structures of capitalist firms and their relations to each other is one aspect of the concentration and centralization dynamic. Marx maintained in most of his mature writings, however, that the most profound impact of progressive accumulation is the stripping of pre-capitalist producers from direct access to the means of production. If he is correct, then the obverse side of the rise of the transnational corporation is the proletarianization of the mass of laborers, for as Marx argued in [126, pp. 776–7]:

With the increasing mass of wealth which functions as capital, accumulation increases the concentration of that in the hands of individual capitalists, and thereby widens the basis of production on a large scale and *extends the specifically capitalist*

---

[25] ... It (the industrial corporation) converts what had been an occasional, accidental occurrence in the individual enterprise into a fundamental principle: namely, the liberation of the industrial capitalist from his function as industrial entrepreneur (See [89, p. 107].)

[26] The late Stephen Hymer deserves credit for being one of the first to make this compelling argument. (See [94, pp. 113–140].)

methods of production . . . Accumulation therefore presents itself on the one hand as increasing concentration of the means of production, *and of the command over labor*; and on the other, and as repulsion of many capitals from one another. (my emphasis)

Since Marx's time, new theories have developed which suggest several intermediate stages between the uprooting of pre-capitalist-contact social relations and the formation of a wage-labor class. Rosa Luxemburg, for example, recognized in [121, pp. 368–418] that capital penetration creates several different "economies" before finally dissolving all pre-capitalist social relations. And, more recently, a complex literature has emerged which attempts to trace out the articulation of different modes of production within a social formation. There is an important debate within this literature about the stability of these linkages—whether capitalism tends to dissolve these social relations, or whether, instead, precapitalist modes of production intensify in order to maintain political order and even enhance exploitation.[27] The intensification of certain exploitative pre-capitalist social relations may have been one result of previous periods of capital penetration. Today, however, subsistence agriculture is rapidly declining; the relative share of the urban population has increased in all sectors of the world; and a new caste of low-wage workers from the periphery of Europe and North America has migrated to the more dynamic sectors of the metropolitan capitalist economies. There can be little doubt that we are currently living in an epoch of global proletarianization.[28]

Hand in hand with this generation of a new working class (with its attendant reserve army) has been the appearance of a much larger professional elite in the Third World. Once again, good, direct evidence of this phenomenon is not available. Nevertheless, both the enormous rise in higher education and the staffing of the expanding Third World state with indigenous peoples are clear indications of this class's important position in the Third World.[29] Indeed, most recent theories of the peripheral, post-colonial state

---

[27] For the most detailed English-language discussion of this issue, see [175].

[28] For information on immigration to the advanced capitalist world, see [109 and 52].

[29] Between 1970 and 1980, enrollments in higher education in the Third World increased in most countries by well over 100 percent. See [182, pp. 248–78].

TABLE VIII

	Urbanization rates and urban population growth, 1950–2000					
	Urban population as percentage of total population			Average annual percentage growth or urban population		
	1950	1975	2000	1950–60	1970–80	1990–2000
Developing countries	20.6	31.1	45.8	4.0	4.0	3.5
Industrial capitalist countries	62.4	74.4	83.6	2.0	1.2	0.8
World	29.0	39.3	51.5	3.5	2.8	2.6

Source: OECD, *World Economic Interdependence and the Evolving North-South Relationship* (Paris: OECD, 1983): 81.

focus on the politically ambiguous class relation of this group to metropolitan imperialism.

Conclusion

This quantitative and qualitative analysis of post-war capital expansion provides the basis for a more thorough understanding of contemporary imperialism. More specifically, there are five key findings to keep in mind.

1) The internationalization of capital is presently associated with the multilateralization of economic life. Spheres of national capitalist influence are in decline, both within most metropolitan economies and in the capitalist Third World.

2) As in previous eras, capital evolution is linked to uneven development. In particular, the leading role of the United States economy in the world accumulation process has quantitatively declined, while the relative levels of capitalist production in Europe and Japan have correspondingly risen.

3) This dynamic of uneven development has strikingly extended itself to the Third World. Money and productive capital have predominantly flowed between the "Newly Industrializing Countries" (NICs) and the metropolitan economies, while the more "backward" territories are still primarily integrated into the capitalist world economy through "foreign assistance."

4) The international capitalist firm has taken on more of the attributes first delineated by Rudolf Hilferding in *Finance Capital*. The global extension of the operations of private enterprise is associated with the consolidation of the transnational corporation. And these industrial and financial combines are now directly involved in managing all aspects of the circuit of expanded reproduction.

5) The intensified expansion of capital into the periphery has created a proletarianized laboring population and an enlarged professional class. These social transformations have profound significance for any explanation of contemporary capitalist imperialism.

B. Capital expansion and post-war theories of capitalist state formation

Introduction

The preceding analysis of post-war capital export is not controversial. Many contemporary theorists have noted the same trends, and even Marx's initial discussion of capitalism's international impact can be read as an analysis of the rise of monopoly capital and the spread of the proletariat. At this most abstract level of understanding the expansion of capital, much of the tradition of Marxian economics need not be altered radically. Rather, Marxism remains a powerful analytic method.

This consensus breaks down, however, when the impact of capital export on politics within metropolitan and peripheral national social formations is considered. Here, theoretical and ideological debates are quite intense; it is difficult to investigate the connections between capital internationalization and nation-state formation dispassionately.

The first step in a systematic study of this problem is to assess the relative power of capital internationalization in determining the political structures and actions of capitalist social formations. Although the premise of such an exercise is that a regional economy's position within the global accumulation process will significantly determine local and inter-regional political interventions, I am not claiming that *all* key characteristics of the political within the world economy should or can be deduced from the logic of accumulation. Rather, the argument is that opening the analysis with a study of the political impact of capital expansion is crucial to the development of a materialist understanding of capitalist imperialist politics. On a more general level, it is not possible to explain the interrelations between the "political" and the "economic" without first conceptually separating these two arenas of social practice. For this reason, determining the level of abstraction appropriate for studying metropolitan and peripheral state formations is one of this section's key tasks.

Capital expansion and metropolitan state formation
During the post-war period, Marxist explanations of the imperialist state have been most fully developed by the state monopoly capitalist, radical dependency and world systems schools. There are two tendencies in accumulation emphasized by the state monopoly capitalist paradigm. On the one hand, it is posited that the centralization of capital has permitted the articulation of Keynesian welfare and directly corporatist mechanisms of national political regulation. As a result, the links between national monopolies and the state have become even more tightly forged than during the pre-World War I era of monopoly capitalism. When considered alone, this hypothesized process has few implications for a theory of imperial state formation. Indeed, some have used this tendency to argue for the possibility of a progressive Social Democratic or Eurocommunist exit out of imperialist capitalism.[30]

The second strand of the state monopoly analysis, however, takes issue with this Kautskyist conclusion; it is argued that uneven development or the anarchy of global competition prevents such a reformist consolidation. Instead, shifts in political-economic power force individual advanced capitalist states, or alliances of capitalist states, to take measures to protect the integrity of "its" or "their" units of finance capital. The result of these struggles determines the overall mechanism of global capitalist regulation, and it is possible on this basis to periodize capitalist imperialism. For this project, the key task is to note accurately the crucial historically-significant shifts in advanced capitalist nation-state relations.[31] More will be said

---

[30] Carl Boggs provides an interesting review of this perspective in [27].
[31] For a sample of this regulatory approach, see Alain Lipietz in [118].

about this method in the discussion of imperial crisis. For now, it is most important to note that these state monopoly capitalist approaches represent a partial elaboration of the original Leninist theory. Imperialist practices are derived from the interaction of the national centralization of capital with global uneven development.

The world systems and radical dependency schools address this issue from a different perspective. Rather than focussing on the centralization of national capitals under the aegis of rival metropolitan nation-states, Samir Amin, Andre Gunder Frank and Immanuel Wallerstein all place their emphasis on the extraction of surplus from the periphery. In this perspective, imperial structures and practices are linked to the dynamics of center-periphery exploitation; the Keynesian welfare state is an epiphenomenon of the creation of a privileged mass of workers in the core. Amin, in particular, argues that parliamentary democracy in the West masks the brutalization and impoverishment of the mass of productive workers in the periphery.[32]

One distinct result of this approach is a slackening stress on nation-state structures and an increased concern with transnational metropolitan institutions—from the private multinational corporation to international organizations. It is implicitly posited that the centralization of capital does not lead to the strengthening of individual nation-state units; instead the interpenetration of capitals stimulates the construction of new unifying regulatory mechanisms. For this approach, the fundamental contradiction within global capitalism lies between North and South, rather than within rival centers of the advanced capitalist world.

It is possible to synthesize the state monopoly capitalist and world systems dependency perspective. In speculating about global imperialism's future, Frank and Wallerstein both maintain in [69 and 186] that uneven development combined with Third World resistance makes political economic rivalry among metropolitan capitalist political entities more likely. In this scenario, the decline

---

[32] But with the advent of imperialism, whether in the form of imperial preserves or of a world ostensibly open to all, the international division of labor between centers and peripheries takes on a new dimension. My basic thesis is that this new division of labor ushers in the era of the social-democratic alliance in the imperialist center. (See [6, p. 26].)

of the United States will unleash a new round of competitive alliance building, and the Third World will play a key role in determining the nature of a reorganized global system.

Unfortunately, this synthesis represents the worst of both worlds. It combines the dubious premise that the centralization of finance capital is coterminous with the territorial authority of the nation-state with the questionable assumption that the politics of Third World nationalism is necessarily resistant to the prerogatives of metropolitan capital.

The first premise clearly flies in the face of the data presented in the previous section. The international interpenetration of capitals suggests that capitalist interests in the integrity of a given national economy have declined rather than advanced, and the recent macroeconomic policies of most advanced capitalist states strongly confirm this intuition. The abandonment of investment and price controls throughout the metropolitan capitalist world, the anarchic coming of a flexible exchange rate regime, and the related explosion in international currency movements all signal an era far different from the state monopoly capitalist school's presumptions. Rather than viewing separate national political processes as fundamentally involved in the imperialist protection of national capitalists from the vagaries of the world economy (the classic Leninist presumption), metropolitan state politics is actually more concerned with success-fully inserting the national economy into the internationalization process. In this context, a government is successful if its policies promote the importation and exportation of domestic *and* foreign capital.

This alternative to state monopoly capitalism has two advantages. In the first place, its focus on the global economy permits a more adequate analysis of post-war international organizations, especially the International Monetary Fund. The second advantage springs from the first. It is important to recognize that metropolitan imperialism cannot always be explained through an analysis of the policies of the major advanced capitalist nation-states. Depending on the circumstances, other institutions may play a much more active role in regulating the subordinated periphery or in coercing imperial antagonists. The rupture between capital centralization and nation-state authority demands this more flexible methodological approach.

The internationalizing process I have outlined should not be interpreted as causing an inexorable decline in the domestic power of the nation-state. In fact, pressures on any government to reorganize industry and discipline labor may be even greater than during an era of "liberal corporatism." Moreover, politicians and bureaucrats still must respond to discordant popular demands for economic regulation and security. Governments' attempts to soften capitalism's contradictions have often been interpreted by the state monopoly capital and world systems schools as the effort to construct a metropolitan national interest in economic expansionism and Third World exploitation. A more adequate interpretation would see the relevant political agents as responding to social pressures for capital's regulation within the constraints of promoting a region's ability to adapt to the demands of the world economy.

This structural/capital-logic synthesis (which both Fine and Harris [65] and Jessup [99] suggest in their works) represents an advance over the state monopoly capitalist school because it takes account of presently evolving global economic processes. It thereby frees us from the archaic pre-World War II premise of national capitalist centralization. This advantage is not unique to the approach I have outlined. The dependency world systems schools also emphasize the importance of analyzing the international structures of accumulation. On the other hand, I hope to demonstrate in the next section that the national capitalisms which have emerged in the periphery deserve an analysis different from the world systems dependency framework—one which is more sensitive to the variety of political processes which can integrate the Third World into the world capitalist system.

Capital penetration and the rise of the peripheral state

The explosion of Third World liberation movements and the subsequent formation of post-colonial states throughout Asia and Africa have attracted the interest of Marxist and non-Marxist social scientists alike. And most theorists have begun their academic explorations of these processes by examining the contradictions that arise between capitalist and precapitalist mechanisms of social reproduction.[33] This approach presents obvious difficulties for any

---

[33] Non-Marxist schools of thought often do not use this terminology, but a dichotomy is still drawn between "traditional" and "modern" societies.

theorist hoping to develop a general theory of Third World state formation. Given the variety of pre-capitalist political-economic forms of social organization, it would be unreasonable to expect the emergence of one type of peripheral state. Indeed, we have already noted that in certain regions (North America and parts of Oceania), where international commercial exchange was associated with the nearly complete elimination of indigenous peoples and large-scale human migration from the metropolis, capital penetration resulted in the eventual enlargement of the advanced capitalist world rather than the emergence of subordinated economic territories. For these reasons, analysts have long recognized the need to modify Marx's assertion that capital expansion must create a world after its own image.[34]

With this proviso in mind, it is important to recognize that there is more than a kernal of truth to *The Communist Manifesto's* buoyant claim. The internationalization of capital has not created a homogeneous capitalist world, but it has imposed a political-economic logic on the peripheral territories of the world economy. This is a key argument for any Marxist theory of imperialism. Certain structural features of the Third World state can be explained by considering abstractly the impact of capital penetration on a pre-capitalist society. In fact, without this general framework, the distinct particularities of a subordinated social formation's history and politics are impossible to decipher.

A schematic "historical" account best captures the key common features in the evolution of contemporary Third World states.[35]

1) Capital penetration initially results in the introduction of new social forms of production and exchange without this process necessarily dissolving the old. The array of modes of production within a territory thus becomes more complex.

2) Political institutions and practices must eventually emerge to preserve this unstable social arrangement if capital expansion is to continue. This, however, does not necessarily imply that the state

---

[34] The Manifesto actually contains a quite complex vision of capitalist evolution. The bourgeoisie "creates a world after its own image" but it also makes "barbarian and semi-barbarian countries dependent on the civilized ones, nations of peasants on nations of bourgeois, the East on the West." See [130, p. 477].

[35] Much of this analysis is stimulated by John G. Taylor's work in [175].

always acts to facilitate accumulation. It may be that contradictory social pressures prevent the pursuit of "rational" pro-bourgeois policies.

3) The commercialization of economic life and the concomitant attempt to extend new forms of political authority eventually give rise to what Marxists often label the petty-bourgeois intelligentsia (and what non-Marxists might call the modernizing elite). The proper name is not so important.[36] Rather, it is the key role which this non-bourgeois grouping plays in the creation of the peripheral state. Placed at the center of competing demands of metropolitan capital, a growing native bourgeoisie, a pre-capitalist oligarchy (which may or may not be merging with the bourgeoisie) and increasingly articulate laboring classes (the proletariat and the peasantry), the actions of the intelligentsia are central to Third World political struggle.

4) The rise of this new class parallels the key role which the peripheral state plays in the organization of the territory's economic life. This often implies the backing of infra-structural building projects and the creation of certain state capitalist enterprises.

5) Even more fundamental is the introduction of a "modern" repressive apparatus that is able to monitor and control the actions of the popular classes. Because of this imperative, military institutions become central to the integrity of most peripheral social formations. The spread of capitalist social relations is integrally connected to the flourishing of nationally-based military institutions.[37]

6) All of these developments point to the emergence of distinct nationalities as a reference point for political action. Coincident with the rise of literacy, nationalist activists draw on metaphors and

---

[36] The name that one gives to a social grouping can be important. Terminology normally betrays a complex set of theoretical presumptions about historical evolution. Nevertheless, nearly all social analysts agree that the "new petty bourgeoisie" or "modernizing elite" are central to the revolutionary transitions of the "capitalist," "socialist" or "modern" world. For an orthodox, sociological view, see [53]. John S. Saul provides an excellent summary of Marxist views on the "new middle class" in [162]. Few deny the importance of this social grouping, but there is a vigorous debate about its "progressive" historical role.

[37] For a controversial, non-Marxist account of the military's central role in Third World state formation, see Irving Louis Horowitz in [93, pp. 89–186].

key cultural symbols to separate the indigenous society from the imperial one, while simultaneously appropriating some core practices and ideologies that permit the legitimation of capitalist nation-state practices.[38]

7) The creation of a new nationalist ideology has its parallel in the attempt by leaders of a Third World state to reorganize its economic relations with the surrounding regional and world economy. This can take many different forms, but the instability of global capitalism constantly reproduces the need for peripheral state action. Relations between center and periphery thus are chronically problematic.

This schematic accounting of peripheral state formation has drawn implicitly on a key concept developed by Marxist theorists in the early twentieth century. Trotsky used the term "combined and uneven development" and "permanent revolution" both to analyze the sources of social instability in the Tsarist state and to argue for the possibility of socialist revolution. He maintained that capital penetration inevitably produces economic, political and ideological anomalies that the pre-capitalist state proves increasingly unable to manage. Moreover, the weakness of indigenous capitalist interests (as a result of imperial domination) can combine with the proletarianization of the national economy to generate a powerful socialist revolutionary movement. Trotsky and Lenin linked this vision of successful socialist revolution in Russia to the spread of proletarian upheaval in the more advanced West. They did not forsee the stabilization of an anti-imperialist regime without such a development.[39]

It is necessary to modify Trotsky's argument to account for certain historical developments that are now, in the late twentieth century, much easier to discern. In the first place: anti-imperialist, national revolutions have resulted in the establishment of more politically autonomous peripheral states without socialist revolution in the West. The rise of the Soviet Union is the clearest early example of this process, but one should also interpret the formation

---

[38] Benedict Anderson is one of the few to have grappled directly with the theoretical complexities of this phenomenon. (See [10].)

[39] Michael Loewy in [119] presents an insightful commentary on the history of the term *permanent revolution*.

of the Turkish and Mexican states during the early twentieth century within the same general framework.[40] More recently, events in Nicaragua and Iran confirm the power of this modified combined and uneven development hypothesis: imperial capital penetration generates intense destabilizing pressures against a compradore imperial regime. The heterogeneous political structures that correspond to the initial states of capital penetration become increasingly difficult to maintain, but the new states which do emerge in the aftermath of revolution or intense reformist pressures must survive in a capitalist world economy. Their successes do not signal the disintegration of global capitalism.

This last point leads to a second crucial modification to Trotsky's analysis: an abstract consideration of the political effects of combined and uneven development cannot account for the variety of recent historical experiences in Third World social formations. The character of economic contradictions facing a society, the global political economic context of imperial domination and the actual evolution of peripheral political structures all interact to shape the oppositional political traditions and programs of a peripheral society. The very different post-colonial experiences of the Ivory Coast and Ghana, or the sharp distinction between the post-revolutionary Iranian and Nicaraguan regimes cannot be explained without a more historically sensitive attention to details.

A Marxist theory of peripheral state formation cannot deduce all political processes from the impacts of capital penetration. Nevertheless, it is important to recognize that there already is a framework embedded within the combined and uneven development model that can help explain variations across space and time. The implicit message of this analysis is that the peripheral state emerges from an interaction of imperialist state actions, the demands of metropolitan capitals, the complex processes of resistance and collaboration among Third World economic elites, and the similar dynamic that takes place within the indigenous governing institutions of the periphery. This approach does not neglect the actions of the subordinated classes, for all governing authorities must attempt to channel or repress the political energies of outcaste

---

[40] Trotsky himself implicitly recognized this perspective in his analysis of Mexico. See [119, p. 92].

groups. Nevertheless, a focus on the elites is especially important if we are to understand the political-economic reproduction of a Third World World social order. A stable "quadruple alliance" among the political and economic elites in the periphery and center is a prerequisite for the security of most Third World states.[41]

In this approach, there is wide scope for a variety of political structures within the Third World. Parliamentary democracy can become consolidated in certain nations, while military dictatorship remains chronic in other neighboring states. The terms of imperial subordination can also differ—from a framework in which local capital and the Third World state have very little room for negotiation (Puerto Rico) to one in which the Third World state and local capital possess a surprising ability to direct the terms of metropolitan capital penetration, even if, in military and diplomatic terms, these local elites are firmly dependent on metropolitan imperial powers (South Korea). This analysis also suggests that the terms of the "quadruple alliance" can also change over time. The evolution of the Brazilian state during the 1970s and 1980s is an important case in point.

This analysis has taken us a long way from Marx's simplistic claim that capital penetration must create a homogeneous capitalist world. But, in another sense, we are not that distanced from his and Engels' mid-19th century intuitions. The *Communist Manifesto* prediction was incorrect. On the other hand, the emphasis on the need to analyze peripheral state formation in the context of international capital penetration remains valid. It is for this reason that the early twentieth century combined and uneven framework is still cogent today.

Conclusion

These dual discussions of metropolitan and peripheral state formation are unified in their attempts to trace the recent evolution of political structures and capabilities to the internationalization of capital. In the case of the advanced capitalist social formation, I argued that the explosive interpenetration of capitals has generated new "a-national" regulatory structures and thereby lessened the

---

[41] The term "quadruple alliance" is a modification of Evans' "triple alliance" formulation in [41].

plausibility of state monopoly capitalist analysis. Indeed, the new advanced capitalist nation-state's integrity depends on the relatively effective functioning of these transnational mechanisms, not on the perfection of centralized mechanisms of control within the nation-state.

This discovery of the importance of world economic processes in metropolitan nation-state formation is not new. On the other hand, the virulence of nationalist and capitalist imperialist conflict in the early twentieth century led to the articulation of a particularly compelling theoretical vision that links uneven development to imperialist war. The contemporary obsolescence of this framework forces us to reformulate the nation-state/capital internationalization dialectic.

This theoretical uncertainty does not exist in the same degree for analyses of the Third World state. Few would argue that this entity is solely formed by national forces, and most Marxists—either consciously or unconsciously—have continued to use the combined and uneven development model to explain the "peculiar" nationalist/internationalist mixtures in the state structures and political cultures of the Third World. The difficulty with this theoretical borrowing lies not in the actual skeleton of the argument, but rather its sometimes too ambitious application.

For example, the effort to explain the inevitability of successful anti-imperialist revolution neglects the symbiotic alliances that normally emerge between peripheral and metropolitan states and capitals, and the attempts to deduce a single authoritarian structure of political dominance fail to account for the immense chronological and cross-sectional variety in Third World politics. In both of these cases, there is a tendency to neglect those particular "quadruple alliances" which influence the trajectory of any given social formation. Wallerstein in [186], for example, attempts to trace all shifts in political fortunes to the secular, long-wave rhythms in accumulation. It should be obvious by now that this approach claims too much for economic forces. The Marxist analysis of global accumulation provides a basis for understanding the processes of state formation; it cannot abolish the study of political and cultural processes altogether.

Making this argument need not indicate a significant modification of Leninist theory—if it could be shown that the peripheral states' own actions are a straightforward result of capital expansion. Unfortunately, this is not the case. The combined and uneven development perspective can be used to anticipate the emergence of bureaucratic and repressive peripheral states that often dominate local bourgeois interests and sometimes clash with advanced capitalist state demands. On the other hand, we cannot predict the precise political configurations that emerge from this process without doing considerable violence to history. As E. P. Thompson noted in [176, p. 343].

Do the categories of "class struggle on a world scale" really explain to us the course of the Iranian revolution? The degeneration of the regime of Pol Pot? The adversary relations of China and the USSR? The generational shifts in political consciousness in Europe, East and West, associated with the peace movement and the movement for civil rights? Or the imperial atavism of the British government's response to the Falklands crisis? By attempting to explain it all in one global mouthful we end with everything left to be explained.

The indeterminancy in this metropolitan and Third World state analysis can be traced to the same source. Neither imperial nor subordinate state behavior can be explained without reference to more specific national and international historical processes.

No narrow focus on the tendencies of capital can by itself explain state behavior. The method does account for certain general structural trends in the evolution of the global polity, but these findings only provide a basis for understanding the subject of imperialism proper. It is still necessary to develop a framework that can model the interactions among core and peripheral nation-states and international organizations. Otherwise, it will not be possible to anticipate the shifting contours of political-economic subordination and conflict so basic to the capitalist world.

C. Explaining capitalist imperial oppression

Introduction: Why imperialism? The Liberal challenge
It is always tempting to argue that contemporary political and economic structures of the capitalist world economy are the direct expression of an unfolding logic in capital expansion. The arguments of the preceding two sections, however, need not evoke this ineluctable magic. The strikingly different pattern of post-war capital internationalization is a result of an advanced capitalist

political settlement after World War II, which itself was formed by three qualitatively new developments: the hegemonic position of the United States, the emergence of the Soviet Union as a major world power and the intensifying strength of national liberation and anticolonial struggles in the periphery.

As Figure 2 suggests, in order to discuss the impact of capital expansion on metropolitan and peripheral state formation in the modern period (A), it was necessary to presume a knowledge of the general political framework of the economy (B, C, D, and E). If we had remained at this most general theoretical level, it would not have been possible to reach any general findings. Starting with capital expansion presupposes a necessary, but arbitrary, theoretical entry into an interconnected process.

This methodological conclusion poses a strong challenge to the Marxist theory of imperialism. If capitalist state structures and political practices are only indirectly regulated by accumulation dynamics, then in what sense can it be argued that imperialism is an essential part of capitalism? A skeptical answer to this straightforward question is the basis of most liberal rejections of radical theory. Instead, it is claimed that imperialism is a result of unique historically-based factors which presumably can be expurgated from the body politic by an enlightened citizenry.

It is the central task of this section to answer this challenge. The key claim will be that the undeniable presence of metropolitan economic interests in peripheral territories has combined with powerful political tendencies within the center and periphery to sustain and even strengthen the practices of capitalist imperialist coercion. In the abstract, this oppression is not necessary for the maintenance of capitalism; in the sphere of historical reality, the capitalist organization of material life and imperialism cannot be decoupled.

In arguing for this materialist perspective, it is important to acknowledge that a key aspect of the liberal criticism is granted. Marxists have often incorrectly maintained that metropolitan capital survives on constant transfusions of economic surplus that are coerced from the periphery. This parasitism argument was a central aspect of the early Comintern's analysis of capitalist evolution, and it still plays a key role in many post-World War II theoretical and rhetorical formulations. For this reason, it is first necessary to dispose of this argument. Understanding why capitalist imperialism is *not* an *economic* inevitability is key to determining why imperialist coercion and conflict are such inevitable features of the capitalist global economy.

Post-Leninist theories of economic parasitism

The focus on economic exploitation and parasitism has acquired a more sophisticated theoretical and empirical apparatus since the World War I period, but it would be incorrect to suggest that one single radical paradigm predominates. One school has placed special emphasis on surplus value extraction through trade (unequal exchange); another places more weight on the institutional regulation of primary product pricing; a third argues for the emergence of a multinational-directed international division of labor; while a fourth attempts to document Hobson's and Lenin's original stress on debilitating financial surplus extraction. None of these perspectives are at all mutually exclusive; in fact they all suffer from similar theoretical weaknesses. Nevertheless, it is useful to examine each hypothesis separately.

Institutionalized Exploitation Through Trade: The Unequal Exchange Model.

The assertion that international exchange itself is exploitative marks an important departure from traditional Marxian theory.[42] In volume I of *Capital,* exploitation is viewed as the appropriation of surplus value generated by the "extra" productive labor of wage workers—where value is defined as the socially necessary abstract labor time associated with the production of a given commodity.[43] World systems and unequal exchange theorists dispute this assertion. In his seminal statement on unequal exchange, Arghiri

---

[42] Note that Marx stressed the non-exploitative character of trade in [126, p. 258]: The sphere of circulation or commodity exchange, within whose boundaries the sale and purchase of labor-power goes on, is in fact a very Eden of the innate rights of man. It is the exclusive realm of Freedom, Equality, Property and Bentham.

[43] This is the standard definition of value, but, as shall be seen, the unequal exchange debate revolves around the quantification of *abstract* labor time. For this discussion to have any meaning, it must be supposed that value does have a quantitative dimension—even if the determination of this "quantity" depends on the act of exchange. For the seminal, qualitatively-oriented discussion of this issue, see I. I. Rubin in [159].

Emmanuel maintains in [54] that there are two mechanisms within the social accounting rules of capitalism that facilitate a transfer of value from one capitalist sector to another. Marx himself demonstrates (although in an inadequate fashion) that those sectors with a relatively high "organic composition of capital" receive additional surplus value through trade with low "organic composition of capital" sectors. In developing this point, Marx assumes a national social formation characterized by free capital mobility and a customary social subsistence wage for all workers. In other words, he assumes a tendency for both profit and wage rates to equalize.

Emmanuel notes these dual assumptions and then argues that it would be more realistic to assume capital mobility and labor immobility. He accurately notes that wage differentials within the world economy are enormous, while there is a rough equality among profit rates. If Emmanuel's assumptions are adopted, then it can be shown through similar reasoning to Marx's that the profit rate equalization process will result in a transfer of value to the high wage sector—since both low wage and high wage workers are assumed in this model to produce roughly the same amount of value in any working day, and yet prices in the low wage area will be lower because capital costs are lower. In this analysis, it is crucial to assume that all countries have access to the same technology.[44]

Despite the logical plausibility of this argument, there is reason to question Emmanuel's analysis. Does trade between high wage and low wage sectors really represent exploitation or unequal exchange? Many have argued that this thesis rests on a misunderstanding of Marxian value theory.[45] According to this perspective, all commodites within any given sector of production must have the same value (the same socially necessary abstract labor embedded within them). Otherwise, one would have to dismiss the law of value—the thesis that capital carries with it a coercive logic forcing production to correspond to the value relations associated with generalized

[44] John Roemer recently provided a generalization of Emmanuel's argument in [158]. He demonstrated that a country experiences unequal exchange if it imports capital and/or exports labor.

[45] The following argument rests heavily on Alain de Janvry and Frank Kramer's analysis in [46]. Although resting on different methodological foundations, a similar critique of unequal exchange has recently been presented by Susan Himmelweit in [90].

commodity exchange. This implies that there can be no unequal exchange associated with the trade of non-specific commodities; that is, goods which can be produced in both high-wage and low-wage sectors of the world economy. Further, if we assume capital mobility (as does Emmanuel), wages in the non-specific production sectors will correspond to differential labor productivities. Otherwise, production would be only located in that sector where wages were lower relative to labor productivity.[46] These points reduce the unequal exchange argument to a consideration of the trade of specific commodities—goods which for geographical and historical reasons can only be produced in a defined region of the globe.

Even in this case, it can plausibly be argued that the transfer of value which Emmanuel asserts to be exploitative is a further misinterpretation of Marxian theory. The key to determining whether or not an economic process (either in the sphere of exchange or production) is exploitative depends on a conceptualization of less coercive social relations (or property distributions) which allow the particular practice (or result) to be eliminated.[47] In the case of Marx's focus on the labor process and wage labor, it is possible to construct an alternative social arrangement which eliminates the coercive value relations that are basic to capitalism. It is more difficult to maintain in a similar way that the *pure* pricing mechanism of capitalism is exploitative. In any complex society in which market relations are still important, prices most probably would reflect the cost of tying up resources in fixed means of production. Moreover, to the extent that wage differentials remain, prices of the final products should bear some relation to wage costs. It is not the price formation process which is exploitative in capitalism, but the capital-labor relation that lies behind it.

Ernest Mandel and Charles Bettelheim agree with this last criticism in [124] and [54] and thus maintain that Emmanuel should have attempted to explain the wage differentials between the core and periphery rather than treating these variables as exogenous to the dynamics of accumulation. For Mandel, in particular, unequal exchange is caused by the differential development of labor

---

[46] Note that this analysis abstracts from transportation costs.

[47] John Roemer provides a concise explanation of this approach in [157].

productivities throughout the world economy. While this formulation fits more easily into the confines of Marxist value theory, it, for this reason, fails to demonstrate that trade leads to the extraction of value from low wage to high wage sectors. Mandel is thus unable to prove that metropolitan capital receives a boost from the unequal exchange mechanisms that he hypothesizes. This particular post-war theoretical development has reached a dead end.

A deterioration in the terms of trade?

One alternative to the unequal exchange thesis also attempts to unearth an inherently exploitative mechanism in metropolitan/ periphery trade. This structuralist approach, however, does not rely on the obscurities of value theory. Rather, the deterioration in the Third World terms of trade is explained by positing unequal power relations in the world economy.

Raul Prebisch first articulated this approach in the early 1950s in [148]. During times of prosperity, both workers and capitalists in the advanced capitalist countries are able to raise their wages and prices relative to those of the Third World; while, during recessions, primary product prices actually deteriorate in absolute terms while those of manufactured goods stabilize. This framework crucially depends on the argument that the economic agents of advanced capitalist countries possess greater economic power during all phases of the world economy; it predicts a continuing deterioration of the terms of trade. The radical version of this thesis does not really take issue with Prebisch's hypothesized mechanisms. Rather, dependency and world systems theorists note that ready access to cheap raw materials permits the consolidation of the imperialist welfare state.

With respect to the terms of trade between manufactured and primary commodities, the empirical evidence for the structuralist claim is strong during most periods of the post-war epoch. The World Bank reports in [195, p. 11] that from the Korean War until the early 1970s, the relative prices of raw materials slumped. During the OPEC crisis of 1973–4, this trend was sharply reversed for nearly all raw material exports; moreover, in 1979, petroleum prices again rose sharply. Nevertheless, by the early 1980s, the terms of trade for primary commodities had again deteriorated. A Prebisch supporter could claim that the underlying trend predicted by this model has been verified. Indeed, because structuralists drew the policy conclusion that only the formation of raw material cartels could reverse the deterioration in relative Third World export prices, one could reasonably argue that the OPEC experience was the exception to commodity price movements that proved the rule.[48]

There is, however, an important anomaly in this prediction. A major result of the international trading dynamic was presumed to be the lack of economic diversification within the Third World economies. This dependence on one or two primary commodities does remain true for most of Africa and certain Latin American countries. On the other hand, other national economies of South America and a series of East Asian countries experienced an impressive industrialization during the 1970s.[49] Despite the relatively poor performance of the traditional exports of the less developed territories, other mechanisms have been at work to reorganize the international structure of production. Indeed, it is striking that (with the important exception of Mexico) those countries which have experienced the most dramatic industrial transformation of their economies are petroleum product importers. Undoubtedly, the determination of primary product prices plays an important role in regulating the accumulation prospects of many social formations, but the dynamics of raw material/manufactured trade between North and South cannot explain the evolving structure of the world economy. Nor is there a necessary correspondence between the reality of this dynamic and the general material interests of metropolitan capital.

A new international division of labor?
The failure to anticipate the changing organization of international trade has led to a general reconsideration of the possible dynamics of international exploitation. As a result, new theories have been articulated which focus on the establishment of productive enterprises under the control of Northern capital. A greater number of Marxist theorists are now suggesting that this process has

---

[48] This was certainly the basis for the UNCTAD program for the formation of producers commodity associations, as outlined in [181, 134–54].

[49] See [196] for information on the development prospects of the Third World.

established a new international division of labor allowing metropolitan capital to intensify the rate of exploitation over all wage workers. Raw material/manufactured trade has been replaced by out-sourcing and the proliferation of assembly operations in low-wage, "platform" regions of the Third World.[50]

To the extent that this posited tendency is an accurate description of present trends, this analysis also suggests an important change in the material interests that citizens of a metropolitan social formation might have in maintaining contemporary imperial structures of accumulation. In the short run, certain sectors of the industrial proletariat will oppose the diversification of the world economy, and to the extent that the new productive enterprises of the Third World also breed worker resistance, it might be possible to hypothesize an internationalist upswelling of resistance to the rule of capital. On the other hand, a longer-run perspective could lead to less sanguine conclusions. Industrial displacement could eventually culminate in the establishment of "clean" service jobs that monitor and regulate production in the Third World. Metropolitan workers may acquire an even more direct interest in the maintenance of the global economy, since the peoples of the "tropics" could come to labor at subsistence wages directly under their supervision. Hobson in warning against this possibility [92] may have erred only in being premature.

The new international division of labor hypothesis (NIDL) is intimately linked to two empirical claims: (1) that transnational corporations are progressively establishing their grip over all sectors of the capitalist world economy, and (2) that subsidiaries established in the Third World primarily exist to service metropolitan needs. This latter argument bears a close relationship to the earlier structuralist hypothesis that metropolitan capital forces the Third World to produce raw materials for metropolitan consumption. With respect to the first point, there is no doubt that transnational

---

[50] Froebel, Heinrich, and Kaye [74, p. 403] state this perspective most sharply: Although a new international division of labor has been brought into existence by the new and increasingly dominant process of the world market oriented industrialization of these countries, this form of industrialization has not meant any change in the historical process of underdevelopment but in fact in its deepening.

For a critique of this perspective as well as the presentation of useful statistical data that warns us against over-stressing the general industrialization tendency in all of the Third World, see Rhys Jenkins' analysis in [98].

corporate activity is entering into new fields of accumulation in both the metropolitan and Third World. The earlier discussion of the internationalization of capital strongly supports this argument. On the other hand, it is also true that the Third World state and even some Third World capitalist combines have come to play an important role in the regulation of certain productive enterprises. Co-partnership agreements and employee training pacts are now a common feature of much transnational activity.

Peter Evans, in an important study of Brazilian state capitalism [57], argues that the state does attempt to force metropolitan capital to divest itself of control in certain mature industries which no longer possess the most advanced technology. On the other hand, in those sectors where local capital has little ability to compete either domestically or internationally, management remains firmly in the hands of Northern corporate headquarters. Given the heavy involvement of the state in the economic organization of most Newly Industrialized Countries, Evans' findings can be generalized. Charles Barone, for instance, stresses the important influence of the South Korean government in regulating (within the constraints already noted) multinational and domestic capitalist behavior [21].

This modification of the first aspect of the New International Division of Labor hypothesis would not really be relevant if the second claim of this perspective could be sustained: that global production and trade is organized to service the needs of metropolitan social formations, while those of the Third World are ignored. Is it true that capitalist production in the periphery is mainly outward-oriented?

Throughout the 1970s, this was not uniformly the case. Per-capita domestic consumption levels rose relatively rapidly in most Third World countries. Moreover, high rates of growth in internal production were strongly linked to intensified inward flows of metropolitan capital.[51] Note that it is not being claimed that the

---

[51] Between 1974 and 1978, the East Asian and Latin American/Caribbean LDCs imported an average of $28 billion dollars of capital per year. This represented 78% of all capital flowing to oil-importing LDCs. More significantly, the much smaller sample of high-income LDCs (grouped in East Asia and Latin America imported $19 billion annually, or 53% of total capital imports to oil-importing LDCs. For more data on this experience, see [141].

peasants and workers of these previously expanding Third World countries necessarily enjoyed improved living standards. In certain important cases (such as Brazil) the absolute consumption and income levels of low income citizens stagnated or declined over the 1960s and 1970s. On the other hand, this period of rapid growth did permit the substantial enrichment of a considerable Third World professional and managerial class.[52]

The return of financial parasitism?
If the 1970s experience does not provide strong support for the NIDL perspective, the 1980s debt crisis does appear to buttress this neo-dependency thesis. The IMF austerity programs that Brazil and Mexico have accepted, for instance, are specifically designed to immiserate all sectors of the domestic economy in order to increase the relative share of production that services the export market. At the same time, these states are under pressure to moderate their controls over foreign investment and thereby encourage the increased penetration of metropolitan capital. There is clearly a logic at work which links the continued expansion of international capital to the subordination of Third World productive effort—both in terms of the direct macroeconomic control over Third World policy management and in terms of an intensified "servicing" of the metropolitan market. In other words, the instability of international capitalism during the 1970s seems to have culminated in a process that closely corresponds to the perspectives that have just been rejected. The Leninist financial parasitism thesis appears much more prescient.

Before concluding, however, that the deep capitalist slump has created subservient and stagnant economic appendages throughout the Third World, it is important to note that the impact of metropolitan capitalist stagnation has not been uniform. Most East Asian countries, for instance, have maintained surprisingly stable financial relations with the advanced capitalist world. In fact, their debt-service ratios (with respect to exports) remain well under twenty percent, while many major South American and African nations are experiencing interest and principal payment demands that are well above that level. It is true that 1983 represented the

---

[52] For a debate on these issues see Fishlow and Fields in [66] and [64] respectively.

first year since 1966 that the GDP rate of growth for developing countries fell below the advanced capitalist world's. (See [196, p. 12].) But past history suggests that this trend will continue only if stagnation in the total world economy persists. The general instabilities of global capitalism may doom much of the Third World, but, in this case, the advanced capitalist nations will also experience chronic economic difficulties. Certainly, the relative social pain cannot be compared; the prospect of permanent stagnation for the periphery is disastrous. The theoretical point, however, is that the parasitism analysis cannot coherently explain the booms and slumps of the world economy, nor can it discern the economic differentiation of the periphery that has continued through all phases of the global business cycle.

The four hypotheses we considered all posit somewhat different realities. On the other hand, they are all unified in presuming that particular exploitative mechanisms doom the Third World to stagnation and subservience. It is this monolithic vision which reveals the inadequacy of these radical theories. They simply cannot allow for the variability in the political economic trajectories of different sectors of the Third World.

This inadequacy is unfortunate. By claiming too much for the power of purely economic mechanisms, the rhetoric blinds the skeptical reader to more prosaic economic realities. It is not necessary to claim that imperial exploitation is associated with an always unequal and subordinated international division of labor. The evolution of capitalism has never yet been characterized by a stabilized distribution of productive activities, and new centers of accumulation have regularly emerged throughout the nineteenth and twentieth centuries. On the other hand, the export of money and productive capital does necessarily establish metropolitan claims on the future productive effort of the periphery. And, as Hobson and Lenin note, these claims could conceivably lead to the development of a nation in which there is a strong bourgeois interest in maintaining the already existent circuits of accumulation.

This argument does not rely on the notion that metropolitan-peripheral economic relations are *uniquely* exploitative. Sectors of metropolitan capital do extract surplus from peripheral workers by directly setting their labor in motion within subsidiary enterprises and by appropriating a portion of the surplus product in the form of interest and dividend payments. These processes, however, are also familiar to the advanced capitalist world. Many advanced capitalist workers labor for foreign subsidiaries, and the present U.S. dependence on short-term capital flows for the financing of its trade and budgetary deficits could, in another context, easily be interpreted as typical of an unstable Third World country. For this reason, it is difficult to use the structure of capital flow patterns to differentiate advanced capitalist from peripheral social formations.

In this discussion, I have rejected a key premise in many Marxist theories of imperialism. It is not true that global capitalism must coerce the Third World into a position of permanent economic backwardness. This conclusion is at sharp variance with much radical work on this subject, but recognizing its validity is essential for the development of a more adequate theory of imperialism. *On the level of the abstract theory of capital expansion and exploitation,* it is not possible to argue for the inevitable necessity of the North-South divide.

Towards an alternative materialist framework: Conceptualizing imperialist oppression and its mechanisms
A theory of imperialism must, above all, identify and account for mechanisms of territorial and/or national subordination. An abstract definition of this form of oppression has two dimensions. A nation experiences political-economic domination if: (1) its political and economic life is largely determined and regulated by decisions and forces subject to the control of foreign, non-indigenous interests; and (2) its own politics and culture regularly resist basic aspects of this dependence. This latter aspect of imperial oppression is less familiar, but is in fact more crucial to a proper understanding of this phenomenon.

Canada's economy, for instance, is thoroughly subject to US control: an extremely high percentage of its foreign assets are owned by US nationals and its macroeconomic health largely depends on favorable conditions of accumulation within the US. On the other hand, Canada is also an important member of NATO and plays a significant role in political-economic negotiations among the Northern capitalist powers. Because its polity is relatively unproblematically integrated into this imperial apparatus, it cannot be claimed that Canada is an oppressed peripheral social formation.

On the other hand, Argentina's economy is subject to more national ownership than Canada's.[53] In addition, its crucial agricultural exports are partly regulated by the Soviet Union's demand for grain. These economic facts, however, do not mean that Argentina is subject to less coercive foreign direction. On the contrary, Argentina's peripheral status is due to the *incomplete* material and cultural integration of its politics into imperial structures.[54] Because Argentina's political struggles regularly focus on the legitimacy of metropolitan capitalist interests, external institutions are more likely to intervene forcefully to regulate the nation's domestic political fortunes. Economic dependence on the global capitalist economy is a necessary condition for the exercise of imperial power. Otherwise, there would be little incentive for the implementation of oppressive measures. Nevertheless, this factor does not by itself permit a differentiation of the world's polities. Every social formation within the world economy has interests in others. More important in distinguishing the center from periphery is identifying the separate processes of class formation that underlie the exercise of global imperialist politics.

This framework has the advantage of allowing the anticipation of changing patterns of imperial subordination. If shifting conditions of accumulation helped to create a Canadian mass movement agitating for a disengagement from imperial structures and the establishment of new, anticapitalist mechanisms of regulation, this would undoubtedly stimulate a US imperial intervention. Canada could become transformed into a peripheral social formation by this political process. In other words, the emergence of a mass-based anti-imperialist politics could lead the Canadian social formation to have more in common with Argentina than its present NATO allies.

Another example that may be illuminating is the case of Puerto Rico. Gordon Lewis has noted in [116] that no nation in the Caribbean has been more thoroughly integrated into the U.S. polity and economy, and yet this fusion is not complete. Puerto Rican

---

[53] See [183] for some comparative, if dated, data.

[54] This perspective seems far different from Franz Fanon's emphasis on cultural imperialism in [59]. Nevertheless I would view his works as a powerful text expressing the problematic ideological nature of Western capital penetration. A more precise articulation of this problematic can be found in analysis Albert Memmi's in [133].

culture and politics have regularly produced oppositional currents that promote the disengagement of this island society from U.S. capitalism. At the same time, the massive movement of Puerto Ricans to and from the United States, the participation of its young adults in the American armed forces, the huge transfer payments to the island all create an alternative politics and culture that evoke the "hope" of complete integration. In this case, the dream is to overcome imperial subordination by joining the imperialist power. This is a possible, if not likely, development for Puerto Rico. Just as Canada might find itself disengaged from and subordinated to the United States, the peoples of other nations may participate in the construction of political/cultural processes that render the term *imperialism* irrelevant as an analytic description of a particular international relation.

The potential political-economic malleability in the core-periphery distinction has its counterpart in the wide array of international policies that reinforce metropolitan control. In times of relative stability, "normal" diplomacy predominates. Political support is traded for subsidized assistance, programs that encourage capital penetration and the forging of closer links among state and quasi-state bodies. Military assistance, bilateral foreign aid, training in educational institutions, government-sponsored trade union communications, and some international aid programs all fall within this category. It is the utopian goal of metropolitan diplomacy to forge such effective programs of this type that there will never be any need to initiate "dirtier" practices of coercion. In a sense, the task of these policies is to eliminate the need for imperial oppression altogether, thereby eliminating the core-periphery distinction.

This liberal attempt to banish the need for imperialism is illusory. Nevertheless, the dream of capitalist peace does provide the basis for conflicts within the imperial state. When economic conditions deteriorate, the developmental goals of some aid programs conflict with the demands of international capital for increased direct control over production and circulation. When social "disruptions" intensify, attempts to strengthen the repressive apparatus seriously strain ties with social institutions (labor unions, universities, peasant organizations) that were formerly seen as fundamental to political-economic stability. In the most extreme cases, imperial-sponsored counter-insurgency war destroys all attempt to construct a stable, liberal capitalist form of regulation.

There is, however, a larger unity behind this liberal/conservative conflict. As long as imperial control is basic to the reproduction of global capitalism (in a historical sense), the effectiveness of "liberal" intervention depends on its reversibility. Economic aid and capital penetration should integrate an economy so that international destabilization is possible. The sponsoring of social reforms should divide political coalitions so that repression can be systematically directed towards the elimination of more intransigent opposition. The sharp conflicts that sometimes arise within the imperial state should not mask the essential continuity that runs between advanced capitalist economic and military interventions.[55]

It should be clear that this conceptualization of the instruments of imperial oppression is predicted on the assumption that the more "extreme" practices of domination are fundamental to the organization of contemporary global capitalism. Otherwise, one could interpret foreign assistance and programs of institutional cooperation between metropolitan and peripheral states as anti-imperialist initiatives. Because these programs do anticipate the creation of friendly states through external manipulation, commentators such as Hayter [88] have argued that all granting of foreign aid is imperialistic. For our purposes, however, this approach is too broadly focussed. If *imperialism* is to have a precise meaning, it must imply systematic political-economic domination that ultimately rests on the use of coercive force. Making such a judgment requires a historical perspective that links shifting conditions of accumulation to the emergence and continuation of coercive global political relations.

Towards an alternative materialist framework: The historical logic of imperial oppression
A materially-based theory of imperialism need not prove that international coercion and conflict is optimally functional to global capitalism's reproduction. It is not even necessary to assume that the ultimate result of imperialist behavior is rational from the perspective of capital. On the other hand, such an approach does

---

[55] Louise FitzSimons reports in [67, pp. 173–214] that the Kennedy Administration had a particularly clear conception of the continuity running between foreign aid and counter-insurgency efforts. It pushed vigorously and successfully for both—although its dual commitment was never really tested by a breakdown in imperialist structures (as the Johnson Administration was shaken in Vietnam.)

require a step-by-step explanation which indicates how a series of responses to certain inherent social contradictions can culminate in the systematic expression of imperial politics. In this way, an analyst can develop a general framework that is able to explain and anticipate tendencies in political-economic behavior within and among dominant and subordinate polities. In developing this "historical" (as opposed to structural-functionalist) logic of imperialism, I will begin by drawing on the "economic-level" and "political-level" conclusions of the preceding two sections.[56] This method is subject to the earlier methodological warnings: beginning with a study of economic contradictions does not imply that this "base" exerts causal primacy (even in the last instance) over all other forms of social action. Rather, this grounded approach more easily permits the theoretical construction of the structure and movement of imperialism's essential aspects.

Capital expansion and the differentiation of the world economy
The traditional beginning of most Marxian theories of imperialism is still adequate: a fundamental aspect of capitalism as a mode of organizing material life is its qualitatively more forceful expansive power. Accumulation leads to the consolidation of capitalist social relations within a home, national territory and the creation of new production relations on the nation's commercial periphery. The internal process does not come prior to the external. Rather, this analysis suggests that the social and political differentiation of territories is a fundamental feature of the beginnings of capital expansion.[57]

These new forms of economic organization have immediate political ramifications. On the one hand, the ruling classes of the newly-created peripheral social formations must respond to the intensified commercial demands on their social order. Compradore merchants and landholders arise to raise demands for more autonomy and power. Resistance to these foreign and local bourgeois

---

[56] This concept is taken from E. P. Thompson [177]. On a more abstract level, I have attempted to employ Anthony Giddens' theory of structuration—the non-functionalist accounting of the reproduction of structures of domination through time and space (or what Giddens calls *time-space distanciation*). This is outlined in [81].

[57] Wallerstein is the theorist best known for pursuing the implications of this analysis. For a relatively abstract presentation of his method, see [187].

pressures is often prolonged, but the result of this process has normally been either the formation of political structures clearly subordinated to metropolitan capital,[58] or the creation of independent political orders that have the capability of "joining" the metropolitan world.

Peripheral state formation and the intensification of imperialist politics in the metropolitan world
The earlier discussion of peripheral state formation stressed the importance of studying "non-economic" factors. The construction of new national ideologies, the pivotal position of the "modernizing intelligentisia," the emergence of national military institutions were all interpreted as essential aspects of the capital penetration dynamic.

But what of the metropolitan world? It is inadequate to leave political and cultural analysis in the periphery, for capital export has a generalizing impact on metropolitan life as well. Marxists have occasionally addressed this issue, particularly in discussions of the aristocracy of labor. Nevertheless, the analysis has been quite scattered and incomplete. This is unfortunate. *Understanding the reasons for the emergence of an imperialist politics and culture within the advanced capitalist nation-state is key to uncovering the historical logic of imperialism.*

Resistance to capital expansion from the periphery has a profound effect on the metropolitan political order. Already emerging economic, diplomatic and military interests agitate for support against the external challenge, and complex ideologies supporting the moral need for national intervention into and control over external territories become popularly elaborated. The almost uniform success of modern imperialist ideology is poorly understood,[59] but I would argue that there are three material reasons (which do *not* depend on the argument that imperialist exploitation is essential to the viability of an advanced capitalist social formation) why

---

[58] Braudel notes in [30, p. 102] that:
It is only a step from market to colony. The exploited have only to cheat, or to protest, and conquest immediately follows.
[59] The most persuasive account of British imperial ideology can be found in Anthony Barnett's *Iron Britannica* [20]. William Appleman Williams has been the primary investigator of this issue in the US context. (See [191].)

metropolitan publics so often enthusiastically embrace the politics of international coercion. First the advanced capitalist state response to anti-imperialist struggles has often been successful, and the consequent involuntary integration of peripheral populations into the global capitalist order requires the intensified participation of metropolitan citizens. As a result, a significant sector of the national population develops a corporate interest in the maintenance of coercive international economic structures. Indeed, given the imperial state's pivotal role in the economy, even a failure to control anti-imperialist challenges can strengthen the public's support for imperialism. A popular revulsion against the "enemies of the state," a search for a resurgence of "lost" national honor and pride become all too common characteristics of an imperialist nation on the defensive.

This popular identification with the state can, however, be traced to more than the immediate interests that significant sectors of the population have in the maintenance of imperial ties. Beyond this particularity lies a generalized support for national economic power and security. The internationalization of capitalist competition does not weaken this tendency. Rather, the expanded scope of accumulation places added pressures on the state to guarantee the national population's accustomed standard of life. In this context, any disruption of the normal international order—even if this order has secularly weakened the nation-state's ability to construct and maintain the national economy—can increase general support for imperialist politics. And this is buttressed by the legitimating ideologies of national power and prestige that have evolved in response to past international tensions.[60]

Beyond these two relatively narrow economic reasons, the strengthening of statist/imperialist ideologies may also rest on other fundamental materialist bases. Marxist-Feminist theorists have long noted that the exercise of male privilege is at the root of all military institutions and that the definitions of maleness and thus the social order of most complex societies depend on the maintenance of a

---

[60] There is an important exception to this process. We would not expect small metropolitan states with few military resources to experience the same sort of imperialist mobilization. Different historically-conditioned possibilities for state action do shape popular ideology.

strong state.[61] If this is true, then any challenge from the periphery threatens more than political-economic stability. Other fundamental institutions of social reproduction—particularly the family—also fall under implicit attack. This admittedly speculative hypothesis may help explain why militarist and familialist ideologies often seem so closely intertwined. It may be that, like the Tsarist state in pre-revolutionary Russia, the state and those leaders that personify the state are still our "little fathers."

A similar argument can be made with respect to race. Certainly, the Western imperialist past has relied on virulent ideologies of racial and national supremacy. The exact character of this chauvinism has varied with the domestic and international historical environment, but few could deny the extent to which racial and/or national bigotry have solidified the concept of "the national interest" and thereby justified the continued maintenance of enormous material divisions between the world's peoples.

Conclusion

Throughout the post-war era, radical political economists have attempted to analyze those political-economic processes in the periphery that help reproduce subservient Third World social formations. Within this general framework, debates have raged fiercely: Has metropolitan capital simply imposed its will on dependent, but resistant national populations? If not, what is the nature of the collaboration and conflict within the "quadruple alliance" of advanced capital, the imperialist state(s), peripheral capital and "its" governmental structures? The studies spawned by these controversies have yielded important new conceptualizations of the nature of imperialist subordination, but they cannot by themselves unravel the most basic theoretical question: Why is it appropriate to assume an internationally coercive metropolitan impulse?

Imperialism and capitalism are intimately related, but not because there is a necessity for the super-exploitation of external territories. Rather, the real benefits that individual corporations and

---

[61] This does not mean that women are morally superior or inherently more peaceful than men. Rather, women and men's participation in imperialist institutions is strongly conditioned by oppressive gender relations. See Enloe and di Leonardo [56] and [50] on this subject.

institutions receive from capital expansion are transmitted politically and culturally to the population as a whole. State agents, often
utilizing racially and sexually charged rhetoric, are able to induce
large sectors of the population to support the politics of oppression.
The success of the advocates of imperialism is not due to especially
clever manipulations. The expansion of capital, by permitting the
integration of large sectors of the populace into metropolitan-
sponsored foreign activities, makes large sectors of the population
susceptible to this politics. Moreover, during non-revolutionary
times, there is a clear general interest in national economic security,
and such a mass desire can lead to popular support for efforts by
center powers to "stabilize" the global environment.

Despite this compelling historical logic, the reproduction of
imperialism is a problematic process. The ideology of control can be
challenged on the basis of other strands within incoherent national
cultures. Furthermore, the material interest in foreign activities is
not uniform and, indeed, during certain periods of history, one can
argue that the prosperity of most citizens is actually harmed by
foreign entanglements. The forces producing capitalist imperialism
are certainly strong and deeply rooted, but the possibility of the
economic and political collapse of imperialist structures is nevertheless real.

D. The Future of Imperialism

International crisis and the Marxian tradition
At the root of imperial oppression lies the permanent anticipation
of social crisis. Moreover, this fear has a powerful rational core:
from the perspective of the pervasive imperialist interests that form
within the metropolitan social formation, "things" threaten to "fall
apart" in the periphery far too often.

A chronic expectation of crisis, however, should not imply that
the world is always *in* crisis. If this word is to have a sharp meaning,
it should refer to particular historical conjunctures—periods in
which a specific social order is called into question by political
struggle. As Andre Gunder Frank suggests in [69, p. 109], this
perspective implies that crisis is a time of transformation as well as
conflict.

The crisis is a period in which a diseased social, economic, and political body or system cannot live on as before and is obliged, on pain of death, to undergo transformation that will give it a new lease on life.

Even within this more focussed approach some ambiguities remain. It is still necessary to form qualitative, historically-informed judgements about the nature of social conflict and the possibilities of transformation. Moreover, *crisis* is often used to refer to a sectoral difficulty, which may or may not threaten the entire social order. A financial crisis—in which, as a result of institutional failure, there is intense struggle to change the workings of the banking system—may lead to significant reform without the whole framework of society being either called into question or fundamentally changed.[62]

The general Marxian approach to crisis recognizes the possibility that serious sectoral difficulties can remain isolated and contained. On the other hand, interruptions in the normal functioning of political economic mechanisms are always potentially disruptive of the entire social fabric; the prolongation of economic instability erodes those political and ideological practices that sustain the material order. As with the specific explanation of imperial oppression, however, an explanation of generalized crisis requires the specification of those processes which connect the contradictions of accumulation to social consolidation or disintegration.

Theorists, not surprisingly, disagree on the relative weight which should be given to economic and political processes. Makoto Itoh, for example, stresses the importance of analyzing the contradictions of accumulation abstractly; that is, separately from the political divisions of the world economy. He suggests in [95] that the fundamental starting-point for Marxian theory is the recognition that crisis is both a response to and a mechanism for overcoming the overproduction of capital in relation to the laboring population. In a different way, Wallerstein also stresses in [186] the importance of an

---

[62] The perspective on sectoral crisis—as distinct from general crisis—permits a more subtle interpretation of certain periods of social breakdown. The Great Depression in the United States, for instance, could be better interpreted as an era in which a series of quite sharp sectoral crises were partially contained by Roosevelt's New Deal. At no point, however, could it be reasonably maintained that the whole framework of the social order was in jeopardy. This could be contrasted with the general political crisis in Germany immediately after World War I.

underlying economic focus. The hypothesized divisions among the core, semi-periphery and periphery can only shift during particular "moments" of crisis—moments that are stimulated by downturns in the Kondratiev cycle.

An alternative method is to posit that any given period of capital expansion is governed by a particular political structure of the world economy. During the beginning phase of expansion, certain mechanisms of regulation effectively guarantee the expanded reproduction of capital. This stability, however, is presumed to rest on certain relations of power that are eventually eroded by the uneven development dynamic basic to global accumulation.[63]

Despite the sometimes eclectic nature of regulation theories, this approach is superior to those which place major emphasis on deriving the economic mechanisms of crisis. This is true for two reasons: no narrow economic explanations of economic rupture have succeeded in establishing a compelling empirical or theoretical account of capitalist crisis; and second, all Marxian descriptions of prolonged economic and social disruption must eventually focus on those political and ideological processes that stimulate regulatory breakdown and its reconstruction.

The first point—that crisis theory has failed in deriving economic mechanisms of breakdown—is controversial and deserves more extensive consideration than I can offer here. Nevertheless, the general argument is straightforward: either the theoretical claims for the economic theories of breakdown are logically flawed, or it has not been effectively demonstrated that the key economic contradictions highlighted by these theories must culminate in a political-economic rupture. The excess commodities theories of underconsumption or disproportionality, for instance, can in principle be overcome by Keynesian policy. Taken by themselves, these perspectives cannot explain why the state might not intervene. If, as Baran and Sweezy maintained in [18], capitalist social relations prevent the state from rationally readjusting demand, then we are no longer considering a theory of crisis which derives breakdown from the "pure" logic of capital.

---

[63] This perspective can and has been related to Kondratiev or long-wave analyses. See [186] for an example of this synthesis. For our purposes, however, it is best to keep these "political" and "economic" approaches conceptually separate.

The excess capital theories also suffer from theoretical and empirical ambiguities. On the one hand, there is no logical reason to suppose that the general rate of profit must fall as a result of a rising organic composition of capital—quite the contrary.[64] Furthermore, those who instead derive a cyclical pattern or imminent tendency from Marx's law of the tendency of the rate of profit to fall fail to explain why the state cannot devalorize backward capital through the promotion of a planned expansion. As with the excess commodity perspective, a full explanation of economic rupture requires a theory of state action and reaction. Finally, the alternative excess capital theories of Itoh in [95] and, to some extent, Arrighi in [15]—that capital expands beyond the supplies of labor and raw materials—also lack empirical and theoretical persuasiveness. It is not clear why, with the internationalization of capital, shortfalls in raw material production could not be overcome.[65] The thesis of labor shortage is more compelling because capital does not directly regulate the production of labor power. Nevertheless, it has not been convincingly demonstrated that this "shortage" has been a prime cause of economic stagnation—especially since the expansion of capital has bred (with the exception of Japan) an enormous flow of labor from the near-periphery to the advanced capitalist world.

This theoretical disarray is a matter of serious concern. On the other hand, few Marxist (and non-Marxist) explanations of specific crisis periods have ever solely focussed on economic variables. The central theme of nearly all analyses of the Great Depression, for example, is that the 1930s troubles were partially caused and then prolonged by international political disorganization. As Kindleberger notes in [105], the unwillingness of the US to provide long-term credit to the exhausted European World War I combatants was a major source of the economic collapse, and this failure in turn stemmed from the inability of the most powerful nation-states to control inter-imperialist rivalries.

---

[64] See John Roemer's analysis in [156, pp. 87–133].

[65] For a brief discussion of raw material supply constraints and capital accumulation, see Albert Szymanski's analysis in [171, pp. 152–168]. This does not imply that the competition for raw materials is an unimportant aspect of international competition. Michael Tanzer provides impressive documentation of this process in [173]. Rather, the claim is that this problem cannot comprise a general explanation of imperialism.

This pragmatic appeal to past scholarly findings does have a theoretical basis. While the disruption of an international order is rooted in intensified capitalist competition and uneven development, global disintegration cannot simply be explained by referring to erratic rhythms of accumulation. The expanded reproduction of capital does not inevitably generate divisive tendencies; it also can unify previously separate accumulation units. Only a study which unravels the connections among global economic contradictions, nation-state formation and international regulation can hope to determine whether integration or disintegration trends will predominate. A theory of crisis, then, involves a complex analysis of economic and political contradictions. Without this focus, Marxian efforts in this area of study lack all conjunctural specificity and, for this reason, fail to provide useful political guidance.

Orthodox crisis scenarios
It is most useful to begin any discussion of the breakdown of global capitalism by elaborating a series of alternative scenarios—the probability of each depending on the analyst's assessment of the "balance of class forces." Unfortunately these speculative exercises often seem quite arbitrary; the reader is sometimes treated to an ad-hoc analysis in which the possible outcomes of crisis multiply indefinitely and all options appear equally likely. The failure to question the theoretical status of the nation-state especially strengthens this scatter-shot tendency. Instead of grasping what may be fundamentally new in the present order (in this case, the possible decline of the nation-state as an economic regulator) the temptation instead is to employ vague metaphors that refer back loosely to past international difficulties which were dominated by nation-state conflicts.

Nevertheless, the advantages of assessing the plausibility of distinct trajectories of global regulation outweigh these flaws. Without this approach, it would be difficult to assess the possible future directions of global capitalism. Moreover, this approach has the advantage of permitting an escape from a deterministic analysis which considers only one or two cataclysmic results from a breakdown in the mechanisms of imperialist reproduction. A systematic analysis of the future requires a well-articulated understanding of past trends in the evolution of global capitalism.

The challenge to capitalist unity: A breakdown within the advanced capitalist west?

In the early twentieth century, most theorists of imperialism assumed that the periphery would be oppressed whether or not the advanced capitalist countries were unified. Indeed, the general argument was that intensified rivalry would stimulate more oppressive forms of colonial rule over sectors of the Third World. Thus, Kautsky was able to represent his model of ultra-imperialism as a preferable, more benign framework for capitalist development.[66] Today, the tables have been turned. It is generally agreed that some form of advanced capitalist coherence greatly facilitates the North's predominance within the world economy. Without some metropolitan nation-state understandings, it would be possible for the more autonomous Third World states to play off rival imperial claimants against each other and thereby exercise more political-economic power. A break-up of the Western alliance, for example, might lead the European powers to extend a much more liberal package of economic assistance to the Lomé countries in order to maintain some influence in the former colonial territories. Or perhaps Japan would expand its military and economic aid in East Asia in order to buttress its predominant capitalist presence. Unlike the early twentieth century, the competition for influence might so strengthen the position of Third World countries that metropolitan nation-state imperialism might cease altogether.[67]

Despite this shift in the implications of advanced capitalist rivalry, there are certain elements of contemporary economic evolution which do confirm Lenin's central presumptions about the erratic nature of capitalist growth. In particular, neo-Leninists often maintain that the process of uneven development must eventually erode the US state's ability to maintain itself as the hegemonic capitalist power. At this point, presumably during a crisis period, one could expect an outbreak of prolonged intrametropolitan conflict, as the more robust capitalist economies compete for their place in the political sun.

---

[66] See Salvadori's analysis in [160, pp. 322–3] for the full statement of Kautsky's unity perspective.
[67] Kidron in [103] was one of the first post-war Marxist analysts to address this possibility.

The data supporting the thesis of US economic decline are, at first glance, compelling. Earlier sections have documented the decline in the US share in global economic activity. But even if this particular manifestation of the uneven development thesis is granted, two further questions still have to be answered before the capitalist rivalry thesis can be accepted:

1) Does a decline in economic competitiveness really indicate a decline in US political economic hegemony?

2) Even if it does become impossible for the United States to maintain its global influence, does this "fall from grace" necessarily imply a breakdown in advanced capitalist cohesion?

The first question arises because US predominance in the advanced capitalist world has rested on much more than American economic supremacy. The construction of military alliances and other agreements of "defense" cooperation have been just as important for the maintenance of the US empire, and there are short-term and long-term reasons why such understandings might continue even as economic relations of power shift. The emergence of autonomous peripheral Third World capitalist states and the construction of a hostile non-capitalist bloc of nations under the domination of the Soviet Union provide a strong impulse for military cooperation. In this geopolitical context, the United States is very well placed to exert its influence. And to the extent that issues of economic and military coordination fuse, subordinate allies will be under strong pressure to promote commercial cooperation as well.

On the economic level, the deepening of the internationalization of capital has also given further impetus to advanced capitalist unity. Recent developments make it possible to imagine a system of economic regulation that no longer rests on the actions of a single nation-state, but rather, on a series of negotiations coordinated through new international negotiating fora. The International Monetary Fund, for instance, has played a key role in disciplining both certain advanced capitalist and Third World economies, and the OECD has also increasingly served as an important site for sectoral economic discussions. Even United States policy has been subject to some global restraints. The dramatic turn-around in monetary policy in the late 1970s and early 1980s has been widely interpreted as a partial response to intensifying European pressures to halt the devaluation of the dollar.[68]

This last argument will seem counter-intuitive to some. Many European Marxist theorists have suggested that the collapse of fixed exchange rates during the early 1970s signalled the beginning of a period of economic chaos that cannot be resolved until a new hegemonic power is able to restore discipline within a new Bretton Woods.[69] It is undoubtedly true that the economic world is more subject to erratic movements than it was during the 1950s and 1960s. In addition, shifts in competitive relations have led to a sharp increase in the governmental management of international trade. Some analysts, for example, have estimated that as much as thirty-five percent of US manufactured imports are now subject to non-tariff controls.[70] Fewer theorists have noted, however, that these orderly marketing agreements and unilateral import quota arrangements have been consistently linked to the further *integration* of the world economy. In almost every case, such measures have encouraged the international movements of productive capital either into the protected country directly, or towards countries whose exports are not being restricted. And even in those cases where foreign investment patterns have not been significantly affected, workers in the protected industries have had to adjust their work practices and wage benefits in order to respond to the devalorizing threat from the outside world.[71]

This pattern reflects an underlying continuity in the world economy. Since the late 1940s, finance and productive capital movements have become progressively less subject to direct governmental regulation. The advent of floating exchange rates has reduced even further the likelihood that any individual capitalist

---

[68] During the late 1970s and early 1980s, international financial concern about the future of the dollar intensified markedly. European business and political leaders increasingly placed pressure on the United States to reform its policies, although this advice was not particularly coherent.

[69] Ricardo Parboni in [145] is best known for this position, and Block provides in [25] an historical accounting of the rise and fall of Bretton Woods from a similar perspective.

[70] Lawrence in [108, pp. 120–1] cites this figure and refers to an article by Bela and Carol Belassa, "Industrial Protection in the Developed Countries."

[71] For a general overview of these relations, see Andreef's analysis in [12].

state will impose unilateral trade and capital controls. This does not mean that the nation-state is now powerless; monetary and fiscal policy can be used to engage in "dirty floating" and subidies can be granted in order to attract capital flows or increase the competitiveness of exports. These actions do increase nation-state antagonisms. Nevertheless, these contradictions take place within the context of progressive capital internationalization. Today, the struggles among the advanced capitalist states are about the nature of the insertion of each national economy into this process. As a result, private capital movements, backed by occasional interventions by the IMF, have become increasingly important in determining the nature of exchange and production relations within the advanced capitalist economies. This is not because national capital has lost power in some unspecified sense, but rather results from the stability of those basic political understandings that have permitted the increasing multilateralization of all sectors of capital throughout the metropolitan world.[72]

The new dynamics of capital expansion and the "a-national" regulatory institutions that have emerged with this internationalization process raise a major challenge to the post-Leninist model of international collapse. Unlike the pre-war and inter-war periods of the early twentieth century, the assessment of any national economy's strength requires the drawing of a sharp distinction between the material circumstances of the general population and the position of capital owned by national citizens. The declining competitiveness of the U.S. economy, for example, has not inhibited the most important sectors of U.S. capital from adapting themselves to new economic conditions. As long as the social pain of capital restructuring does not produce new forms of anti-capitalist struggle, the domestic base for US capital internationalization can remain strong. This is one more reason why we should not mechanistically expect a breakdown in advanced capitalist coherence.

The collapse of metropolitan domination: The revolt of the Third World?
The political autonomy of the Third World has clearly restrained

---

[72] Radice makes a similar argument in [151].

the options of metropolitan capitalist states. Western attempts to resolve internal tensions of uneven development can no longer replicate earlier colonialist struggles for territory, and this is one of the major factors making a significant intensification of metropolitan rivalry unlikely. Paradoxically, this weakening in the power of individual nation-states has strengthened the position of metropolitan capital as a whole. Capital penetration and the corresponding consolidation of capitalist social relations has rarely slackened in the post-war period.[73]

Nevertheless, it is possible to argue that this strong position rests on unstable political and economic foundations. The drive for Third World political autonomy must eventually challenge capitalist prerogatives, and the contradictions of capitalist growth in the periphery will permit an anti-imperialist revolutionary breakthrough that cannot be contained by the advanced capitalist world. This perspective, which can draw on both Maoist and Trotskyist traditions, is a Third Worldist mirror image of Luxemburg's thesis of capitalist crisis: instead of capital expansion shrinking the non-capitalist areas of production available for exploitation, the capitalist sectors of the Third World will transform themselves through political struggle into non-capitalist entities.

During the heady days of Chinese cultural revolution, little thought was given to the alternative. A nationally-based anti-imperialist revolt might actually strengthen certain contemporary structures of metropolitan domination. In particular, new military ties and new forms of financial and productive capital investment could serve to re-link more politically autonomous national social formations to the logic of capital internationalization. Both the Maoist encirclement and Trotskyist permanent revolution analyses correctly pinpoint the sources of peripheral revolt without noting that the same instabilities may drive triumphant nationalist leaders to form "more favorable" alliances with the imperial center.

The experience of Vietnam provides a good example of this process. During and after the "fall" of Indochina in the early 1970s, many predicted that the whole region of South East Asia would become progressively hostile to metropolitan capital. An examination of US imperial reaction to this setback, however, reveals a

---

[73] O'Connor [140] and Nabudere [138] strongly make this point.

quite different process. After some indecision, new alliances with the Peoples Republic of China and the continuation of close links with the states surrounding Indochina effectively isolated this region—thereby intensifying the starvation of war-devastated masses and forcing Vietnam into an even closer embrace with the Soviet Union. By most accounts, this region today desperately requires infusions of capital and technological assistance for its development projects. If there is to be any shift in geopolitical relations, it is more likely that we will witness a gradual rapprochement with the West, rather than an expanding zone of state-socialist economies in South East Asia.[74]

If national, anti-capitalist revolt by itself is not likely to disintegrate the global capitalist order, it is still possible that the global economy will eventually suffer from a series of irredeemable breakdowns. If this occurred, it could be plausible to hypothesize that local rebellions would spark significant regional unravellings of the capitalist order. Certainly, the oil price shocks of the 1970s and the debt crises of the early 1980s can be interpreted as signalling eventual political-economic collapse. On the other hand, the sectoral crises of the recent past also carry with them a far different implication—one which highlights the unifying and differentiating power of global capitalism.

The OPEC crisis, for instance, reveals the close, interdependent ties that existed between Middle Eastern governments and the global oil companies. The increased autonomy of these Third World states allowed the elites of these regions to command a portion of the enormous oil rents that would have been unheard of twenty years before. This success, however, depended on the continuing operation of the marketing and distribution networks of the global oil companies. Thus, during a period of increased demand, a devaluing dollar and rising production costs in the United States, it was possible for both metropolitan oil capital and the OPEC states to share in the bounty. This is hardly a story of Third World revolt. It is true that the oil shock did severely disrupt the metropolitan domestic economies, but it does not follow that such harm (in the

---

[74] Chomsky and Herman describe U.S. resurgence in South East Asia in [39], while White analyzes Vietnam's recent development experience in [190].

form of inflation and unemployment) represents more than the sharp and erratic adjustment of exchange and production relations between two, increasingly integrated sectors of the world economy.[75]

The shifts in capital flows that resulted from the events of the 1970s are closely connected to the debt crises of the 1980s. Metropolitan banks became able to tap the enormously increased liquidity of the OPEC states and "recycle" these funds to the "Newly Industrializing Countries" (NICs) of South America and East Asia. As the earlier section on the internationalization of capital documents, the Third World today can be classified into at least two distinct categories: those "richer" nations that are primarily dependent on private funds for international liquidity, and those poorer nations which receive the bulk of their foreign finance from the bilateral and multilateral "aid-giving" institutions. Even with the striking fall of OPEC surpluses and the drying up of new bank lending to many of the NICs, this bifurcated pattern has continued. It is unlikely that the countries which became primarily dependent on private credit during the previous decade can ever return to public funds for infusions of additional capital.

The debt burden for Latin American NICs is now intense and the living standards of the bulk of the population in many countries have fallen sharply during the early 1980s. Nevertheless, there is little indication that a unified resistance to metropolitan bank usury is developing. Instead, each nation is taking advantage (or suffering from) its unique status in the global economy. The numerous ad-hoc negotiations coordinated by the IMF and the distinct character of each debt rescheduling agreement reveal this process sharply.[76] The need to import necessary agricultural and industrial products can make even the most nationalistic and anti-imperialist state planner reluctant to break credit links. It is never clear when it would be propitious to take such a drastic step. Despite the present harsh austerity and the strong possibility that it will continue well

---

[75] Tanzer and Zorn suggest this assessment of OPEC in [174].

[76] The 1984 Argentine case is especially instructive. Its efforts to encourage the coordination of global bargaining were essentially undercut by the separate rescheduling agreements of Brazil and Mexico.

into the next decade,[77] any break with metropolitan capital would, in the short-term, impoverish the renegade national economy even further.

There is a dynamic similarity between these general North-South developments and the role which the evolving world economy has played in determining political economic relations within the metropolitan core. Economic difficulties have become associated with the emergence of surprisingly stable *ad-hoc* international capitalist regulatory mechanisms.

It is always possible that continued stagnation will eventually rupture the contemporary practices of the "quadruple alliance." The fragile resurrections of Argentinian and Brazilian parliamentary democracy in the context of severe economic crisis, for instance, could be read as promising this development. This potential, however, should not blind us to contemporary reality. Nation-state relations between North and South have been strained as a result of the early 1980s economic collapse, but, so far, the crisis of material production has not challenged the global capitalist order.

Instead, flows of private capital have increasingly come to determine Third World economic evolution. This development does not eliminate nation-state conflict, nor even the sometimes effective manipulation of some market variables through state policy. But the discourse of North-South nation-state conflict has shifted: since the early 1970s, the New International Economic Order rhetoric of the Group of 77 has focussed on reorganizing market structures by limiting the power of transnational corporations and guaranteeing Third World export earnings. In short, the struggle has been waged over the nature of Third World integration into global capitalism— not the question of integration itself. As in the metropolitan world, the absence of far-reaching shifts in the framework of domestic and

---

[77] The 1980–5 period has been disastrous for most African nations (a 1/6% *per annum* decrease in *per capita* GDP). The "middle income" developing nations also experienced a sustained decrease in *per capita* GDP during this period. The World Bank estimates in [194, pp. 34–6] that if industrial country performance does not improve over the next decade then African *per capita* income will continue to shrink (although at a lower rate) and most other developing nations' growth will be consistently lower than that experienced during the 1970s. Even the optimistic William R. Cline has labelled the 1980s as the lost decade for Latin America. For Cline's analysis, see [40].

international political struggle has so far foreclosed other anti-capitalist options.

A new crisis scenario: The generalization of imperialism and the logic of exterminism
The two orthodox theories of imperial breakdown are not compelling because neither considers the shifting implications of nationality in the contemporary world. The imperial rivalry school fails to note that it is increasingly difficult to identify consolidated and opposed national capitalist interests in each metropolitan social formation. On the other hand, the Third World revolt scenario normally discounts the crucial and divisive role that the nation-state plays in the formation of capitalism in the periphery. Correcting these gaps forces one to conclude that the internationalization of capital continues to rest on strong political-economic foundations.

There are, nevertheless, some unspoken assumptions in this analysis that should be clarified. It has, for instance, been taken for granted that popular opposition to imperialism's workings is unlikely to develop within advanced capitalist societies. There are good reasons for this premise—not the least of which is the formation of powerful, but routinized, imperial cultures in most metropolitan social formations. On the other hand, there have always been signs (especially in Europe and Japan) that popular acceptance of the structures of global politics is unstable. No sweeping assumptions about the future nature of oppositional politics are ever that secure.

A second implicit assumption of the preceding analysis is that the dynamics of imperial oppression—if not challenged effectively by new social movements—can always produce a stable social order. In other words, without a qualitative shift in class politics, imperialism cannot self-destruct. This is a classic Marxian assumption, since it is generally argued that significant social changes can only take place through the conscious or unconscious manifestations of class politics. True, radical theorists from Marx onwards have expressed the premonition that capitalism will collapse under the accumulated weight of intensifying contradictions, even without the direct intervention of the working class. Nevertheless, few Marxian theorists have speculated about the possible mechanisms of disintegration into chaos. The slogan "Socialism or Barbarism" remains a grand theatrical appeal that evokes the prophets of the Old Testament rather than provoking scientific inquiry.

It is no longer necessary to remain on this rhetorical level. The reproduction of metropolitan domination is associated with the spread of capitalist social relations, the emergence of quasi-autonomous Third World states, the intensification of nationalist conflict within the South, and the consequent progressive militarization of global politics. Although a strange sort of peace has reigned within the center, the last two decades in particular have been associated with an intensified arms trade and the regular waging of catastrophic warfare in the periphery.[78] It is, therefore, reasonable to ask whether or not the present structure and practices of global politics can continue. And, given the enormous advances in the technology of warfare, it is now possible to specify the meaning of barbarism more precisely. At stake is the actual elimination of a large portion, if not all, of humanity.

For the purposes of this essay, there are two aspects to the exterminism scenario: the generalization of imperial conflict throughout the Third World and the particular modalities of conflict between the US and the Soviet Union.[79] In both cases, the mechanisms of domination that are inextricably linked to the expansion of metropolitan capital have laid the basis for the consolidation of autonomous imperialist practices within peripheral states.

It is easier to develop this argument with respect to the capitalist Third World than the Soviet Union—where the intensity of cold-war rhetoric often obscures the tight interdependence between metropolitan and Soviet imperialisms. I have already argued that capital internationalization is closely connected to the articulation of new nationalist ideologies and the importation of new and sophisticated mechanisms of military coercion. This combination has often resulted in powerful, expansionist tendencies, and as neighboring

---

[78] For documentation of the rising arms trade to the Third World, growing internal arms production in this region and the chronic waging of warfare, see Ruth Leger Sivard, statistical presentations in [165].

[79] A further exterminist angle that will not be considered here is that articulated by Green Party theorist Rudolf Bahro [16], who foresees the ecological collapse of the globe. The theory of exterminism on which we will focus is largely taken from E. P. Thompson's articles [176] and [177].

Third World states are experiencing the same process, the possibility of fractricidal conflict is great. There is a material basis to this powerful evocation of national integrity: nation-state consolidation takes place in an atmosphere of crisis; distinct social groupings are articulating and struggling for alternative visions of national homogeneity. From these contradictions arise pressures to quell internal "enemies of the state" and meet the challenges posed by external Third World and metropolitan nations. It is not surprising that this process often culminates in the intensified presence and use of military institutions within the peripheral state.

The metropolitan powers have participated in this process; often, their specific actions have sparked intense divisions within the Third World and encouraged the militarization of entire regions. Nevertheless, the periphery is not always manipulated by the North in a straightforward way. This is especially evident in the aftermath of specific social/political revolutions. The case of the 1980s Iran/Iraq war is the most dramatic recent example of metropolitan inability to contain political and military conflict. Although new tentacles of political-economic control are reorganized by the imperial powers, there is always the possibility that this exercise of imperialist politics will fail. This potential for breakdown beomes more pronounced as Third World states acquire the ability to manufacture sophisticated military equipment for themselves. The generalization of imperialist politics leads the metropolitan social formations into an ever more dangerous round of global politics that can eventually threaten the security of the citizens of the metropolitan world.[80]

As a starting point, this analysis of the derivative imperialisms of Third World states can be applied to the Soviet Union. Trotsky himself pointed out that the extreme backwardness of inherited economic and social conditions combined with external imperial pressure to stimulate a renewal of an authoritarian Russian nationalism that centered on the imprecise slogan: "Socialism within One Country."[81] It is also necessary to add the centrifugal threat of

---

[80] Nowhere is this process clearer than in the Middle East. The US is an active participant in and thus responsible for an evolving politics that seems increasingly uncontrollable and life-threatening. See the analysis of Noam Chomsky in [38].

[81] For an analysis of Trotsky's perspective, see [48, pp. 34–5].

non-Russian nationalist politics after 1917. This led to an eventual Bolshevik breaking of Lenin's promise to grant self-determination to all minority nationalities within the borders of the old empire. Finally, the internationalist commitment to export the revolution was transformed at a quite early stage into a justification for practices of external and internal coercion. The explicitly imperial Brezhnev doctrine of "proletarian internationalism" has its origins in the aborted Red Army invasion of Poland in 1920.[82]

The radical reorganization of social life in the Soviet Union combined with this new expression of imperial state power led to a predictable metropolitan response; after World War I joint policies were introduced to isolate the "socialist cancer" through the construction of new alliances with anti-Soviet regimes immediately around its borders. Until World War II, Soviet-Western relations can be interpreted within the framework already developed for metropolitan-peripheral relations during the post-war period. And if this global conflict had not occurred, the concerted pressures on this non-capitalist territory might have eventually culminated in a clearer subordination of the USSR to capitalist imperialism.

Mid-twentieth century history, however, turned out quite differently. Despite the staggering devastation of the war in the USSR, Stalin was able to redraw the map of Eastern Europe to give the Soviet Union a much larger field of autonomy. In addition, the technological independence of the USSR allowed it to compete with the United States on a military level—at first symbolically and then practically. These two breakthroughs signalled a qualitative shift for the nature of capitalist imperialism. In the periphery, a bi-polar world of global tension became the political framework under which

---

[82] Charles Bellelheim describes in [23, pp. 419–28] Lenin's deathbed concern about Stalin's development of policies that would subordinate non-Russian nationalities. But Lenin was not blameless in this matter. Deutscher in his account of the 1920 invasion of Poland notes that Lenin was an enthusiastic proponent of this action (against the isolated Trotsky). While the decision could be justified as a legitimate response to the Polish invasion of the Ukraine, Lenin did eventually admit his error in attempting to export revolution by arms. As Deutscher notes in [47, p. 471]:
The error was neither fortuitous nor inconsequential. It had its origin in the Bolshevik horror of isolation in the world, a horror shared by all leaders of the party but affecting their actions differently . . . The march on Warsaw had been a desperate attempt to break out of that isolation. The idea of revolution by conquest had been injected into the Bolshevik mind; and it went on to ferment and fester.

the accelerated expansion of both capitalist social relations and anti-imperialist revolts in the Third World took place. In Europe, the newly-found capitalist unity of the West was purchased at the expense of a rigidly divided Europe—a freezing of autonomous socialist and nationalist politics in this region. As Thompson notes in [176], this is the real social meaning of the Cold War.

This unstable framework of co-existence is associated with the unprecedented stockpiling of weapons of extermination. The detente so hailed during the 1970s quickly collapsed—as both the United States and the Soviet Union were forced and encouraged to respond to new eruptions of Third World unrest and new technological breakthroughs in nuclear arms competition. Thus, Third World contradictions have interacted with U.S.–Soviet conflict to expand all aspects of the arms race. Given the complex interconnections of regional and global imperial tensions, and the sophistication, sensitivity and power of all new weapons systems, it is not difficult to imagine how a technological or political miscalculation could culminate in a generalized global conflict beyond the control of any nation-state leadership.

In short, the exterminist thesis of imperial breakdown rests on strong theoretical and empirical foundations. The religious intimations of a collapsing world now have a scientific basis. The ever expanding "advances" in the forces of destruction can only be temporarily and imperfectly controlled by contemporary political institutions; society's continued existence requires a transformation in the social organization of economic and political life. The revolutionary implications of this analysis present all of humanity with unprecedentedly cruel choices. Either we work to interrupt and reverse the dynamics of imperial conflict in the hope that such a politics is not in itself destabilizing, or we watch the exterminist logic of today's international conflicts unfold while praying that the universally recognized danger of nuclear war somehow imposes constraints and rationality on the global political order.

3. CONCLUSION

In this essay, I have taken issue with many of the fundamentals of the classic Leninist theory of imperialism. Imperialism does not represent a special stage in the development of capitalism; uneven development does not always culminate in the breakdown of capitalist order; there is no necessity for the super-exploitation of the periphery by metropolitan capital; and, consequently, it is possible for some Third World economies to develop sophisticated industrial capitalist structures.

Rejecting the familiar nostrums of the dominant Marxist theory is essential if a materialist framework is to address the evolving dynamics of capitalist imperialism. Leninist theorists have been able to explain a set of cyclical processes—war and economic division and degeneration being the major ones—with some superficial plausibility. On the other hand, the standard analyses of qualitative change, of those macroscopic anomalies that Arrighi referred to in this essay's opening passage, have been much less successful. The declining significance of inter-metropolitan capitalist war, the rise of "a-national" capitalist regulatory mechanisms, the growing power of expansionist impulses in certain key Third World and non-capitalist states—and the increasing possibility that these processes will bring about the end of human life itself—all of these shifts in the imperialist experience can be better explained by an alternative Marxist framework.

This alternative recognizes that:

1) Capital expansion has always been a powerful force behind the global differentiation of the world economy.

2) This economic differentiation is simultaneously linked to the rise of imperialist and subordinated national social formations within the capitalist world economy.

3) The resulting polarities of the world economy are not frozen, but continually evolving as a result of shifts in class structures and technological capabilities. In particular, the populations in each Third World capitalist social formation must contend with the constantly changing contours of a quadruple alliance among metropolitan capitals, metropolitan states, local peripheral capitals and the Third World state.

4) These disruptions have tended to strengthen imperialist politics and culture in the major states of the capitalist world, even while threatening the ongoing frameworks of capitalist political-economic management.

5) Imperialism is not a feature of capitalist nation-state behavior that is unique to the metropolitan world. Nevertheless, the imperialistic impulses that exist in non-capitalist and peripheral nation-states have been largely structured by the histories of metropolitan capital and nation-state expansion.

This alternative sustains one key finding of the Leninist theory: that capitalism and imperialism are inextricably linked. On the other hand, it rejects the stage-theoretic framework and its attendant attempt to describe the static characteristics of capitalism in each hypothesized historical epoch. If there is one aspect of capitalist imperialism that all analysts should recognize, it is its heterogeneous character—both in history and in the contemporary world. The concepts exist within the Marxist framework to embrace this variety. Indeed, no other economic theory can as effectively describe and explain shifts in the capital accumulation process, and no political theory has as persuasively linked these economic tendencies to the formation of contemporary political and ideological practices. The detour of the Leninist tradition notwithstanding, this rich analytic heritage provides a key foundation for any analysis of contemporary international oppression and conflict.

References

[1] Abdel-Malik, A., *Nation and Revolution*. Albany, N.Y.: State University of New York Press, 1982.

[2] Adelman, I., and C. T. Morris, *Economic Growth and Social Equity in Developing Countries*. Stanford: Stanford University Press, 1973.

*[3] Aglietta, M., "World Capitalism in the Eighties," *New Left Review* **136** (November-December 1982).

[4] Alavi, H., and T. Shanin (Eds), *Introduction to the Sociology of Developing Countries*. New York: Monthly Review Press, 1982.

[5] Alexander, R. J., *The Tragedy of Chile*. Westport, Conn.: Greenwood Press, 1978.

**[6] Amin, S., *Class and Nation: Historically and in the Current Crisis*. New York: Monthly Review Press 1980.

[7] Amin, S., "The Class Structure of the Contemporary Imperialist System," *Monthly Review* **31** (January 1980).

[8] Amin, S., *The Law of Value and Historical Materialism*. New York: Monthly Review Press, 1978.

[9] Amin, S., *Unequal Development*. New York: Monthly Review Press, 1976.

*[10] Anderson, B., *Imagined Communities: Reflections on the Origins and Spread of Nationalism*. London: Verso, 1983.

[11] Anderson, P., *Lineages of the Absolutist State*. London: Verso, 1979.

*[12] Andreef, W., "The International Centralization of Capital and the Re-ordering of World Capitalism," *Capital and Class* **22** (Spring 1984), 59–80.

*[13] Andreef, W., *Les Multinationales hors la Crise*. Paris: Le Sycomore, 1982.

*[14] Arrighi, G., "A Crisis of Hegemony," in *Dynamics of Global Crisis*. New York: Monthly Review Press, 1982.

*[15] Arrighi, G., *The Geometry of Imperialism*. London: NLB, 1978.

**[16] Bahro, R., *Socialism and Survival*. London: Heretic Books, 1982.

[17] Baran, P., *The Political Economy of Growth*.

**[18] Baran, P., and P. Sweezy, *Monopoly Capital*. New York: Monthly Review Press, 1966.

[19] Barnet, R., and R. E. Muller, *Global Reach: The Power of the Multinational Corporation*. New York: Simon and Schuster, 1974.

*[20] Barnett, A., "Iron Britannica," *New Left Review* **134** (July–August 1982).

[21] Barone, C. A., "Dependency, Marxist Theory, and Salvaging the Idea of Capitalism in South Korea," *Review of Radical Political Economics* **15 (Spring 1983), 43–67.

[22] Barratt Brown, M., *Essays on Imperialism*. Nottingham, Eng.: Spokesman Books, 1972.

**[23] Bettelheim, C., *Class Struggle in the USSR: First Period: 1917–23*, trans. by Brian Pearce. New York: Monthly Review Press, 1976.

[24] Bleaney, M. F., *Underconsumption Theories: A History and Critical Analysis*. New York: International Publishers, 1976.

**[25] Block, F., *The Origins of International Economic Disorder*. Berkeley: University of California, 1977.

[26] Bluestone, B. and B. Harrison, *The Deindustrialization of America*. New York: Basic Books, 1982.

**[27] Boggs, C., "The Democratic Road: New Departures and Old Problems," in *The Politics of Eurocommunism*, ed. by C. Boggs and D. Plotke. Boston: South End Press, 1980, 431–76.

[28] Brandt Commission: *Common Crisis*. London, Pan Books, 1983.

[29] Brandt Commission: *North-South: A Program for Survival*. Cambridge, Mass., The MIT Press, 1981.

**[30] Braudel, F., *The Structure of Everday Life: Civilisation and Capitalism, 15th-18th Century*. New York: Harper and Row, 1981.

*[31] Brett, E. A., *International Money and Capitalist Crisis: The Anatomy of Global Disintegration*. Boulder, Colo.: Westview Press, 1983.

*[32] Brewer, A., *Marxist Theories of Imperialism: A Critical Survey*. London: Routledge and Kegan Paul, 1980.

**[33] Bukharin, N., "Imperialism and the Accumulation of Capital," in *Imperialism and the Accumulation of Capital: Rosa Luxemburg and Nikolai Bukharin*, ed. by K. J. Tarbuk. London: Allen Lane, Penguin, 1972.

*[34] Bukharin, N., *Imperialism and World Economy*. New York: Monthly Review Press, 1973.

[35] Bunkina, M. K., *USA versus Western Europe: New Trends*. Moscow: Progress Publishers, 1979.

[36] Calleo, D. P., *The Imperious Economy*. Cambridge, Mass.: Harvard Press, 1982.

[37] Cardoso, F. H., "Associated-Dependent Development: Theoretical and Practical Implications," in *Authoritarian Brazil*, ed. by A. Stepan. New Haven: Yale University Press, 1973.

**[38] Chomsky, N., *The Fateful Triangle: The United States, Israel and the Palestinians*. Boston: South End Press, 1983.

**[39] Chomsky, N., and E. S. Herman, *After the Cataclysm*: *Postwar Indochina and the Reconstruction of Imperial Ideology*. Boston: South End Press, 1979.

**[40] Cline, W. R., *International Debt*: *Systemic Risk and Policy Response*. Washington, D.C.: Institute for International Economics, 1984.

[41] Cohen, B. J., *The Question of Imperialism*: *The Political Economy of Dominance and Dependence*. New York: Basic Books, 1973.

**[42] Cottrell, P. J., *British Overseas Investment in the Nineteenth Century*. London: Macmillan Press, 1975.

[43] Corrigan, P. (ED.), *Capitalism, State Formation and Marxist Theory*. London: Quartet Books, 1980.

*[44] Cypher, J., "The Internationalization of Capital and the Transition of Social Formations: A Critique of the Monthly Review School," *Review of Radical Political Economics* **11** (Winter 1979), 33–49.

[45] Cypher, J., "A Prop Not a Burden," *Dollars and Sense* **93** (January 1984).

*[46] de Janvry, A., and F. Kramer, "The Limits of Unequal Exchange," *Review of Radical Political Economics*" (Winter 1979), 3–15.

**[47] Deutscher, I., *The Prophet Armed*: *Trotsky*: *1879–1921*. London: Oxford University Press, 1954.

[48] Deutscher, I., *The Prophet Outcast*: *Trotsky*: 1929–40. New York: Vintage Books, Random House, 1963.

[49] de Vroey, M., "A Regulation Approach Interpretation of Contemporary Crisis," *Capital and Crisis* **23** (September 1984), 45–66.

[50] di Leonardo, M., "Morals, Mothers and Militarism," *Feminist Studies*, **11 (Fall 1985), 599–618.

*[51] Dobb, M., "Imperialism," in *Political Economy and Capitalism*. New York: International Publishers, 1945.

**[52] Easterlin, R. A., "American Population since 1900," in *The American Economy in Transition*, ed. by M. Feldstein. Chicago: NBER, University of Chicago Press, 1980.

**[53] Eisenstadt, S. N., *Revolution and the Transformation of Societies*: *A Comparative Study of Civilizations*. New York: The Free Press, Macmillan, 1978.

*[54] Emmanuel, A., *Unequal Exchange*: *A Study of the Imperialism of Trade*, trans. by B. Pearce. New York: Monthly Review Press, 1972.

[55] Emmanuel, A., "White Settler Colonialism and the Myth of Investment Imperialism," *New Left Review* **73** (May–June, 1972), 35–57.

*[56] Enloe, C., *Does Khaki Become You? The Militarization of Women's Lives*. London: Pluto Press, 1983.

*[57] Evans, P., *Dependent Development*: *The Alliance of Multinational, State and Local Capital in Brazil*. Princeton: Princeton University Press, 1979.

[58] Evans, P., "Reinventing the Bourgeoisie: State Entrepreneurship and Class Formation in Dependent Capitalist Development," in *Marxist Inquiries*: *Studies of Labor, Class and States*, ed. by M. Burawoy and T. Skocpol. Chicago: University of Chicago Press, 1982.

**[59] Fanon, F, *The Wretched of the Earth*. New York: Grove Press, 1963.

[60] Fann, K. T., and D. C. Hodges (Eds.): *Readings in U.S. Imperialism*. Boston: Porter Sargent, 1971.

[61] Farhang, F., *U.S. Imperialism*: *From the Spanish American War to the Iranian Revolution*. Boston: South End Press, 1981.

[62] Feinberg, R. E., *The Intemperate Zone*: *The Third World Challenge to U.S. Foreign Policy*. New York: Norton, 1983.

84   J. WILLOUGHBY

*[63] Fieldhouse, D., *Economics and Empire: 1830–1914*. Ithaca, N.Y., Cornell University Press, 1973.
[64] Fields, G. S., "Who Benefits from Economic Development? Reply," *American Economic Review* **70 (March 1980), 250–262.
**[65] Fine, B., and L. Harris, *Rereading Capital*. New York: Columbia University Press, 1979.
[66] Fishlow, A., "Who Benefits from Economic Development? Comment," *American Economic Review* **70 (March 1980): 250–262.
**[67] FitzSimons, L., *The Kennedy Doctrine*. New York: Random House, 1972.
[68] Frank, A. G., *Capitalism and Underdevelopment in Latin America: Historical Studies of Chile and Brazil*. New York: Monthly Review Press, 1967.
**[69] Frank, A. G., "Crisis of Ideology and Ideology of Crisis," in *Dynamics of Global Crisis*. New York: Monthly Review Press, 1982.
**[70] Frank, A. G., *Latin America: Underdevelopment or Revolution*. New York: Monthly Review Press, 1969.
[71] Frank, A. G., *Lumpen-Bourgeoisie and Lumpen-Development: Dependency, Class and Politics in Latin America*. New York: Monthly Review Press, 1972.
[72] Frank, A. G., *On Capitalist Underdevelopment*. Oxford: Oxford University Press, 1975.
**[73] Frank, A. G., *Reflections of the World Economic Crisis*. New York: Monthly Review Press, 1981.
**[74] Froebel, F., J. Heinrich, and O. Kaye, *The New International Division of Labor*. Cambridge, Eng.: Cambridge University Press, 1980.
**[75] Furtado, C., *Economic Development of Latin America: A Survey from Colonial Times to the Cuban Revolution*, trans. by S. Macedo. Cambridge U. Press, 1970.
**[76] Gadgill, D. R., *The Industrial Evolution of India in Recent Times: 1860–1939*. Bombay: Oxford University Press, 1971.
[77] Gallagher, J., and R. Robinson, "The Imperialism of Free Trade," in *Imperialism*, ed. by W. R. Lewis. New York: New Viewpoints, 1976.
**[78] Gerschenkron, A., "Economic Backwardness in Historical Perspectives" in *Economic Backwardness in Historical Perspective: A Book of Essays*. Cambridge, Mass.: Harvard University Press, 1962.
**[79] Gerschenkron, A., "Notes on the Rate of Industrial Growth in Italy: 1881–1913," in *Economic Backwardness in Historical Perspective: A Book of Essays*. Cambridge, Mass.: Harvard University Press, 1962.
**[80] Gerschenkron, A., "Russia: Patterns and Problems in Development," in *Economic Backwardness in Historical Perspective: A Book of Essays*, Cambridge, Mass.: Harvard University Press, 1962.
**[81] Giddens, A., *A Contemporary Critique of Historical Materialism: Power, Property, and the State*. Berkeley: University of California Press, 1981.
[82] Gilpin, R., *U.S. Power and the Multinational Corporation: The Political Economy of Foreign Direct Investment*. New York: Basic Books, 1975.
*[83] Goulbourne, H. (ED.), *Politics and State in the Third World*. London: Macmillan, 1979.
[84] Gould, S. J., "Between You and Your Genes," *New York Review of Books* **31** (August 16, 1984), 30–2.
[85] Hamilton, N. L., "Mexico: The Limits of State Autonomy," *Latin American Perspectives* **2** (Summer 1975), 81–108.
[86] Hargreaves, J. D., *The End of Colonial Rule in West Africa: Essays in Contemporary History*. New York: Harper and Row, 1979.

[87] Harris, N., *Of Bread and Guns: the World Economy in Crisis.* Harmondsworth, Eng.: Penguin Books, 1983.

**[88] Hayter, T., *The Creation of World Poverty: An Alternative View to the Brandt Report.* London: Pluto Press, 1981.

*[89] Hilferding, R., *Finance Capital,* trans. by M. Watnick and S. Gordon. London: Routledge and Kegan Paul, 1981.

[90] Himmelweit, S., "Value Relations and Divisions Within the Working Class," *Science and Society* **48 (Fall 1984), 323–43.

**[91] Hinton, J., "The Rise of a Mass Labour Movement: Growth and Limits," in *A History of British Industrial Relatives,* ed. by C. Wrigley. Amherst, Mass.: University of Massachusetts Press, 1982.

**[92] Hobson, J., *Imperialism: A Study.* London: George Allen & Unwin, 1954.

**[93] Horowitz, I. L., *Beyond Empire and Revolution: Militarization and Consolidation in the Third World.* New York: Oxford University Press, 1982.

*[94] Hymer, S., "The Multinational Corporation and the Law of Uneven Development," in *Economics and World from the 1970s to the 1990s,* ed. by J. Bhagwati. Basingstoke, Eng.: Macmillan, 1972.

**[95] Itoh, M., *Value and Crisis: Essays on Marxian Economics in Japan.* London: Pluto Press, 1980.

[96] Jalee, P., *The Third World in World Ecomomy.* New York: Monthly Review Press, 1969.

[97] Jelavich, C., and B. Jelavich, *The Establishment of the Balkan National States, 1804–1920.* Seattle: University of Washington Press, 1977.

[98] Jenkins, R., "Divisions over the International Division of Labour," *Capital and Class* **22 (Spring 1984), 28–57.

**[99] Jessup, B., *The Capitalist State.* New York: New York University Press, 1982.

*[100] Keat, R., and J. Urry, *Social Theory as Science.* London: Routledge and Kegan Paul, 1975.

*[101] Kemp, T., *Theories of Imperialism.* London: Bookprint Ltd., 1967.

[102] Kidron, M., *Capitalism and Theory.* London: Pluto Press, 1974.

*[103] Kidron, M., "Imperialism: Highest Stage But One," *International Socialism* **61** (June 1973).

*[104] Kiernan, V. G., "The Marxist Theory of Imperialism and Its Historical Formation," in *Marxism and Imperialism.* New York: St. Martin's Press, 1975.

*[105] Kindleberger, C. P., *The World in Depression.* London: Allen Lane, 1973.

[106] Kirsanov, A., *The USA and Western Europe: Economic Relations after 1975.* Moscow: Progress Publishers, 1975.

[107] Kolko, J., and G. Kolko: *The Limits of Power: The World and United States Foreign Policy, 1945–54.* New York: Harper and Row, 1972.

*[108] Lawrence, R. Z., *Can America Compete?* Washington, D.C.: The Brookings Institution, 1984.

*[109] Lebon, A., and G. Falchi, "New Developments in Intra-European Migration since 1974," *International Migration Review* **14** (Winter 1980), 539–79.

*[110] Leiken, R. S. (ED.), *Central America: Anatomy of Conflict.* New York, Pergamon Press, 1984.

[111] Lenin, V. I., "Address to the Second All-Russia Congress of Communist Organizations of the Peoples of the East," in *Collected Works, Vol. 30.* Moscow: Foreign Languages Publishing House, 1965.

[112] Lenin, V. I., *The Development of Capitalism in Russia,* in *Collected Works,* vol. 3. Moscow: Foreign Languages Publishing House, 1960.

*[113] Lenin, V. I., *Imperialism: The Highest Stage of Capitalism*. Moscow: Progress Publishers, 1970.

[114] Lenin, V. I., "Preliminary Draft Theses on the National and the Colonial Questions: For the Second Congress of the Communist International," in *Collected Works, Vol.* 31. Moscow: Foreign Languages Publishing House, 1966.

[115] Lenin, V. I., "Report of the Commission on the National and the Colonial Questions, July 26, 1920," in *Collected Works,* vol. 31. Moscow; Foreign Languages Publishing House, 1966.

**[116] Lewis, G. K., *Puerto Rico: Freedom and Power in the Caribbean*. New York: Monthly Review Press, 1963.

[117] Lewis, J. P., and V. Kallab (Eds.): *U.S. Foreign Policy and the Third World Agenda 1983.* New York: Praeger, 1983.

*[118] Lipietz, A., "Imperialism or the Beast of the Apocalypse," *Capital and Class* **22** (Spring 1984), 45–66.

*[119] Loewy, M., *The Politics of Combined and Uneven Development: The Theory of Permanent Revolution*. London: Verso, 1981.

[120] Lotta, R., *America in Decline* (Chicago: Banner Press, 1984).

*[121] Luxemburg, R., *The Accumulation of Capital*, trans. by A. Schwarzchild. New York: Monthly Review Press, 1964.

*[122] Magdoff, H., *Imperialism: From the Colonial Age to the Present*. New York: Monthly Review Press, 1975.

*[123] Magdoff, H., "Is Imperialism Really Necessary?" in *Imperialism: From the Colonial Age to the Present*. New York: Monthly Review Press, 1978.

**[124] Mandel, E., *Late Capitalism*. London: Verso, 1978.

[125] Marcussen, H. S., and J. E. Torp, *Internationalization of Capital: Prospects for the Third World: A Re-examination of Dependency Theory*. London: Zed Press, 1982.

**[126] Marx, K., *Capital, vol. I*. New York, Vintage Books, 1977.

[127] Marx, K., *Capital, vol. II*. London: New Left Review, 1978.

[128] Marx, K., "Future Results of British Rule in India," in *Karl Marx and Frederick Engels, Selected Works, vol. I*. Moscow: Progress Publishers, 1969.

**[129] Marx, K., *The Grundrisse: Introduction to the Critique of Political Economy*. Middlesex, Eng.: Pelican Books, 1973.

**[130] Marx, K., and F. Engels: "The Communist Manifesto," in *The Marx-Engels Reader,* ed. by R. Tucker. New York: W. W. Norton, 1978.

[131] Melman, S., *The Permanent War Economy: American Capitalism in Decline*. New York: Simon and Schuster, 1974.

[132] Melotti, U., *Marx and the Third World*. London: Macmillan Press, 1977.

**[133] Memmi, A., *The Colonizer and the Colonized*. New York: The Orion Press, 1965.

[134] Mills, C. W., *The Power Elite*. New York: Oxford University Press, 1959.

[135] Mommsen, W. J., *Theories of Imperialism: A Critical Assessment of the Various Interpretations of Modern Imperialism*, trans. by P. S. Falla. New York: Random House, 1980.

[136] Moore, B., *Social Origins of Dictatorship and Democracy*. Boston: Beacon Press, 1966.

[137] Murphy, C., *The Emergence of NIEO Ideology*. Boulder, Colo.: Westview Press, 1984.

**[138] Nabudere, D., *The Political Economy of Imperialism*. London: Zed Press, 1977.

**[139] North, D. C., *Growth and Welfare in the American Past: A New Economic History*. Englewood Cliffs, N.J., Prentice Hall, 1966.

*[140] O'Connor, J., "The Meaning of Economic Imperialism," in *The Corporations and the State: Essays in the Theory of Capitalism and Imperialism*. New York: Harper and Row, 1974.

**[141] OECD: *World Economic Interdependence and the Evolving North-South Relationship*. Paris: OECD, 1983.

[142] Olle, W., and W. Schoeller, "Direct Investment Monopoly Theories of Imperialism," *Captial and Class* 16 (Spring 1982), 41–60.

[143] Owen, R., and B. Sutcliffe (Eds.), *Studies in the Theory of Imperialism*. London: Longman Group, 1972.

*[144] Palloix, C., "The Self-Expansion of Capital on a World Scale," *Review of Radical Political Economics* 9 (Summer 1977), 1–28.

*[145] Parboni, R., *The Dollar and Its Rivals*, trans. by Jon Rothschild. London: NLB, 1981.

[146] Parsons, H. L. (ED.), *Marx and Engels on Ecology*. Westport, Conn.: Greenwood Press, 1977.

[147] Petras, J., F. and M. H. Morley, "The Imperial State," in *Class, State and Power in the Third World*. London: Zed Press, 1981.

[148] Phillips, R., "The Role of the International Monetary Fund in the Post-Bretton Woods Era," *Review of Radical Political Economics* 15 (Summer 1983), 59–81.

**[149] Poulantzas, N., *Political Power and Social Classes*. London: NLB, 1975.

**[150] Prebisch, R., "Commercial Policy in the Underdeveloped Countries," *American Economic Review* 49 (May 1959).

*[151] Radice, H., "The National Economy: A Keynesian Myth?" *Capital and Class* 22 (Spring 1984), 111–140.

[152] Rainnie, A. F., "Combined and Uneven Development in the Clothing Industry: The Effects of Competition on Accumulation," *Capital and Class* 22 (Spring 1984), 141–156.

[153] Rhodes, R. I. (Ed.), *Imperialism and Underdevelopment*. New York: Monthly Review Press, 1970.

**[154] Robinson, J., "Introduction," in *The Accumulation of Capital*, by R. Luxemburg. New York: Monthly Review Press, 1964.

[155] Rodney, W., *How Europe Underdeveloped Africa*. Washington, D.C.: Howard University Press, 1974.

**[156] Roemer, J., *Analytic Foundations of Marxian Economic Theory*. New York: Cambridge University Press, 1981.

**[157] Roemer, J., "New Directions in the Marxian Theory of Exploitation and Class," *Politics and Society* 11 (1982), 253–88.

**[158] Roemer, J., "Unequal Exchange, Labor Migration, and International Capital Flows: A Theoretical Synthesis," in *Marxism, Central Planning, and the Soviet Economy: Economic Essays in Honor of Alexander Erlich*, ed. by P. Desai. Cambridge, Mass.: MIT Press, 1983.

**[159] Rubin, I. I., *Essays on Marx's Theory of Value*. Montreal: Black Rose Books, 1973.

**[160] Salvadori, M., *Karl Kautsky and the Socialist Revolution*, trans. by J. Rothchild. London: NLB, 1979.

[161] Sampson, A., *The Arms Bazaar, From Lebanon to Lockheed*. New York: The Viking Press, 1977.

*[162] Saul, J. S., "The State in Post-colonial Societies: Tanzania," in *Politics and State in the Third World*, ed. by H. Goulbourne. London: Macmillan, 1979.

*[163] Schumpeter, J., "The Sociology of Imperialisms," in *Imperialism and Social Classes,* ed. by P. Sweezy. New York: Augustus M. Kelley, 1951.

[164] Shirer, W. L., *The Rise and Fall of the Third Reich.* Greenwich, Conn., Simon and Schuster, 1960.

**[165] Sivard, R. L., *World Military and Social Expenditures.* Leesburg, Va., World Priorities, various annual editions.

[166] Smith, D., and R. Smith, *The Economics of Militarism.* London: Pluto Press, 1983.

[167] Smith, D. M., *Italy, A Modern History.* Ann Arbor, University of Michigan Press, 1959.

**[168] Smith, T., *The Pattern of Imperialism: The United States, Great Britain and the Late Industrializing World since 1815.* Cambridge, Eng.: Cambridge University Press, 1981.

**[169] Stalin, J., "Problems of Leninism," in *Selected Works.* Davis, Calif.: Cardinal Publishers, 1971.

**[170] Sternberg, F., *Der Imperialismus.* Berlin: Malik-Verlag, 1926.

*[171] Szymanski, A., *The Logic of Imperialism.* New York: Praeger, 1981.

[172] Tanzer, M., *The Political Economy of International Oil and the Underdeveloped Countries.* Boston: Beacon Press, 1969.

**[173] Tanzer, M., *The Race for Resources: Continuing Struggles over Minerals and Fuels.* New York: Monthly Review Press, 1980.

**[174] Tanzer, M., and S. Zorn, "Opec's Decade: Has It Made a Difference?", *Monthly Review* 3 (May 1984), 31–43.

**[175] Taylor, J. G., *From Modernization to Modes of Production: A Critique of the Sociologies of Development and Underdevelopment.* London: Macmillan Press, 1979.

*[176] Thompson, E. P., "Europe: The Weak Link in the Cold War," in *Exterminism and Cold War,* London: Verso, 1982.

*[177] Thompson, E. P., "Notes on Exterminism, The Last Stage of Civilization," in *Exterminism and Cold War.* London: Verso, 1982.

**[178] Thompson, E. P., and D. Smith (Eds.), *Protest and Survive.* New York: Monthly Review Press, 1981.

[179] Thornton, A. P., *Imperialism in the Twentieth Century.* Minneapolis, Minn.: University of Minnesota Press, 1977.

[180] Thurow, L., "Losing the Economic Race," *New York Review of Books* 31 (September 27, 1984), 29–31.

**[181] UNCTAD, "An Integrated Programme for Commodities and Indexation of Prices," in *The New International Economic Order: Confrontation or Cooperation between North and South.* Boulder, Colo.: Westview Press, 1977.

**[182] UNESCO: *Statistical Yearbook 1983, vol. III.* Paris: UNESCO, 1983.

**[183] United Nations: *Multinational Corporations in World Development.* New York: United Nations, 1973.

**[184] Veblen, T., *Imperial Germany and the Industrial Revolution.* New York: Macmillan, 1915.

**[185] Vernon, R., *Sovereignty at Bay: The Multinational Spread of U.S. Enterprises.* New York: Basic Books, 1971.

*[186] Wallerstein, I., "Crisis in Transition," in *Dynamics of Global Crisis.* New York: Monthly Review Press, 1982.

*[187] Wallerstein, I., "The Rise and Future Demise of the World Capitalist Systems: Concepts for Comparative Analysis," in *The Capitalist World*

Economy: *Essays by Immanuel Wallerstein*. Cambridge, Eng.: Cambridge University Press, 1979.

[188] Warren, B., *Imperialism*: *Pioneer of Capitalism*. London: NLB, 1980.

[189] Weber, M., "Structures of Power," in *From Max Weber*, ed. by H. H. Gerth and C. W. Mills. New York: Oxford University Press, 1958.

[190] White, C., "Recent Debates in Vietnamese Development Policy," in *Revolutionary Socialist Development in the Third World*, ed. by G. White, R. Murray and C. White. Brighton, Eng.: Wheatsheaf Books, 1983.

[191] Williams, W. A., *Empire as a Way of Life*. New York: Oxford University Press, 1980.

[192] Willoughby, J., "The Changing Role of Protection in the World Economy," *Cambridge Journal of Economics* 6 (June 1982), 195–211.

[193] Willoughby, J., "The Lenin-Kautsky Unity-Rivalry Debate," *Review of Radical Political Economics* 11 (Winter 1979), 91–101.

[194] Willoughby, J., "Must Monetarism Persist? The Internationalization of Capital and the Future of Macroeconomic Policy," *Science and Society*, **49** (Fall 1985), 287–314.

[195] World Bank: *World Development Report* 1983. Washington, D.C.: IBRD, 1983.

[196] World Bank: *World Development Report* 1984. Washington, D.C.: IBRD, 1984.

Indicates books and papers considered by the author essential to the understanding of the topics covered in this book.

Indicates all publications mentioned in the text but not covered by a single asterisk.

References not preceded by an asterisk are books and papers considered by the author to be interesting and relevant.

INDEX

For Product Safety Concerns and Information please contact our EU representative GPSR@taylorandfrancis.com Taylor & Francis Verlag GmbH, Kaufingerstraße 24, 80331 München, Germany

Printed and bound by CPI Group (UK) Ltd, Croydon, CR0 4YY
08/05/2025
01864410-0001